EARLY CHILDHOOD EDUCATION

SOCIETY AND CULTURE

Edited by

ANGELA ANNING, JOY CULLEN AND MARILYN FLEER

Los Angeles • London • New Delhi • Singapore • Washington DC

First published 2009

SAGE Publications Ltd
1 Oliver's Yard
55 City Road
London EC1Y 1SP

SAGE Publications Inc.
2455 Teller Road
Thousand Oaks, California 91320

SAGE Publications India Pvt Ltd
B 1/I 1 Mohan Cooperative Industrial Area
Mathura Road
New Delhi 110 044

SAGE Publications Asia-Pacific Pte Ltd
33 Pekin Street #02-01
Far East Square
Singapore 048763

Library of Congress Control Number: 2008926858

British Library Cataloguing in Publication data

A catalogue record for this book is available from
the British Library

ISBN 978-1-84787-452-8
ISBN 978-1-84787-453-5 (pbk)

Typeset by C&M Digitals (P) Ltd, Chennai, India
Printed in Great Britain by Cromwell Press Ltd, Trowbridge, Wiltshire
Printed on paper from sustainable resources

CONTENTS

NOTES ON CONTRIBUTORS

Angela Anning is Emeritus Professor of Early Childhood Education at the University of Leeds, UK. She has a background of teaching and management in early childhood and primary education, and further and higher education. Her research interests include curricula for young children, art and design education, professional knowledge-sharing in multi-agency teams working with young children, and family intervention programmes. She was a principal investigator in the National Evaluation of Sure Start team and for an ESRC-funded project on Multi-Agency Teamwork for Services for Children (MATCh). Publications include: with Anne Edwards, *Promoting Young Children's Learning Birth to Five*, 2nd edition; with Kathy Ring, *Making Sense of Children's Drawings*; and Anning et al., *Developing Professional Teamwork for Integrated Children's Services*, all published by the Open University Press; and with Mog Ball, *Improving Services for Children: From Sure Start to Children's Centres*, published by Sage.

Margaret Carr is Professor of Education in the Wilf Malcolm Institute of Educational Research at the University of Waikato, New Zealand. She was a co-director of the Curriculum Development project that developed *Te Whāriki*, the New Zealand early childhood national curriculum. Since the publication of this curriculum, she has been involved in a number of research projects that have explored assessment in the early years, as well as projects on learning dispositions in early childhood centres and key competencies in schools. Relevant publications include *Assessment in Early Childhood Settings* (2001, London, Paul Chapman/Sage) and (for the Ministry of Education) *Kei tua o te pae: Assessment for Learning: Early Childhood Exemplars* (2005 and 2007 Wellington, Learning Media).

Bronwen Cowie is the Director of the Wilf Malcolm Institute for Educational Research, School of Education, University of Waikato, New Zealand. She has worked as a secondary science and mathematics teacher and lectured in science and mathematics education. Her research interests include assessment for learning, science and technology education, the role of ICTs in teaching and learning, and the implications of sociocultural views of learning. She was a member of the advisory team for *Kei tua o te pae*: *Assessment for Learning: Early Childhood Exemplars.*

Joy Cullen has recently retired as Professor of Early Years Education at Massey University, Palmerston North, New Zealand. She has conducted national contract research on early intervention services for the NZ Ministry of Education and qualitative studies on sociocultural pedagogy in inclusive early years settings.

Marilyn Fleer is Professor of Early Childhood Education at Monash University, Australia. She began her teaching career working with children in childcare and preschool. She has worked as a curriculum developer, early childhood adviser and researcher. Her PhD was in the area of early childhood science and technology education. Marilyn's research interests include science, technology, environmental education, and human development and learning. She is particularly interested in learning theories within the context of culture and gender.

Susan Hill is an Associate Professor at the University of South Australia and has written more than twenty books for teachers on literacy-related topics. She was the project director for two Australian national literacy projects entitled *100 Children Go To School: Connections between Literacy Development in The Prior To School Period and The First Year Of Formal Schooling* and *100 Children Turn 10: Literacy Development in the Early Years: A Longitudinal Study from the Year Prior to School to the First Four Years of School.* Her current research explores children learning with information technology in a project titled *Children of the New Millennium: Using Information and Communication Technologies for Playing and Learning in the Information Age.*

Barbara Jordan is a Senior Lecturer at Massey University College of Education, New Zealand, teaching in the pre-service BEd(Tchg) Early Years (birth to age eight) programme and teaching in and co-ordinating the GradDipECE, which qualifies primary teachers as early childhood teachers. Her research interests include early childhood curriculum, learning, teaching and action research with teaching teams, supporting teachers as researchers, and in the implementation of sociocultural theory and the New Zealand early childhood national curriculum, *Te Whāriki.*

Glenda MacNaughton is a Professor in the Faculty of Education at the University of Melbourne, Australia, where she established and now directs the Centre for Equity and Innovation in Early Childhood. She has published widely on issues of equity and social justice in early childhood education and is regularly invited to present her research nationally and internationally.

Christine Merrell has worked as a research associate on the Performance Indicators in Primary Schools (PIPS) project at the Curriculum, Evaluation and Management

Centre, University of Durham, UK, for several years. She has helped to develop PIPS assessments for preschool children and year groups throughout the primary phase. She has also researched the academic achievement and progress of young children who are severely inattentive, hyperactive and impulsive.

Susan Nichols is a key researcher at the Centre for Literacy Policy and Learning Cultures at the University of South Australia. Her research interests include home–school connections, literacy pedagogy, gender and cultural diversity.

Valerie N. Podmore is engaged as an Associate Professor part-time in early childhood research, and in doctoral supervision, at Victoria University of Wellington, New Zealand.

Carmel Richardson is the preschool teacher and acting Director of Wiradjuri Preschool and Childcare Centre at the University of Canberra. Australia. She lectures in the Bachelor of Early Childhood Education programme. She has been actively researching sociocultural theory over a number of years and has presented numerous conference papers and keynotes on this topic over that time.

Iram Siraj-Blatchford is Professor of Early Childhood Education at the Institute of Education, University of London, UK. She has been an educational researcher for 17 years. Her current research projects include developmentally appropriate technology for early childhood in Europe and pedagogy in early years settings. She was co-Director of the major Department for Education and Skills five-year study on the Effective Provision of Preschool Education (EPPE) Project (1997–2003) and of the Effective Pedagogy in the Early Years project. She is particularly interested in undertaking research that aims to combat disadvantage; and to give children and families from these backgrounds a head start.

Peter Tymms is the Director of the Performance Indicators in Primary Schools (PIPS) project at the Curriculum, Evaluation and Management Centre, University of Durham, UK. After taking a degree in natural sciences he taught in a wide variety of schools from Central Africa to the north-east of England before starting an academic career. He was 'Lecturer in Performance Indicators' at Moray House, Edinburgh before moving to Newcastle University and then to Durham University where he is presently Professor of Education. His main research interests are in monitoring, assessment, school effectiveness and research methodology. He is Director of the PIPS project within the CEM Centre, which involves monitoring the progress and atti-tudes of pupils in about 4000 primary schools. He has published many academic arti-cles and a book, *'Baseline Assessment and Monitoring in Primary Schools'*.

Denise Williams-Kennedy describes herself as an Indigenous Australian who has worked for more than twenty years as a teacher across various levels of education including childcare, preschool, primary, secondary and adult education. She has spent the past ten years working in an independent Indigenous school in Central Australia.

Elizabeth Wood is Professor of Early Childhood Education at the University of Exeter, UK. She has researched and published widely on early childhood teachers' theories of play, progression and continuity in early childhood education, young children's learning, and gender and underachievement in primary and secondary schools.

CHAPTER 1

RESEARCH CONTEXTS ACROSS CULTURES

Angela Anning, Joy Cullen and Marilyn Fleer

In the first edition of *Early Childhood Education: Society and Culture* we argued that 'early childhood education has been challenged by a theoretical sea change that has seen individualistic developmental explanations of learning and development replaced by theories that foreground the cultural and socially constructed nature of learning'. In 2008 the continuing evolution of theory has increasingly highlighted the significance of cultural-historical explanations of learning and development and accordingly we have altered our theoretical framework of *socio-cultural* theory to use the more explicit term of 'sociocultural-*historical* theory', for the second edition. We argue that foregrounding historical contexts in this revised term represents a natural progression as the early childhood field is now more conversant with sociocultural theory. The book uses sociocultural-historical theory as an umbrella term that incorporates the various theoretical developments that reflect Vygotskian and post-Vygotskian explanations of development and learning. These include: sociocultural, social constructivism, cultural-historical, activity theory, cultural-historical activity theory (CHAT) as well as aspects of postmodernism/post-structuralism that have highlighted the significance of shared discourses and practices in early childhood education.

This second edition maintains the cross-national focus of the first edition to explore the different ways of constructing learning in early childhood settings in the United Kingdom, Australia and *Aotearoa* New Zealand. These analyses are situated in each country against the historical dominance of the play-based, developmental tradition in early childhood education. Variation in each country's response to the challenges posed by sociocultural-historical theory to early childhood practice is itself an indicator of the importance of acknowledging culture and history within societies and educational systems. The cross-national focus further illustrates the embeddedness of learning in current early childhood practices and policies. The second edition comments on the development of such influences since 2004.

The following sections introduce sociocultural-historical theory as a framework for the subsequent chapters. We argue that an in-depth understanding of theory is necessary to minimise superficial interpretations of sociocultural-historical theory by practitioners that can serve to maintain the dominance of practices grounded in individualistic developmental perspectives. This analysis is followed by an overview of early childhood policies, research and practice in the UK, Australia and New Zealand, within the four broad themes of the book that are pivotal to understanding early childhood practice from a sociocultural-historical perspective:

- conceptualisation of learning and pedagogy in early years settings;
- the nature of knowledge in early years settings;
- assessment in early years settings;
- evaluation and quality in early years settings.

Psychology's legacy in guiding early years education – a sociocultural-historical reading

> One of the reasons that so many Western psychologists are reading the writings of a long-dead Russian may be that they are seeking to extend the insights of the so-called cognitive revolution and yet are painfully aware of the shortcomings of so many of its products (e.g. Hirst and Manier, 1995; Sampson, 1981). The research practice of experimentation in artificial situations has provided valuable insights but incurred significant costs. Context, however defined, remained under-theorised and its efforts remained under-researched. (Daniels, 2001: 7)

Daniels (2001), in discussing the field of psychology, points directly at problems within the field of early childhood education. Much of our profession is grounded in the research products of the field of psychology. Foundational to our field is the concept of child development. The observational and child study approaches that have been so highly valued and seen to make the field distinct from other areas of education, have been developed and normed by psychologists. Further, these tools have been consistently used in Australia, New Zealand and in the UK for generating knowledge about children so as to inform practice within the field. The theoretical frameworks that have guided our views on how children think, learn and develop also come directly from psychology. How we conceptualise pedagogy, what we look for in terms of expected developmental trajectories or what constitutes knowledge in early years education, have been traditionally framed using the tools and theories from psychology. Similarly, how we measure these is guided by the worldview that has been bequeathed to us from previous early years professionals/researchers who formed their knowledge from their readings of traditional psychology. Importantly, the paradigm in which we work has been built by and maintained through a psychological tradition.

It is timely that we take stock of how we have come to 'know and do' within the field and to critically examine pedagogy, knowledge construction, assessment and evaluation with the 'context lens' in mind. As discussed above 'Context, however defined, [remains] under-theorised and its efforts [remain] under-researched' (Daniels, 2001: 7). This book seeks to foreground context and to put forward research that has been framed from a sociocultural-historical perspective from within the field of early years education. Many prominent researchers from Australia, New Zealand and the UK have contributed to this book, and their writings provide rich examples of how the conceptual base guiding practice is slowly changing.

We can extend Daniel's (2001) argument, and suggest that many early years researchers from Australia, New Zealand and the UK are also reading the writings of a long-dead Russian because they too are looking for insights into dealing with the limitations of the existing theories and practices used in early years education. Much of the discontent has come from the limitations inherent in the interpretations and developments of Piaget's theories. For example, constructivist thinking focuses attention on the individual, and the individual's construction of the world and of knowledge itself. Many researchers and teachers steeped in cross-cultural contexts will argue that learning and knowledge construction is not an individual process. There are many examples within cross-cultural research of how knowledge is collectively and not individually framed and considered (see Rogoff, 2003 for an expansive argument on this with a range of supporting examples). It is interesting to note that in this volume no author claims to be using a constructivist view of learning or has framed their research and writings following the theories of Piaget. This is reflective of the developments in the field of early years education generally.

In the evolution of theory use in the early years, some researchers and practitioners have moved forward and adopted a social-constructivist approach to pedagogy. In many respects this development appears to be a transition away from focusing simply on the individual and in working towards being able to take account of the social and cultural context of the learner. For instance, Tymms and Merrell (Chapter 9), in their presentation and discussion of data gathered across cultural communities in different countries, acknowledge culture as something that researchers and practitioners must pay attention to in their analysis of pedagogical and curriculum planning. However, to simply 'add culture' to the set of variables being explored could universalise complex and diverse cultural communities into a single category, leading to inappropriate conclusions and ultimately to positioning many children and their families into deficit (see Gutierrez and Rogoff, 2003 for a full discussion of this problem). Similarly, MacNaughton (Chapter 4) moves the theory lens beyond constructivism and uses a critical constructivist perspective in order to cast the lens from a simple reading of the individual to engage critically in how the individual has appropriated (or not) the social discourses which surround them. MacNaughton argues that 'Critical theorists reject the idea that meaning, knowledge and, therefore, learning is a uniquely individual, value-free cognitive pursuit'.

Researchers and practitioners in the early years interested in capturing 'context' have looked to sociocultural theory (later to become known as cultural-historical theory) in order to help them think and act differently about their work. For example, Fleer and Richardson (Chapter 10) have used sociocultural theory with practitioners in order to document how sociocultural assessment moves away from documenting the individual and captures the dynamic relations between the individual and the social context. Both Podmore (Chapter 12) and Cowie and Carr (Chapter 8) give examples of national curriculum and assessment approaches in New Zealand which draw upon sociocultural theory. Hill and Nichols (Chapter 13) and Williams-Kennedy (Chapter 7) provide similar examples of more localised curriculum development in Australia which has been informed by sociocultural theory. Anning (Chapter 5), in using activity theory for shaping the directions of a curriculum for the childcare sector in the UK, demonstrates another important theoretical development. Activity theory, discussed fully in Anning's chapter, treats the context as an activity system, and seeks to understand the motives, goals and needs of the participants as they work towards specific outcomes (agreed or unarticulated).

Running in parallel with the theoretical evolutions that have been adopted and briefly discussed has been a keen interest in the role of the adult in children's learning. Once again, the legacy of child development theory (notably Piaget) has seen the de-emphasising of the role of the adult in children's learning. With a move away from simply studying or observing children's development, and on to studying children's learning, we have seen a focus on researching how adults interact with children (see Jordan, Chapter 3) and how professionals construct knowledge about learning (see Cullen, Chapter 6). Theoretically different ways of framing research and methodologically different approaches were needed for this renewed attention on the practitioner as pedagogue (see Siraj-Blatchford, Chapter 11). In line with this evolution, many researchers and practitioners have adopted a sociocultural-historical approach for informing their work. This is exemplified in this book. Others have blended across theories; for example, Wood (Chapter 2) uses post-structuralist theory to examine the cultural implications of play, but does so with a view to building a new pedagogy of play. Through her interest in pedagogy and culture, she brings together both post-structual theory and elements of sociocultural-historical theory in order to deconstruct, understand and re-build new pedagogical approaches.

Sociocultural-historical theory offers one way of addressing the limitations that our profession has inherited because it specifically deals with context. In order to appreciate the complexity of the chapters that follow, the next section will examine Vygotsky's theoretical ideas in relation to foundational knowledge of early years education, with the view to building a new basic framework for pedagogy, knowledge, assessment and evaluation – the four themes that contributing chapter authors have researched from within the field of early years education. The final chapter in this book, takes up this challenge more explicitly. Taken together, the chapters presented here provide the basis for the much-needed theorisation of 'context' as outlined by Daniels (2001), but specifically for the early years of education.

Vygotsky's legacy in relation to recent developments in early years education

Child development

The assessment of learning and development, and the evaluation of early years programmes have traditionally been designed on the premise of 'child development' principles focused on the ages of children and a correspondingly linear set of stages for progression. That is, assessments are benchmarked against the expected norms for children. This has traditionally been framed in relation to the age of a child – as an indicator or point of progression to be expected. In his time Vygotsky (1998) argued against this kind of developmental trajectory which relied upon the child's chronological age. He suggested that age 'cannot serve as a reliable criterion for establishing the actual level' of a child's development (Vygotsky, 1998: 199). This critique is exemplified in the work of Jordan (Chapter 3), who examined teacher interactions with children, noting the differences and the interplay between teacher scaffolding and teacher co-constructing with children in order to determine children's actual level of development for informing the teaching–learning process. The children's chronological age was not discussed, but rather the focus of attention was on how the teacher and the children interacted and what types of intersubjectivity were being built through a focus on children's interests. Although Jordan's focus of attention was indirectly on the assessment of actual developmental levels, her sociocultural-historical framework represents a significant move away from a traditional view of *child development,* where development is seen as a naturally evolving process. Mapping interactions has also been featured in the work of Podmore (Chapter 12), who nicely shows how evaluation models in early childhood education can be reconceptualised in relation to child-focused questions. That is, teachers projecting their minds to the interests, activities and interactions of the children, through questions such as Do you engage my mind? Can I trust you? – generating a new framework for evaluation. This approach, they argue, creates a new space for the evaluation of children's learning in relation to teacher-initiated programmes. Once again the sociocultural-historical approach that Jordan and Podmore draw upon marks a significant change in teacher thinking and assessment of children's development from that traditionally used in early childhood education.

Vygotsky suggested that the dominant concept of child development sees 'development as nothing other than realisation, modification, and combination of deposits. Nothing new develops here – only a growth, branching, and regrouping of those factors that were already present at the very beginning' (Vygotsky, 1998: 190). A linear path is generated which positions children who do not meet the development expectations in deficit; or as Vygotsky stated, they are viewed as '"diseases" of development' (1998: 191). Cullen (Chapter 6), has explored in her research the tension that arises when different theoretical orientations of staff working with children come together. She states that 'it is in this area of professional knowledge that differences in the perspectives of early childhood teachers and EI [Early Intervention] professionals can most clearly be seen. Although they share a common philosophy of authentic assessment, the more specialised professional knowledge of the speech language therapist, physiotherapist or psychologist can be in conflict with the holistic interests-based planning of the early childhood programme' which is reliant upon a more sociocultural-historical framework. Cullen's research demonstrates that whilst a sociocultural-historical curriculum is clearly being promoted and used, teacher professional knowledge needs to move beyond simply *creating a community* of practice to generating a *community for improving* practice. In using sociocultural-historical theory to frame her research, Cullen has been able to identify two significant problems in early years education. First is the tensions that are generated when an interest-led practitioner base – that focuses on processes and context – works together with a group oriented toward content and disembedded context. Cullen's research provides new knowledge on the significance of the theoretical orientation of professionals and how this generates particular sets of expectations which are looked for and measured by the two groups. The second dimension of Cullen's work relates to the difficulty of professionals in appreciating fully the complexity and depth of understandings needed to use sociocultural-historical theory for informing practice. The latter is noteworthy because the profession has not closely examined the challenge for the field in moving from a traditional evolutionary view of development towards a sociocultural-historical framework for thinking and working with children. This point is also taken up by Fleer and Richardson (Chapter 10), who show how difficult it is for teachers to change how they undertake their observations of children. It is not surprising that Vygotsky (1998) wrote about the need for a revolutionary approach for transforming thinking on 'child development'.

In line with Vygotsky's revolutionary view of development the authors in this book with their focus on 'context' demonstrate the signification of the 'social situation of development'.

> The social situation of development represents the initial moment for all dynamic changes that occur in development during the given period. It determines wholly and completely the forms and the path along which the child will acquire ever newer personality characteristics, drawing them from the social reality as from the basic source of development, the path along which the social becomes the individual. Thus, the first question we must answer in studying the dynamics of any age is to explain the social situation of development. (Vygotsky, 1998: 198)

This view of development moves away from internalising development as a feature of the child where a particular developmental milestone is not achieved, and towards viewing development as the relations between the social context and the biological child. The social situation of a child is dependent upon the society and cultural context in which the child is embedded. Different cultural contexts foreground particular social situations, which in turn position children to actively engage and take up particular participation structures for learning. Williams-Kennedy (Chapter 7) illustrates how some Indigenous families foreground different ways of reading – such as, reading the land, reading body language – and how traditional literacy benchmarks capture Western and not necessarily Indigenous knowledges, particularly, in relation to progression and expectations at particular year levels. Through documenting the everyday practices of Indigenous families, and through family examination of these practices, different views on literacy and learning were ascertained. This sociocultural-historical study further problematises the traditional view of development that has been used to generate knowledge of literacy learning in Australia. This problem is further explored by Hill and Nichols (Chapter 13), who map literacy learning in the home and literacy learning in school. Their work suggests that a complete view of learning in literacy can be gained only when the relations between school and home are built into not just the teaching–learning process, but also the assessment framework. Through their research, Hill and Nicols show that traditional assessment frameworks have become institutionalised in Australia, and as Cullen argues in discussing practice in New Zealand, institutionalised practices require a major paradigm shift for approaches to assessment to change.

Together, these studies show how the view of child development as a naturally evolving process is embedded within the institutionalised thinking of early childhood education in Australia, New Zealand and the UK. The construction of childhood and development within the framework of the institution, the society and the individual, has been researched by Hedegaard (2008), who draws extensively upon Vygotsky's (1998) seminal critique of child development, but specifically examines contemporary contexts, where cultural and linguistic diversity feature. In line with Vygtosky's work on the dialectical approach to development, and the social situation of development, Hedegaard views development as a relationship between the child and society. Development is not something that exists within the child, but rather takes place when the child participates in the activities of his/her cultural community. When the development of the child within their cultural community does not match what is expected or accepted as the 'normal' developmental trajectory by the institution, conflicts arise. Hedegaard (2008) argues that the *problem lies not within the child, but rather within the institution*. In this situation, the pedagogue is blind to the possibilities of both the diversity among children and the potential for creating different developmental trajectories within the institution. This latter point is also taken up in Cullen (Chapter 6).

Institutionalisation based on age

Rogoff (2003) has argued that learning institutions, such as nursery schools, preschools and schools, are organised in relation to age. Spaces are created and boundaries are formed based on the criterion of 'age'. Age as a 'defining' variable for organising learning is problematic. However, 'age' as a key variable for 'development' is also problematic. Vygotsky (1929a/1998) illustrates the limitations of positioning 'age' as the key variable in development, through the example of expecting 'older children to remember more' because remembering is a psychological function inherent *in* the child: that is, it is an individual act that a child does alone. Vygotsky (1929a/1998) suggested that culture plays a very important part in memory. He states: 'The child who remembers by means of a geographical map or by means of a plan, a scheme or a summary, may serve as an example of such cultural development of memory' (pp. 57–58). The cultural development of memory will vary across families and communities, and this illustrates the significance of the social situation of development in shaping how that development is supported. Memory is not an individual construction held in the mind of the individual. Wertsch (2007) exemplifies this when he asks who is doing the remembering when a child cannot find its jumper and the adult asks the child to recount their day in order to determine when and therefore where the jumper may have been left. Is remembering an individual act? In Chapter 8, Cowie and Carr 'take the view that learning and development, rather than being primarily about individual achievement, is distributed over, stretched across, people, places and things'. The dynamics of the context – places, people and things – shape how a child responds. Their research into assessment exemplifies the dialectical relations between places, people and things. Podmore (Chapter 12) has also argued that the evaluative framework that she has generated, which involved questions of 'Is this place for me?' is enacted in practice, as 'Is this place fair for us?', demonstrating a collective rather than an individual orientation to teachers' work. Similarly, Fleer and Richardson (Chapter 10) move the assessment lens away from the individual and to the group. This refocusing lies in direct opposition to the traditional practices of observing, documenting and reporting upon individual children in early childhood centres. Cowie and Carr (Chapter 8) and Podmore (Chapter 12) draw upon the theoretical work of Lave and Wenger (communities of practice), and Fleer and Richardson (Chapter 10) use Rogoff's three planes of analysis for informing the paradigm shift needed in assessment for professionals who are currently working in early childhood education. Podmore also draws upon Rogoff's work, but specifically makes use of her writings on the 'transformation of understanding through participation'. Significantly, Fleer and Richardson show through their research that a paradigm shift from the individual to the collective is exceedingly difficult for practitioners and requires a great deal of reorientation and intellectual effort to transform thinking. Anning (Chapter 5) thoughtfully summarises the growing conflict between a traditionally oriented developmental trajectory, the government agenda for standards and measurements of quality, and a sociocultural-historical 'paradigm shift to the social (Vygotskian) and situated nature of learning (Lave and Wenger, 1991; Resnick et al., 1991), and to the central importance of reciprocity in learning episodes between adults and young children (Schaffer, 1992)' (also see Jordan, Chapter 3).

A sociocultural-historical research orientation

In this book there are significantly different approaches to taking account of the social situation of development or the cultural context being investigated. Tymms and Merrell (Chapter 9) describe a baseline assessment approach known as Performance Indicators in Primary Schools (PIPS), which was originally developed to measure performance in literacy and numeracy, but which has been used in practice as an opportunity for teachers to come to know their children in these areas, but also in social, emotional and physical development.

However, development towards more qualitative research designs has been noted in some areas of psychology, with this approach dominating early years education research. Sakharov (1930/1998: 75) suggests that 'the main flaws in the [quantitative] method ... [are that] it fails completely to take into account the process of concept generation in children and works only with finished concepts'. This approach to research 'cannot tell us how the child uses concepts in solving different life tasks. Indeed, an index of the qualitative characteristics of a concept is, in the particular case, not the child's practical use of this concept in his responses to objects in the world around him, but the verbal description of the content or the scope of the concept. We obtain this description under experimental or test conditions. However, this index is not only incomplete: it is not even clear' (Sakharov, 1930/1998: 74). In this book most researchers have sought to study early childhood policy and practice from within a dynamic and dialectical framework. In their writings authors have foregrounded context and worked towards understanding the cultural-historical context of their research through exploring a range of dimensions at the one time. Those researchers who have drawn upon Rogoff's (2003) three foci of analysis have concentrated on the child, but in relation to interactions (see Jordan for a nice example of this). They have also concentrated upon the broader context, such as the theoretical perspectives different groups bring to the research context (see both Cullen, and Fleer and Richardson for examples), or the cultural nature of learning (see Williams-Kennedy for a rich example of this).

In this book a dynamic rather than a static view of research is considered. For example, Fleer and Richardson specifically seek to capture the dynamics of the research context and work towards supporting staff in early childhood centres to move beyond a traditional view of development, but also an individualised and static documentation of children. Through mapping the transformation of understanding, rather than focusing on only an end point, their work operationalises how early childhood professionals can move outside of the constraints portrayed by Vygotsky:

> An exceptionally important methodological problem arises that consists, naturally, of basic points of formulating the problem we are interested in: how can we in the process of research differentiate cultural from biological development and isolate cultural development which, in fact, cannot be found in a pure and isolated form? Does not the requirement of differentiating both processes contradict recognizing their merging as a basic form of mental development of the child and is not their merging an obstacle that makes comprehending unique features of cultural development of the child impossible? (Vygotsky, 1997: 22)

Through the sociocultural-historically framed studies presented in this volume, we gain insights into the cultural nature of development, with all of the complexities of policy, practice, institutional frameworks and the movement from traditional to a revolutionary theoretical orientation.

The cultural-historical context of early childhood education in the UK

The United Kingdom (UK) includes England, Northern Ireland, Scotland and Wales. Devolution of power from Westminster since 1999 has resulted in national differences related to new legislation and policies emerging in approaches to curriculum design, implementation, testing and training for service delivery. For example, the Welsh Assembly has developed a distinct and more play-based curriculum for children aged from 3 to 7 years old (ACCAC, 2004; Selleck, 2007). In Scotland there has been a discussion about shifting the school starting age to 6 (Macmillan, 2006; Stephen, 2006).

Details can be found at the respective national government websites (www.scotland.gov.uk and www.wales.gov.uk).

However, a common historical legacy across the UK of uneven and underfunded provision for young children and their families has resulted in children attending a variety of settings before the statutory school starting age of 5. A young child in the UK may spend periods of time (sometimes concurrently) with childminders or in privately funded daycare settings (currently accounting for 80% of daycare provision in England, see Penn, 2007), in Children's Centres combining childcare and education with health services funded and managed by local government children's services directorates, in playgroups run by voluntary agencies, in nursery schools (increasingly becoming Children's Centres with so-called 'wrap-around care' before and after school hours and in school holidays) or in nursery classes and Reception classes in primary schools managed under local authority children's services systems. Yet, despite a raft of government reforms in the past decade, accessibility to and affordability of services for under-5s is still dependent on national and regional historical/cultural/political priorities (Pugh, 2001).

The discourse and infrastructure of UK services for children and families have changed dramatically. Two Green Papers, *Every Child Matters: Change for Children* (DfES, 2004a) and *Every Child Matters: The Next Steps* (DfES, 2004b) (www.everychildmatters.gov.uk) led to the seminal Children Act of 2004. In the Act five broad outcomes were defined for all children from birth to the age of 18: being healthy; being protected from harm and neglect; being enabled to enjoy and achieve; making a positive contribution to society; and achieving economic well-being. The Act marked a radical change of direction from single agency service delivery to integrated services. The concept of responding to the 'whole child' within his/her family and community context underpinned the vision of reforming children's services. Traditionally distinct departments of Education, Health and Social Services were charged with working together to deliver the five *Every Child Matters* (ECM) outcomes. At local levels practitioners working with young children and families were also charged with working together, and sometimes reconfigured into multi-agency teams. The shifts in roles and responsibilities and changes in working patterns and practices have been problematic for many early childhood education, health, family support and care workers (Anning et al., 2006).

In 2003 the first Minister for Children, Young People and Families was appointed. As the push for inter-agency collaboration intensified, funding systems and infrastructures changed. For example, Children's Trusts, bodies responsible for joint commissioning of local children's services and pooled resources across agencies delivering services, were in place in every region by 2008. The infra-structure of Trusts is underpinned by five key principles: child-centred, outcome-led vision; integrated front-line delivery of services; integrated processes; joint planning and commissioning strategies; and inter-agency governance. Trusts are required to demonstrate effective leadership at every level, including front-line delivery, performance management driving an outcomes focus (from local inspections to rewards and incentives for individual staff), and strategies to listen to children and young people.

In England, the Department for Education and Skills became the Department for Children, Schools and Families (DCSF) when Gordon Brown succeeded Tony Blair as

Prime Minister in 2007. The Department published a radical new agenda for re-thinking childhood (DCSF, 2007). Schools will be expected to address many of the new government targets for enhancing the lives of children and their families under an Extended Schools initiative. Extended Schools will offer out-of-school recreation and childcare services, family support programmes, liaison with a range of services for families and career and employment advice for parents as well as young people.

All 3- and 4-year-olds in England are now entitled to a free, good-quality, part-time education place (currently 12.5 hours a week for 38 weeks of the year, but to be increased to 15 hours). Parents can choose to access the free places from the wide range of early years settings listed above, provided the settings are registered and demonstrate that they deliver the Foundation Stage Curriculum. All such settings are inspected by a unified inspection system, under the control of the Office for Standards in Education (Ofsted).

Childcare has been expanded rapidly in order to ensure that parents (particularly those on benefits) can get back to work. In 2000 the Neighbourhood Nursery Initiative was launched to increase the supply of daycare in 'poor' neighbourhoods, but with a requirement that their funding be commissioned from the private sector. A *Ten-year Strategy for Childcare* was set out by the government in 2005 (DfES, 2005). But the new Early Years Foundation Stage in England sets standards for *combined learning, development and care* of children from the age of birth to 5 (www.everychildmatters.gov.uk). The principles guiding the work of all practitioners charged with delivering services to young children and their families are grouped into four distinct but complementary themes which reflect a sociocultural-historical approach: a unique child, positive relationships, enabling environments and learning and development (DfES, 2007a).

There remains anxiety about the ever-widening gap between the rich and poor in England (Joseph Rowntree Foundation, 2007). Ambitious anti-poverty intervention programmes were modelled in Sure Start Local Programmes set up in 1999 with funding of £1.4 billion over six years. By 2004 Sure Start offered 525 community-based integrated services schemes to support families with under-4s in the most deprived areas of England; but the government decided to rebrand the Sure Start Local Programmes as Sure Start Children's Centres in the face of (perhaps premature?) early anxieties about their effectiveness (Belsky et al., 2007; Anning and Ball, 2008). There was also concern that attention needed to be paid to poor families outside the boundaries of Sure Start Local Programmes. The intention is to roll out core services in education, health and family welfare, drawing on lessons learned from the evaluation of Sure Start Local Programmes. By 2010 there will be 3500 Sure Start Children's Centres as hubs of integrated children's services in all areas, not just those deemed to be 'deprived'. There are also major concerns about the relative underachievement of boys and children from so-called ethnic minority communities (often ex-Commonwealth or refugee populations), which the education and care sector are expected to address.

Generic curriculum guidelines and the related assessment system, the *Foundation Stage Early Learning Goals and Profile*, were introduced to all early childhood settings in 2000 (DfEE/QCA, 2000). In September 2008 this will be combined with the *Birth to Three Matters* Curriculum for under-3s (DfES, 2002), and will form a new *Early Years Foundation Stage* (DfES, 2007a), which will relate to all children from birth up to the age of 5. In many primary schools in England, Foundation Stage units for children under 5 have replaced separate nursery (for 3- to 4-year-olds) and reception classes (for 4- to 5-year-olds). The staffing of these units is now a matter of debate in England. As part of the reform of the children's services workforce initiative a new early years professional (EYP) has been developed, a pedagogue of graduate status trained to work across the sectors of care, learning and child development. There will be an EYP in all Children's Centres by 2010, in daycare settings by 2015 and in every Foundation Stage setting in the long term. The blurring of the distinction between a teacher and an EYP raises the possibility of a distinct (and less well paid) category of educators for early childhood settings. So, for example, there is evidence that head-teachers in primary schools are increasingly saving money by using a teacher as the manager of a team of teaching assistants, rather than employing two teachers, to deliver the curriculum in their combined early years units (Anning and Calder, 2008).

Conceptualisations of learning and pedagogy in the UK

As outlined in the earlier sections of this chapter, the distinct discourse of early childhood education, drawing on the discipline of developmental psychology, emphasises the importance of young children learning through first-hand experiences within a 'child-centred' learning environment. In the UK this discourse exists in tension with statutory schooling discourse which emphasises the preparation of children for 'real' school, in particular their induction into and achievements in the 'basics' of literacy and numeracy, and preparation for the world of work. There are additional tensions from the policy shift to combine staff teams from education and care sectors as their constructs of childhood collide, and from the radical plans to change children's services into multi-agency teams (Anning and Edwards, 2006).

The government commitment to 'evidence-based' policy development was demonstrated in funding a large-scale, longitudinal study, the Effective Provision of preschool Education (EPPE) project (1997–2003) (Sylva et al., 2003). It was designed to investigate the development and attainment of 3000 children between the ages of 3 and 7, initially in their progress through 141 preschool settings (of six main types of provision) in six English local authorities. The project has influenced policy decisions on the future of educating children under 5 in the UK.

In order to pursue evidence of effective pedagogy, two more studies were funded by the government. One was based on case studies in settings in the EPPE study shown to be particularly effective in promoting young children's learning (Siraj-Blatchford, Sylva, Taggart et al., 2002). Their findings were that effective pedagogy was characterised by:

- a judicious mix of adult-initiated group work and freely chosen child-initiated activities;
- the quality of shared, sustained thinking and dialogue between adults/children and children/peers;

- skilful diagnostic assessment of children's learning and strategic planning for a wide range of curriculum experiences;
- practitioners' knowledge of child development and curriculum;
- encouragement for children to represent their understanding in a range of modes.

A second project was based on investigating the perspectives of effective practitioners on pedagogy in early years settings (Moyles et al., 2002). Their findings were that:

- quality teaching and learning is characterised by practitioners' ability to apply knowledge of young children's learning and curriculum knowledge to the planning, implementing and evaluation of children's progression across a range of curriculum areas;
- effectiveness can be identified and measured against agreed criteria.

In English primary schools, where many 4-year-olds receive a version of 'nursery' education, the impact of the National Curriculum (1988) and introduction of Literacy (1999) and Numeracy (2000) Hours resulted in more whole-class teaching, ability grouping, direct instruction and subject-based teaching for 4- to 7-year-olds (Pollard et al., 1994). Currently all registered providers of 'preschool' education must deliver a synthetic phonics scheme to children from birth to 5 (DfES 2007b). Reception class teachers remain confused about pedagogy appropriate to the Foundation Stage within the above constraints (Taylor Nelson Sobres with Aubrey, 2002) and how to use play for learning (see Chapter 2 for a full discussion). Furthermore, the task of training a range of early years practitioners (many of whom have low-level qualifications) in a wide variety of settings to deliver the Foundation Stage and Letters and Sounds curricula remains daunting.

The nature of knowledge in early years settings in the UK

The folklore and practice of designing a curriculum for young children in the UK has been to 'follow the interests of children', though in reality it has reflected the adults' constructs of childhood (Anning, 2007). For practitioners accustomed to plan by themes or projects, the introduction of a subject-based National Curriculum at Key Stage 1 (for 4- to 7-year-olds) was traumatic. Targets set by government for attainments in Literacy and Numeracy, measured by standardised tests for all 7- and 11-year-olds, exacerbated pressures in primary schools to narrow a 'broad and balanced curriculum'. Concerns about the stress levels of young children in primary schools have resulted in a call for a radical review of the primary school curriculum and related systems of assessment (Alexander, 2007).

The English Foundation Stage curriculum outlines six areas of learning: personal, social and emotional development; communication, language and literacy; problem solving, reasoning and numeracy; knowledge and understanding of the world; physical development and creative development. In response to repeated concerns about the negative effects of young children being exposed to too formal a curriculum too soon, guidance notes for the new Foundation Stage Curriculum for 2008 emphasise the importance of learning through play, reciprocity in partnerships with parents, working with other professionals and responding to the diverse needs of children and their families.

Assessment in early years settings in the UK

In England policy and practice in assessment have been driven by the Standards Agenda. Alongside the National Curriculum are related Standard Assessment Tasks (SATs) for 7-year-olds, focused on attainments in reading, writing and arithmetic. Individual child attainments must be reported annually to parents. SATs results are aggregated for schools and reported in league tables. There is pressure on practitioners to teach to the tests. In Scotland and Northern Ireland there are no league tables (though Northern Ireland retains selection tests at 11) and in Wales SATs for 7-year-olds have been discontinued. There is mounting pressure in England to do the same.

Baseline assessment for children as they enter school (sometimes at 4) was made compulsory in 1999 (see Chapter 9). Ninety schemes were accredited against criteria prescribed by the government. The results of these disparate schemes were seen to be unreliable for measuring the 'value-added' of Key Stage 1 schooling. In 2002 a single, centralised statutory assessment of children's progression through the Foundation Stage was introduced based on profiling against 'stepping stones'. Summative scores in personal, social and emotional development, language and literacy and mathematics were returned via local authority systems to central government. The introduction of the detailed, centrally imposed profile for each child has met with some resistance from practitioners. An updated version of the profile for the 2008 Foundation Stage Curriculum includes a set of 13 assessment scales, each of which has nine points. Judgements on each child's attainment must be based on observations over time, and it will mainly be the task of teachers in reception classes to complete the profiles by the time children transfer at age 5 to Key Stage 1.

A Common Assessment Framework (CAF) has been introduced as a standardised tool for assessing the need of children for services (www.everychildmatters.gov.uk/delivering services/caf). It consists of a pre-assessment checklist to identify if a child needs a CAF; a protocol for collecting the views of parents/carers and relevant professionals on the strengths and needs of the child; and where deemed appropriate, a proforma for recording and sharing information across agencies about assessments and treatments. A key professional, probably the child's teacher or social worker, will manage each case.

Alongside these centralised systems, practitioners in a range of early years settings continue to operate a variety of detailed profiles, often shared regularly with parents and carers, based on their daily observations of and interactions with children and their grounding in child development.

Evaluation and quality in early years settings in the UK

Moss and Pence (1994) identify two approaches to defining and measuring quality in early childhood settings: one descriptive and relative, the other evaluative and quasi-objective. They describe the former as an 'inclusionary paradigm' in which the processes of reaching a common understanding of quality among the various stakeholders are central. Practitioners and users (ideally children and their parents/carers) negotiate for services that are mutually agreed as worthwhile and of good quality. For example, community-led decision-making about services underpinned the vision of the Sure Start intervention programme (Anning and Ball, 2008).

The second approach identified by Moss and Pence stipulates benchmarks of quality for services as measured by 'outsiders'. Instruments may be:

- defined locally by local authority systems;
- marketed by independent agencies (such as the voluntary sector preschool Learning Alliance with responsibility for playgroups);
- standardised for research purposes (such as the Early Childhood Environment Rating Scale [ECERS] instruments used in the EPPE and National Evaluation of Sure Start projects [Harms et al., 1998]);
- regulatory (such as the Office for Standards in Education system).

It is the Ofsted machinery in particular that has impacted on early childhood education. Ofsted is nominally independent of the government. However, the emphasis placed in their inspections on attainments in literacy and numeracy reflects the government's standards agenda. Ofsted procedures are based on the notion that there is a universal definition of quality without acknowledging the significance of a particular cultural context at a particular point in its history of a setting. The protocols and procedures have been simplified in recent inspections, but the principles of Ofsted-type accountability sit uneasily alongside those of a self-regulating, professionally driven approach to maintaining high standards in education and care.

The cultural-historical context of early childhood education in Australia

Early childhood education in Australia is the responsibility of each of the states and territories. The Commonwealth provides additional funding to support the sector, but only for specific purposes, such as Indigenous early childhood education programmes. As a result, each state and territory has different ways of structuring education and care provision for children from birth to 8 years. Each state and territory has different nomenclature, school starting age, curricula, approaches to testing and evaluation, support services, policies and mix of private and public funded early childhood education and care programmes (Fleer and Udy, 2002).

Although early childhood education is generally viewed as focusing on children from birth to age 8 in Australia, there has been a tradition for states and territories to place children who are in preschool and childcare under the policy and funding regime of the health sector and children aged approximately 5–8 years into the school sector. However, recent government changes have resulted in the merging of childcare policy and provision from the health sector to the education sector. For example, staff from

Family and Community Services and Indigenous Affairs with responsibility for childcare have physically moved portfolios and are now under the Department of Education and Work Relations. In the state of Victoria, childcare has moved from the Department of Human Services to a newly formed Department of Early Childhood Education and Development within the Victorian Department of Education. These changes are most recent and the flow on effects to centres are yet to be realised.

Most states and territories provide one year of free preschool education. The full cost of childcare resides with the families, although partial subsidies are provided for some disadvantaged groups. The cost of public school education for children aged 6–8 years (and beyond) is provided by states and territories. Private schools receive some funding from the government.

Australia is a multicultural society with a 2% Indigenous community. Indigenous children live all over Australia – urban to remote rural – and have a range of languages and cultures. Most schools and centres in Australia use English as their language of instruction. However, in some remote communities bilingual programmes operate.

Conceptualisation of learning and pedagogy in Australia

As in the UK, in Australia learning and pedagogy have been framed from within a developmental paradigm, mostly influenced by developmental psychology. The enactment of this theoretical perspective in early childhood centres has been mostly shaped by the United States of America through their construction and discourses of developmentally appropriate practice (DAP). The influence of DAP has been strong and this language has found its way into all departmental documentation throughout Australia.

In recent years there has been a growing re-conceptualisation of early childhood pedagogy through the influence of Reggio Emilia. The principles of Reggio Emilia have found their way into some early childhood long daycare centres and preschools, but also into the school sector – mostly private schools. Historically, the school sector has principally adopted a discipline focus alongside a child-centred approach to learning and pedagogy. However, it is mostly the preschool and childcare sector which has followed the interest of the child, while the school sector has followed the interest of the curriculum.

Evidence-based policy imperatives set by the Australian government have principally focused on literacy and numeracy. The government's national literacy and numeracy plan has strongly influenced how learning and pedagogy are enacted in Australian schools and centres, the latter being least influenced by this perspective due to the childcare sector largely being federally funded, and education being funded at the state level. However, the Australian government has recently invested in innovative practices through directing money to research in preschools and childcare centres on how best to support literacy and numeracy in centres. For example, a one million dollar research and development project was funded by the government to support the birth to age 5 sector in adopting a sociocultural-historical approach to literacy and numeracy learning in families and centres. Funding has also been directed towards the research and development of early childhood science programmes through funding informal learning centres, but also through investigating the possibility of developing a national preschool science resource and curriculum programme. However, with a change of government in 2007, it is difficult to know if this new imperative will be maintained.

Generally speaking, government research to support the re-conceptualisation of learning and pedagogy for the early childhood sector has emerged only since 2005. Although the Australian government has targeted early childhood education (Fleer, 2000; Press and Hayes, 2000; Raban, 2000; Yelland, 2000) as a priority area, historically limited funds have been directed towards this sector of education. Consequently, the early childhood profession has tended to look elsewhere – mostly to local small-scale studies (Hill et al., 1998) or to larger research from the UK (e.g. Sylva and Sammons, 2000) and the United States (e.g. Schweinhart and Weikart, 1999) to support its pedagogical practices. The EPPE project and the follow-up effective pedagogical study (Siraj-Blatchford, Chapter 11), and the Sure Start studies (www.surestart.gov.uk at Department for Education and Employment, or NESS@bbk. ac.uk at Birbeck College) are important sources for informing policy and practice in Australia.

The nature of knowledge in early years settings in Australia

Early childhood programmes in Australia in the before-school sector principally operate a domains-based approach, drawing upon developmentally appropriate practice to inform programming. There is no national early childhood curriculum. However, most states and territories now have some form of curriculum. Most have developed an early childhood curriculum for the birth to 8 sector. In this documentation a mix of domains and key learning areas, such as the arts, science and technology, mathematics, literacy, and health and physical education, are evident. In the school sector, each state and territory has developed a curriculum that is centred around the key learning areas. However, most states are now moving away from key learning areas and are beginning to construct curricula that foreground an integrated view of knowledge. For example, Queensland has adopted a 'new basics' view of education, and Tasmania has designed its curriculum in relation to 'essential learnings'. New curricula tend to focus mostly on life-long learning skills, citizenship and a form of futures education. In the past, sociocultural-historical theory has not been influential in informing the early childhood curriculum in Australia. However, some states and territories have examined the New Zealand curriculum *Te Whāriki* (Ministry of Education, 1996a) with a view to framing their documents around principles. The curriculum in Australia is evolving, and research in some states and territories around observations and planning (Horner and Topfer, 2003; Fleer and Richardson, 2003; Fleer and Robbins, 2004a) is acting as a catalyst for change from domains to a broader more sociocultural-historical framing of knowledge.

Assessment in early years settings in Australia

Another major issue that has been raised across all states and territories in recent years has been the policy imperative of raising standards in literacy and numeracy. It has been argued that the focus on these areas has been at the expense of other curriculum areas. Similarly, concerns have also been voiced about outcomes-based education, with some states linking outcomes directly to ages (contrary to the original philosophy of outcomes-based education). For some other states, outcomes-based education has been adopted alongside accountability measures such as testing, benchmarking and reporting. Some educators have reported a negative impact on the quality of child-centred curriculum programmes (Fleer, 2000). However, more recently, some sectors in government and two states have researched and implemented a sociocultural-historical approach to assessment. For example, the Australian government uses an instrument known as the preschool profile to map the literacy, numeracy and social context of all Indigenous preschool children. This tool was developed specifically on sociocultural-historical theory and seeks to capture a dynamic image of children working in collaboration with others. This model has been used by the Western Australian Education system for all preschool children in that state, and preliminary findings indicate that early childhood professionals find the tool to be effective for assessment, but also for changing their own pedagogical practices. In South Australia and in some parts of Victoria teachers are drawing upon Learning Stories (Carr, 2001a; Cowie and Carr, Chapter 8) to inform their assessment practices. These assessment tools have been developed from a sociocultural-historical theoretical framework by early childhood researchers and are proving to be effective for generating change. However, there is a real concern for the development and implementation of assessment tools designed from outside of the field of early childhood education. Recently, there has been a real push by paediatricians and epidemiologists to make use of a Canadian-based Early Education Index. This Index has been trialled in Western Australia and modified for use with Australian preschool children. It is the intention of the new Labor government to roll out this assessment tool so that a picture of the attainments of Australia's young children can be gained.

Evaluation and quality in early years settings in Australia

A significant initiative by the Australian government in 2004 was the release of a paper entitled *A National Early Childhood Agenda*, a series of national consultations in each state and territory, and the release of the consultation paper that resulted from discussions by professionals across the care and education sector. The government brought together health and education professionals from each state and territory, and took an active leadership role in generating evidence-based policy across portfolios and political groups. This document signalled the need for disbanding the division between care and education. It also suggested communication across jurisdictions (Federal and state) and across structural levels (different departments). The traditional divide between sectors has become further entrenched as a result of differing industrial awards, conditions of service and corresponding salaries/wages. Whilst divisions in government jurisdictions are currently being addressed, the industrial awards and conditions, including unions, will continue to be a major issue for Australian early childhood professionals.

Although the concerns regarding the clear divisions between care and education in Australia have been noted in official publications (Press and Hayes, 2000; OECD, 2001) and roundtable sessions organised through the Commonwealth Child Care Advisory Council, we have also seen similar concerns on the international front, as evidenced by reports and initiatives in the UK and New Zealand.

Research evidence (Farquhar, 1999a) suggests that the salary paid (and therefore an assumed increase in qualifications and experience of staff) has been shown to be a significant contributor to outcomes for children. Anecdotal evidence from academic staff across universities in Australia suggests that students who have completed four years of a degree in early childhood education would generally demonstrate greater knowledge and higher interactional patterns with young children than those who had completed only three or two years of a degree. Confirmation of this view has been noted in the international literature (Sylva, 1999). In New Zealand there is general agreement that further education results in higher quality interactional patterns and the implementation of higher quality programmes for young children (Smith et al., 2000). However, extensive research into qualifications has not been conducted in Australia. Over the past five years there has been a general push in some states to reduce the level of staff qualifications in early childhood programmes as one way of reducing costs in the bid for centres to stay financially viable. While the national quality assurance system has been most effective for measuring minimum standards relating to the safety and care of young children, the system was not designed as a tool for making fine-grained judgements on outcomes for children as a result of staff qualifications. The introduction of national professional standards for early childhood teachers has been suggested as one option for raising the quality and status of teaching and the early childhood profession.

The cultural-historical context of early childhood education in New Zealand

Early childhood services in *Aotearoa* New Zealand are primarily community-based and cater for children from infancy to school entry, usually at age 5. With separate curricula, qualifications and histories, there are few links between the early childhood and primary sectors. Currently, licensed and chartered early childhood services are responsible to the Ministry of Education. These services include sessional kindergartens, play-centres (parent co-operatives), childcare, Ngā Kohanga Reo (Maori immersion centres), Pacific early childhood centres, co-ordinated family daycare and the correspondence school early childhood service.

The integration of care and education occurred when responsibility for childcare services was transferred from the Department of Social Welfare to the Department of Education in 1986. In 1988, the Working Group on Early Childhood Care and Education (Department of Education, 1988) proposed that the early childhood sector would have equal status with other education sectors. A change of government interfered substantially with this goal and the 1990s witnessed a 'marginalized and often divided early childhood sector' (May, 1999: 19) as the national government's market-led policies influenced developments in the sector.

Despite tensions resulting from the downsizing of the proposed reforms, the 1990s were marked by a growing sense of professionalism, associated with the implementation of an early childhood curriculum and the growth of a postgraduate research culture. While tensions between market-driven policies and the new professionalism remained, the growth of academic and professional debate generated a culture of inquiry that promoted a focus on quality. At the beginning of the twenty-first century, a change of government provided the policy context to support the focus on quality early childhood education (ECE). The most visible indicator of this emphasis is the ten-year Strategic Plan for Early Childhood, *Pathways to the Future: Nga huarahi aratiki* (Ministry of Education, 2002), which establishes core goals and strategies for the sector. Three core goals are identified:

* to increase participation in quality ECE services;
* to improve quality of ECE services;
* to promote collaborative relationships.

Policy directions associated with these goals include: increased qualification requirements, the implementation of teacher registration, the provision of 20 'free' hours ECE, provision of equity funding and the establishment of research-based Centres of Innovation. Strategies include a specific focus on building a sector that is responsive to the needs of Maori (indigenous New Zealanders) and Pasifika (Pacific Island) peoples.

A consultative approach has characterised development of both the early childhood curriculum and the strategic plan. Widespread consultation with the sector culminated in an innovative bicultural curriculum, *Te Whāriki* (Ministry of Education, 1996a) that has received strong support from practitioners. An anomaly in the current Labour government's goals for early childhood seems likely to maintain tensions in the sector for the foreseeable future, despite government support for quality education. On one hand, there is a liberal, inclusive view of education, encapsulated in the statements regarding quality and diversity; on the other hand, there is a tighter outcomes-focused view of policy analysis and implementation (Scrivens, 2002).

Conceptualisations of learning and pedagogy in New Zealand

A long-standing tradition of informal play-based programmes has influenced the implementation of *Te Whāriki*. In this context, it has not been easy for educators to appreciate the complexity of the *Te Whāriki* curriculum, or to take the more proactive teaching role envisaged by its sociocultural philosophy.

Te Whāriki draws upon a variety of theoretical perspectives but increasingly its sociocultural underpinnings have been stressed in academic debate. Anne Smith (1998), in the fourth edition of her highly influential textbook *Understanding Children's Development: A New Zealand Perspective*, introduced student teachers and practitioners to the principles and language of sociocultural theory, with particular attention to the roles of adults and learners within a relationships model. Other influences were congruence with relationships-based Maori pedagogy (Bishop and Glynn, 1999), and interest in the Italian Reggio Emilia programmes and project learning.

Most contemporary research on learning and pedagogy in New Zealand has adopted small-scale qualitative methodologies that accord with sociocultural perspectives. An exception is the longitudinal Competent Children project, conducted by the New Zealand Council for Educational Research, which has tracked the effects of families and early childhood education on children's competencies at school. Wylie (2001) identified the ECE quality factors that were most clearly associated with competencies as:

- the environment is print-saturated;
- ECE staff are responsive to children;
- ECE staff join children's play;
- ECE staff ask open-ended questions.

The most recent report on the cohort at age 16 points to the lasting effect of quality early childhood education (Hodgen, 2007). The visibility of adult–child interactions in the ECE quality factors is consistent with sociocultural principles. However, the sector cannot be overly complacent about the Competent Children findings. The sample was slanted towards upper socioeconomic levels, did not include Kohanga Reo and only a few Pasifika centres participated. This qualification suggests there could still be much to learn about a pedagogy that is responsive to social and cultural contexts.

The nature of knowledge in early years settings in New Zealand

Te Whāriki's view of the child as a 'competent learner and communicator' reflects a credit view of the child that is guiding current approaches to programming and assessment. The four central principles of *Te Whāriki* support a holistic curriculum philosophy:

Empowerment	*Whakamana*
Holistic development	*Kotahitanga*
Family and community	*Whanau tangata*
Relationships	*Nga hononga*

Whāriki or 'mat' signifies the weaving of the principles, strands and goals that comprise the curriculum. The five strands – well-being, belonging, contribution, communication and exploration – are considered essential areas for learning and development. The goals within each strand highlight ways in which educators can support children rather than specific skills or content areas. The *whāriki* metaphor also encompasses the diverse peoples, philosophies and services that participate in early education.

The holistic approach to curriculum planning has melded with sociocultural principles and the project approach to promote interests-based programming. However, the strong free-play tradition of New Zealand's early childhood programmes has meant that practitioners have been slow to move away from a narrow interpretation of 'interests' as children's self-selection of activities to the stronger sense of interests reflected in project approaches. Projects involve collaborative planning for sustained learning experiences around shared interests in the sociocultural contexts of home, community and centre. Theoretically, project learning should fit well with the *Te Whāriki* principles, but without this deeper understanding of sociocultural principles a *Te Whāriki* programme may look little different from programmes planned under a developmental philosophy (Meade, 2000).

A further issue relates to the place of content learning in the early childhood curriculum and links with the learning areas of the New Zealand Curriculum in primary schools. Concern about downward pressure from primary schools has created nervousness in the sector about acknowledging content learning in an early childhood curriculum. An official pressure for greater continuity between sectors was signalled when the Ministry of Education highlighted literacy and numeracy in the early years through a multi-media campaign aimed at families, and early childhood centres. Promising results from a literacy professional development programme have strengthened interest in the significance of literacy learning prior to school entry for literacy instruction at school. Based on the sociocultural premise that children's early literacy meanings are embedded in the literacy practices of homes and communities, the *Picking Up the Pace* programme (Phillips et al., 2001) worked with early childhood and primary teachers to promote understanding of a co-constructive model of literacy learning.

Postgraduate research from a sociocultural perspective has brought a new dimension to the subject content debate. Jordan (see Chapter 3), Hedges (2002) and Prince (2007) have identified children's interest in content learning, which has challenged their teachers both to upskill their own subject content knowledge and to value community-based 'funds of knowledge' (Gonzalez et al., 2005). The increasing understanding of this sociocultural conception of knowledge in the early childhood sector, together with the 2007 launch of the revised New Zealand Curriculum for schools which proposes key competencies that align more clearly with *Te Whāriki* strands, may help to alleviate early childhood concerns about the prescriptive nature of content learning (see also Chapter 8).

Assessment in early years settings in New Zealand

There has been a limited tradition of assessment in ECE and a 1993 survey of assessment practices found that assessment procedures tended to be problem-oriented (Wilks, 1993). This deficit approach to assessment has been challenged by learning story assessment (Carr, 2001a) which focuses on the child as a learner in specific contexts rather than on achievement objectives and skills. Other practices include the use of portfolios and documentation of children's experiences. These credit approaches are consistent with *Te Whāriki*'s focus on the 'rich child'. The release of early childhood assessment exemplars (developed by Carr and her team) (Ministry of Education,

2005) and associated Ministry-funded professional development have promoted learning stories as a dominant assessment approach in centres.

At school entry, usually at age 5, children are assessed with the School Entry Assessment (SEA) kit (Ministry of Education, 1997). The SEA comprises three performance-based tasks designed to assess concepts about print, story retelling skills, and numeracy skills and concepts. At 6 years a diagnostic net for literacy skills is used to identify children requiring Reading Recovery tuition. To date there has been no move to establish mandatory standards-based assessment for the first years of school, as occurs with older children. Despite this greater flexibility in the early school years, there is little consistency between early childhood and primary assessment approaches.

Evaluation and quality in early years settings in New Zealand

The Education Review Office (ERO) has responsibility for monitoring the standards of early childhood services. Licensing regulations and the Statement of Desirable Principles and Practices (DOPS) are two mechanisms for monitoring quality assurance, but these are usually assumed to constitute minimum standards. Programme evaluation within the holistic curriculum framework of *Te Whāriki* has created considerable challenges for practitioners. The flexibility of *Te Whāriki* can lead to interpretations of quality that are incompatible with its principles (Cullen, 1996).

To assist practitioners to engage in reflective practice, *The Quality Journey* (Ministry of Education, 1997) was developed as a resource for all services. *The Quality Journey* extends concepts and ideas in the DOPs and *Te Whāriki*, and provides a framework for a self-review process. A further publication, *Quality in Action*, has the 'objective of encouraging management and educators to use their professional judgement about the best way to implement the DOPs' (Ministry of Education, 1998: 6). *Ngā Arohaehae Whai Hua. Self-review Guidelines for Early Childhood Education* (Ministry of Education, 2006) provides guidelines for internal reviews by teachers and services that incorporate NZ pedagogical research. As with *Te Whāriki*, these directions, while encouraging professionalism and diversity, place heavy demands on the knowledge base and professional skills of practitioners.

The teacher–researchers in the Ministry-funded Centres of Innovation have documented innovative teaching and learning using the *Te Whāriki* curriculum (Meade, 2007), however there is still a need for research that considers macro and micro factors that influence teachers' implementation of *Te Whāriki* (Hedges and Nuttall, 2008).

Conclusion

Against this cross-national background, the country authors in Chapters 2–13 explore issues that are grounded in specific contexts, but which raise theoretical and practical issues at a cross-national level. The theoretical terms used by country authors (e.g. 'activity theory', 'sociocultural theory') have been retained, reflecting the diverse theoretical strands of post-Vygotskian and post-structuralist research. In the concluding chapter the editors use the umbrella term 'sociocultural-historical' to consider outcomes of sociocultural-historical research in the early years, synthesise debate surrounding the four main themes, and highlight future directions for policy, research and practice. The book concludes with a set of propositions for quality early years education derived from the research evidence debated by contributing authors.

PART 1

CONCEPTUALISATIONS OF LEARNING AND PEDAGOGY IN EARLY YEARS SETTINGS

CHAPTER 2

DEVELOPING A PEDAGOGY OF PLAY

Elizabeth Wood

Introduction

One of the fundamental principles in early childhood education is the importance of play to children's learning and development. The commitment to play can be traced through theory and ideology into early childhood programmes in many different countries (Saracho and Spodek, 2002; Wood and Attfield, 2005). While there is substantial evidence on *learning* through play, there has been less evidence on *teaching* through play. Linking play and pedagogy has long been a contentious area, because of the ideological commitment to free play and free choice (Wood, 2008). However, contemporary theoretical and policy changes have shifted the focus to better understanding the distinctive purposes and nature of play in education settings, and the role of adults in planning for play and playfulness in child-initiated or teacher-directed activities. The aim of this chapter is to examine the pedagogy of play, which is defined broadly as the ways in which early childhood professionals make provision for play and playful approaches to learning and teaching, how they design play/learning environments, and all the pedagogical decisions, techniques and strategies they use to support or enhance learning and teaching through play. This definition can also be extended to include home-based pedagogies of play, and the ways in which children act as playful pedagogues in their self-initiated activities. The main focus in this chapter is on play in early childhood settings that provide care and education (birth to age 7). Three key themes are addressed: the influence of national curriculum policies in the United Kingdom, the validation for a pedagogy of play in a range of contexts (home, preschool and school), critical issues on play in theory and in practice, and future directions in research and scholarship.

Policy contexts

The UK education policy context, outlined in Chapter 1, reflects ongoing concerns with providing guidance on curriculum content, planning and assessment, improving the quality and effectiveness of provision, and developing 'joined-up' provision and services for children and their families. The Early Years Foundation Stage in England (DfEE/QCA, 2000) was broadly welcomed by the early childhood community because of the emphasis placed on the role and value of play in supporting learning at home and in educational settings. This framework was subsequently revised to include children from birth to 5 (DfES, 2007a), and was aligned with wider social policy issues in *Every Child Matters* (DfES, 2004a and b). The curriculum guidance documents articulate the principles that underpin pedagogy, curriculum and assessment with an emphasis on well-planned experiences based on children's spontaneous play (both indoors and outdoors); allowing time for children to become engrossed in their play, and to create and solve problems; engagement between children and adults, and provision of a wide range of creative and imaginative activities to stimulate learning and development. The role of the practitioner includes:

- planning and resourcing challenging learning environments;
- supporting children's learning through planned and spontaneous play activities;
- extending and developing children's language and communication in their play;
- observing and assessing children's learning through play;
- ensuring continuity and progression.

Good quality play is linked to positive learning outcomes in the cognitive, emotional, social and psycho-motor domains, and in the six areas of learning. A commitment to play and talk for Reception children (age 4–5) in the first year at school is stated in both the Literacy and Numeracy Strategies (see Chapter 1). The Foundation Phase in Wales, which is being rolled out across the country from 2008, extends continuity in the commitment to play as a key approach to learning across ages 3–7 (ACCAC, 2004).

There are common principles in UK policy frameworks that endorse a combination of adult-directed and child-initiated activities, including free and structured play. Validation for integrated pedagogical approaches can be found in play scholarship (Wood, 2008) and in the highly influential government-funded study on Effective Provision for Preschool Education (EPPE) (www.ioe.ac.uk/projects/eppe). This large-scale longitudinal study has provided detailed evidence of the impact of pre-school education and family background on children's development. EPPE has demonstrated links between higher quality provision and better child outcomes and explored the specific pedagogical actions that link play with positive learning outcomes (Sylva et al., 2007). In the related study on Researching Effective Pedagogy in the Early Years (REPEY) (Siraj-Blatchford, Sylva, Muttock et al., 2002) the authors distinguish between pedagogical interactions (specific behaviours on the part of adults) and pedagogical framing (the behind-the-scenes aspects of pedagogy which include planning, resources and routines). Their findings show that:

> The most effective (excellent) settings provide both and achieve a balance between the opportunities provided for children to benefit from teacher-initiated group work and the provision of freely chosen yet potentially instructive play activities. (2002: 43)

Indicators of effective pedagogy include opportunities for co-construction between children and adults, including 'sustained shared thinking', joint involvement in child- and adult-initiated activities and informed interactions in children's self-initiated and free-play activities. The practitioner's role is conceptualised as proactive in creating play/learning environments, as well as responsive to children's choices, interests and patterns of learning.

These pedagogical recommendations are informed by sociocultural theories, which also underpin contemporary early childhood curriculum models; for example *Te Whāriki* in New Zealand (Ministry of Education, 1996a), First Steps (Education Department of Western Australia, 1994), Developmentally Appropriate Curriculum (Bredekamp and Copple, 1997; Krogh and Slentz, 2001) and Reggio Emilia (Rinaldi, 2006). A consistent feature of these models is that learning through play is not left to chance, but is sustained through complex reciprocal and responsive relationships, and is situated in activities that are socially constructed and mediated. While children's interests remain central to curriculum planning, the subject disciplines enrich and extend children's learning. Although contemporary curriculum models endorse play within integrated pedagogical approaches, achieving good quality play in practice remains a considerable challenge, particularly in the UK where teachers face competing demands for accountability, performance and achievement, and competing notions of what constitutes effective teaching and learning (Wood, 2007, 2008). The next section examines play in theory and practice and reviews some of the key studies that support a pedagogy of play, as well as those that argue for more critical engagement with the play ethos.

Play in theory and practice

The commitment to play in early childhood is both challenged and reinforced by theory and research evidence, and is reflected in the diversity in play scholarship (Johnson et al., 2005; Sutton-Smith, 1997). Theoretically there has been a shift away from experimental studies rooted in developmental psychology towards broader theoretical and methodological frameworks for researching and understanding play. Contemporary studies have adopted a range of orientations, drawing on post-structural, feminist and critical theories (Blaise, 2005; Yelland, 2005) and sociocultural theories (Broadhead, 2004; Kalliala, 2006). Because the term 'play' encompasses many different activities, research studies have focused on different types of play, different aspects of play behaviours, the influence of contexts on play and interactions in communities or groups of players. There is substantial evidence that through play children demonstrate improved verbal communication, high levels of social and interaction skills, creative use of play materials, imaginative and divergent thinking skills and problem-solving capabilities (Wood and Attfield, 2005). Play and playful forms of activity potentially lead towards increasingly complex forms of knowledge, skills and understanding, particularly in the cognitive and social domains.

In the context of practice, research evidence shows that play is problematic, particularly beyond the preschool phase. In a collaborative study with nine Reception class teachers in England, Bennett et al. (1997) found that play was limited in frequency, duration and quality, with adults adopting a predominantly non-interventionist approach. Good quality learning outcomes were not always achieved, and progression in learning through play was difficult to sustain. The teachers identified instances where they had over- or under-estimated children's competencies (social, cognitive and physical-manipulative). In the episodes that did not provide good-quality learning experiences, the children were frustrated, struggling, lacking a focus or messing about. In more successful play activities children were purposefully engaged and the teachers' intentions were realised, at least in part.

By acting as co-participants in the study, the teachers reconsidered their role in play. They agreed on the importance of supportive frameworks for developing and assessing children's skills as players and learners, while guarding against too much planning and prescription. Where children followed their own interests and agendas, the teachers realised the need to understand the meaning of play in children's own terms, rather than in relation to predetermined learning objectives. Thus a key pedagogical change was that play provides opportunities for teaching and learning. This was not an argument for using play solely for achieving predetermined outcomes, or privileging teachers' rather than children's intentions. Rather, the teachers recognised the importance of understanding children's patterns of learning and interaction which could inform their pedagogy and curriculum planning. In particular, they realised that children need more time to develop sustained bouts of play, and to return to their own themes and ongoing interests. Broadhead's (2004) study of children's social and co-operative skills also reinforces the importance of allowing time for play activities (especially role-play) to develop in complexity and challenge in order to support progression in play.

MacNaughton (2000a) also highlights the importance of evidence-based research in informing professional change. Using a feminist post-structural stance, MacNaughton challenged the theoretical hegemony of developmentally appropriate practice in early childhood curricula specifically relating to gendered preferences in play activities and gendered patterns of play. In an action research study with Australian teachers, it became evident that many teaching practices, as well as free play activities, influenced the gendering and stereotyping of children's identities. For example, boys and girls took an active part in the construction of gender: they regularly chose to play in different areas, and they controlled the space they used in different ways. These practices were challenged and changed through a process of collaborative professional development, resulting in practical guidance on reconceptualising early childhood pedagogies in relation to considerations about equality. In a similar study with teachers in a kindergarten in the United States, Blaise (2005) examined the ways in which young children understand gender discourses and access them in order to construct and regulate gender in their everyday lives. Play activities provided particularly powerful contexts in which children could express or contest gender discourses and roles. Their choices and play preferences were related to the ways in which they positioned themselves in terms of relative power, and the power-effects of those choices. These studies revealed possibilities for new readings of children's identities and cultures and for a deeper understanding of knowledge–power relations between children, and between children and adults. Looking at play through these theoretical lenses demonstrates that play is not simply the child's world, but reflects children's understanding and interpretations of the complex social and cultural worlds they inhabit.

Making role-play real

In spite of the many positive endorsements for play, the benefits are not universally shared across all children, and play is not always a natural or spontaneous activity in children's home and community cultures. In 2006–7 I led an action research study in a large urban primary school in Wales, with a focus on developing a whole-school approach to play, building on the Foundation Phase and ensuring continuity through to Key Stage 2. The school community was very diverse: 87% of the children came from minority ethnic groups, ranging from established second- and third-generation British Asian families, to newly arrived economic migrants from Eastern Europe, and refugees from countries virtually destroyed by civil wars and natural disasters. Around 30 community languages were spoken in the school, with language support assistants working alongside learning support assistants and teachers. In the two Year 1 classes (age 5–6) the team decided to focus on improving the quality of role-play. They were concerned about progression in children's social and communicative skills, particularly for children with English as an additional language. The adults were observing solitary and parallel play, rather than social and co-operative play, with little imaginative interaction, and little evidence of the development of sustained imaginative play. They questioned whether the children were progressing in their play, and whether the role-play provision was appropriate for the children's interests and home/community experiences. The team decided on the theme of the role-play area, with links to the learning outcomes in the curriculum, and put a great deal of energy into planning and preparing resources, and setting up the area ready for the children to use. They also planned related activities to stimulate play (for example by creating a 'garden centre', providing real plants, seeds and related equipment, and modelling buying and selling activities).

Observations were undertaken of children using the role-play area, followed by research conversations within the team, and with myself as co-researcher. I also carried out joint observations with the teachers, which enabled us to talk through events, problems and dilemmas as they arose. The garden centre theme proved to be less successful than the teachers had hoped, although the children did enjoy the tactile play in the wet soil, for planting seeds and filling containers. Children showed little interest in buying and selling activities, or in further developing the theme. The potential for co-operative play depended on the abilities (especially in language and communication) and dispositions of the players. Good language and imagination were observed in child-initiated play where children developed their own interests and agendas. The quieter children were sometimes pushed out of the role-play area by those who were more domineering, which narrowed the potential for the more skilled children to act as co-players. By reflecting on their observations, and discussing possible alternative approaches, the team focused on how they might make role-play more 'real', drawing on children's home- and community-based knowledge and experiences. They decided on the following actions as a result of their research:

1   Children should be allowed to move the role-play in their own direction rather than focusing solely on how the teachers initially planned the area to be used.
2   Adults can act as co-players to model skills with less confident children, especially in communication and language.
3   Making role-play more 'real' to the children involves taking account of their interests, and home and community experiences. The stimulus for role-play needs to be meaningful to the children, and located in the community so that a visit could take place prior to setting up the role-play area.
4   In order to create more meaningful play, children should be involved in planning and developing the role-play areas.

Challenging the concept of the 'universal child'

Further research conversations with the Foundation Phase team revealed their concerns about the different starting points of the children, which reflected their prior experiences, home values and cultures, varied child-rearing practices, parents' orientations to the education system, and their expectations of schooling. In addition, their theoretical knowledge of child development did not serve them well in such a culturally diverse community, and they sought the help of parents and the language support assistants in developing more culturally situated understandings of home and community practices. One teacher remarked that many children starting in the nursery at age 3 were 'under the radar' of the learning objectives in the Foundation Phase. For some children, the freedom and flexibility enshrined in a 'free play/free choice' environment was unfamiliar and difficult to negotiate without support and guidance from the adults. This research underlines the importance of challenging dominant views of the 'universal child', looking more closely at cultural differences and orientations to play, and considering the culturally constituted child (Kuschner, 2007).

Although the findings from EPPE and REPEY reinforce the educational aims for play, the emphasis is on 'freely chosen yet potentially instructive play activities' and 'planned and purposeful play', which raises a number of questions and potential dilemmas. As Kuschner (2007) argues, teachers and practitioners strive to constrain and manage the unpredictability of play that is truly free, and aim instead to engineer children's play choices, activities and behaviours in ways that promote educational outcomes. Thus they are working constantly with pedagogical challenges and dilemmas. For example, how do practitioners maintain a balance between intentional and responsive planning? This question becomes more pertinent in the Reception year (age 4–5) and beyond as there are competing imperatives from other curriculum priorities (notably achieving targets in literacy and numeracy). Which children take responsibility for planning, how do they go about this, and whose interests and needs lead or dominate play? If play is to be purposeful, then whose purposes are privileged, and whose purposes are being served: those of the child, the practitioner or the curriculum?

The foregoing studies indicate that a more secure pedagogy of play needs to be based on detailed theoretical understanding of cultural differences and variations in home-based child-rearing practices, and in orientations to schooling. In addition, practitioners need a more critical understanding of the meaning of play activities to children, the cultural reproduction of power relations in society, the scaffolding strategies embedded in child–child and adult–child interactions, and how the curriculum can be planned in order to combine teacher-directed and child-initiated activities. These integrated approaches require high levels of pedagogical knowledge and skills, flexibility in curriculum planning and the ability to use evidence from observation to inform cycles of planning, assessment and evaluation. Further conceptual advances can be facilitated through sociocultural and activity theories, which propose that play is a social practice and is situated in communities of practice. Learning is socially mediated and constructed as children participate in shared and distributed practices that are based on combining their everyday 'real-world' knowledge with play knowledge. Play activities may facilitate transfer of knowledge across different contexts, with the distinction that play occurs in imagined situations. Players become part of a discourse community in which meanings, intentions and activities are communicated through mediating means: imagined situations, tools, symbolic actions, scripts, roles and rules.

Play activities create transformational possibilities: children can reproduce and go beyond what is given. They transform ideas, materials, resources, media, actions and behaviour from one thing into something else, thereby creating novel meanings, interpretations and combinations. As children learn to negotiate different communities of practice, play provides a bridge between the possible (for example, acting as competent readers and writers) and the actual (being readers and writers). Play provides varied contexts in home and preschool settings for acquiring literacy and numeracy skills as well as acting out the social roles associated with those practices (Roskos and Christie, 2000; Worthington and Carruthers, 2003). Those social roles include media and information technologies and the varied ways in which children use these in their homes and communities (Marsh, 2005; Yelland, 2007). Playful uses of cultural tools and symbol systems are of immediate benefit to the child and provide an essential foundation for more 'formal' learning. The following vignette was recorded by advisory teacher Sheena Wright as part of a professional development module on play. It illustrates some of these theoretical issues, specifically a teacher's pedagogical framing of a role-play activity, the children's co-constructions of events and their use of cultural tools and symbols.

Fire station play

In a Year 1 class (age 5–6), the role-play area was a fire station, and was designed collaboratively by the children and the teacher. The children visited a fire station, and learnt about 'watches' – the rotating pattern of shifts for the firefighters. The role-play resources included:

Wellington boots, wet play clothes, walkie-talkies, two telephones, whiteboards, musical instruments, uniforms and helmets, fire engine, keyboard, tables and chairs, plastic bottles, selection of tools, torches, tubing and hoses, ladder, flashing blue light, wall charts showing rosters for the 'watches', coils of rope, notepads, tape recorded messages, large bricks, large notice board covered in children's paintings of fire engines, signs and symbols (for example, *Keep Clear, Emergency Exit, Fire Station, No Entry, Fire and Rescue Services*).

Extracts from the observation:

Number 98 – there's a fire down town.
What do we have to do today? [*using walkie-talkie to ask chief*]
See if the road is busy.
[*Playing the triangle and bells to alert to the fire. Writing on the whiteboards*]
Number two fire. House number two.
Yes but what street?
This is officer Bradley. Fire. Fire.
There's a baby locked upstairs.
Ssssss [*putting fire out*]
I'll get it …
Fire's gone. I've saved the house …
[*Back in the control centre the chief is reporting*]
OK, a robber has blown up the house.
We definitely need to go.
Go go go. We have to put our fire coats on 'cos we're the ones going in.
And a safety hat. [*selects one with a visor*]
Boss, am I late?
We need you on a job.
I need a safety thing [*harness*] so I don't fall over.
[*Fire bell ringing again*]
Dog stuck up a tree.
Job's not for me – I go at night times. I'm blue watch.
You need your oxygen so you can breathe.
[*Chief writing on the whiteboard*]
I can do a hundred sentences.

This episode reveals knowledge-in-use in a community of practice, with imaginary elements and symbolic exchanges. Shared meanings and identities are embedded within the play script and are dependent on the inter-subjective attunements of the players. The children draw on real-world knowledge about fire-fighting, gleaned from popular culture – the children's cartoon *Fireman Sam* and the (adult) television drama series *London's Burning*. This is combined with their play knowledge, showing new configurations and transformations in a co-constructed social context.

Broadhead (2004) provides further support for the efficacy of play in children's social development and cooperation. Her study investigated the language and interactions children use when being social and cooperative with peers in play contexts. The focus was on child-initiated, contextually situated activities rather than teacher–pupil interactions. Many of the recorded play episodes provided examples of social, emotional and intellectual challenge, with opportunities for building sequences of reciprocal action that were often initiated and sustained by the children. They used a wide range of skills in order to operate sociably and cooperatively, and to develop increasing complexity in their play:

- initiating and sustaining verbal interactions;
- initiating and responding to non-verbal interactions;
- interpretation of others' actions;
- problem-framing and problem-solving with different materials;
- successful entering of ongoing play;
- selecting and operating an appropriate role or degree of involvement;
- developing a shared sense of direction and goal orientation;
- empathising

Affordances for learning

The foregoing studies demonstrate how play activities create different 'affordances' for learning. The concept of affordances relates to the perceived and actual properties of objects and artefacts which determine their possible uses, including how they are understood and used by the learner, what challenges they present and what forms of participation are enabled by their use (Carr, 2000a). Such affordances are situated in how the play/learning environment is planned, the materials and resources that are available, what use is made of these by the children and the children's investment of existing knowledge, expertise and skills. Play resources and activities have different affordances and potential for flexibility, especially where children have the freedom to make their own novel combinations and transformations. Yelland (2007) argues that new technologies have brought additional dimensions and affordances to familiar objects and activities; for example dolls that can communicate their emotions, computer games that enable children to create and interact with characters and scripts, and art and design programmes that enable children to combine their own drawings with pre-made features, and to record and present their creations. Children do not always need resources and games to stimulate their play, but can spontaneously enter a state of playfulness. Playing with knowledge, words and ideas can be seen as a form of 'instant play'. The following vignettes were recorded in research conversations with children during a study of progression and continuity, and show subversive elements of children's playfulness, particularly their playful challenges to dominant power relations (Wood, 2001).

Word play

(Nicky [age 4.5 years] spent over an hour sorting buttons, using different criteria. She talked about sorting into pairs, and invited the adult to make pairs of buttons. Nicky joked about pairs of buttons, and pears that you eat. At the end of the session, she extended this word play further with the researcher).

Researcher: I remember you telling me something about pairs – you said there were pairs of buttons. Can you remember telling me that?
Nicky: Ya.
Researcher: What did you tell me? What's a pair?
Nicky: It's not an apple!

Nicky's joke involved communicating her understanding of the synonym pears/pairs, while at the same time playing with pears/pairs as 'not apples'. Nicky's knowledge was sufficiently secure that it could be played with, and she may have been playfully resisting adult questioning by not giving the expected or correct answer.

Playing with knowledge

(Liam [age 6] was a playful child who often changed [or subverted] the teacher's intentions for an activity):

Researcher: Liam, can you tell me some words that rhyme?
Liam: Hey diddle diddle the cat and the [*hesitates and changes word purposely*] middle. [laughs] ... And the fish went over the moon.

Both vignettes show the children's minds at play: like Nicky, Liam subverted the adult's expectations, an action that could be interpreted as 'naughty' or as imaginative and creative.

These vignettes show that play is varied and complex. From the perspective of sociocultural and activity theories, play needs to be understood in terms of relationships between individuals, their actions and interactions, the meanings they construct and communicate, and the contexts in which play occurs. In terms of the bigger picture of continuing play scholarship, the concluding section argues that developing a pedagogy of play is dependent on a more critical understanding of diversity within play activities, the characteristics of effective pedagogy in early childhood and, in particular, the role of the adult.

Future directions

The foregoing discussion has outlined positive validations, in policy, theory and practice, for developing a pedagogy of play. At the same time, play remains vulnerable to the top-down influences of prescriptive policy directives. So what further progress is needed for developing a more secure pedagogy of play? Vygotsky (1978) warned against the pedantic intellectualisation of play, but at the same time argued that only a profound internal analysis makes it possible to determine its role in young children's development. Contemporary play scholarship is providing the theoretical and methodological frameworks to facilitate such analyses, focusing on a range of contexts as well as the wider social and cultural influences on play. However, in order to develop more critical understanding of the cultural implications of play, greater emphasis needs to be placed on cultural repertoires of practice in homes, communities and educational settings.

Sociocultural theories provide a bridge between fundamentally cognitive and fundamentally social accounts of learning (Schoenfeld, 1999). At an individual level learning is interpretive, recursive and incremental, based on children constructing new knowledge and capacities on existing foundations. Learning is also socially centred and involves dynamic interrelationships between adults and children through joint involvement and social co-participation. Learning and development are channelled through sociocultural activity in which teachers and learners are interdependent. In play contexts the child may be the more (or differently) knowledgeable other, and may provide scaffolding strategies for peers. Play can be seen as a social practice that is distributed across a range of contexts and co-participants, and is influenced by the tools and symbol systems of community cultures, and the affordances that are situated within play/learning environments. Thus multiple perspectives are needed in future studies to examine the interactions between the child as player/learner and the child in the playing/learning contexts. Children are enculturated into play by adults and peers; indeed parents and family members tend to be the child's first co-players and provide a 'home-based' pedagogy of play. Further research might usefully explore home-based pedagogies and child-rearing practices, including what forms of play are encouraged and supported, and how these articulate with cultures of playing and learning in early childhood settings.

In contemporary curricula, there is broad international consensus that the subject disciplines offer powerful means for framing children's learning, as evidenced in the studies reviewed in this chapter. Children's interests are often driven by their fascination with the world of adults, and their motivation to act more knowledgeably and more competently. Future play scholarship should aim to provide empirical understanding of what counts as play in early childhood settings, and how different forms of play have implications for developing discipline-based knowledge, skills and understanding. Research in the field of play and literacy has been conducted from multiple perspectives, and has generated strong evidence of links between developing literacies and play activities (Marsh, 2005; Roskos and Christie, 2000). Similarly detailed and robust studies are needed across the subject disciplines in order to provide an evidence base that can inform policy and practice. Another significant gap in research is knowledge about how play progresses, how children's learning progresses through play within and beyond early childhood. Theories about progression in play also need to take account of the culturally constituted child, and the cultural conditions for learning and development in different contexts. These issues remain pressing in view of the need to improve transitions, continuity and progression across phases of schooling, and to ensure that practices are informed by the social justice agenda inscribed in *Every Child Matters* (DfES 2004a, 2004b) and other policy documents across the UK.

Finally, one of the key themes to emerge from recent studies is the importance of professional knowledge and expertise in early childhood specialists. Teachers and practitioners have a strategic role in planning for play, using playful pedagogical approaches in adult- and child-initiated activities, and engaging with children on their terms and with respect for their meanings. Such pedagogical strategies create the conditions for combining intended learning outcomes with the possible outcomes that emerge from children's interests, engagement and participation. More empirical work is needed on the pedagogical knowledge and expertise that underpins these processes, particularly in relation to influencing policy developments and the design of professional development programmes for early childhood specialists. The twenty-first century holds much promise for developing a pedagogy of play that respects the ideological tradition, and provides a theoretically rigorous underpinning for creating unity between playing, learning and teaching. Finally, lifelong playing needs to be considered as inseparable from lifelong learning. We need to re-value our relationship with play as an essential dimension of human activity across the life-course, and as an infinite source of possibilities for learning and development.

Acknowledgements

With thanks to Sheena Wright for her permission to use the observations of fire station role-play, which she carried out as part of a module.

CHAPTER 3

SCAFFOLDING LEARNING AND CO-CONSTRUCTING UNDERSTANDINGS

Barbara Jordan

Introduction

The focus of this chapter is the work of teachers in four New Zealand early childhood centres as they improved their dialogues with children in support of scaffolding learning and thinking. Their journey led teachers and me to explore similarities and differences in their working definitions of scaffolding learning for children and of co-constructing understandings with them. Each centre's programme of action research involved the teaching team's joint analysis of their own best dialogues with children, enabling teachers to identify and critique their beliefs about children's learning, and especially their own role in this. Teachers identified that children were more empowered when interactions were co-constructive in comparison with the outcomes of scaffolding interactions.

Teachers found that they needed to conduct their own research on topics of the children's interest so that they knew the language and the concepts with which the children sometimes had more expertise than they did. Having developed their own content knowledge the teachers could then use their adult perspectives to pose challenging questions and suggest extending activities for further investigation. My dual role was as facilitator of each team's programme of professional development and as doctoral student.

Theoretical and research foundations of scaffolding learning for children and co-constructing understandings with them

Research in early childhood services demonstrates that staff beliefs are often based on developmental theory, and that their interactions with children tend to be of a superficial nature, seldom succeeding in tapping into children's thinking, let alone challenging and extending thinking through scaffolding learning (Athey, 1990; Meade, 1995; Nutbrown, 1994; Smith and Taylor, 2000). *Te Whāriki* (Ministry of Education, 1996a) (see Chapter 1 for details) has a sociocultural foundation, and its implementation requires teachers to rethink their planning and interaction strategies. The sociocultural paradigm involves both children and teachers working together towards the upper ends of their zones of proximal development (ZPDs), as they co-construct meanings in activities that involve higher order thinking (Vygotsky, 1926/1997, 1929b). Central to the practices of sociocultural theory as it has evolved in the context of early childhood education in New Zealand, is the development of children's dispositions for learning, in which teacher–child dialogues and interactions play a key role.

Dispositions to learn are defined as learning (or coping) strategies that have become habits of mind, tendencies to respond to, edit and select from, situations in certain ways (Carr, 2000b). Dweck and Leggett (1988) and Smiley and Dweck (1994) identified that by the age of 4 or 5 children have settled into one of two major dispositions that influence their approaches to learning; these are a disposition towards mastery of learning, or a disposition towards approval of their performance from others. These goal orientations are independent of ability and predicted understandings or emotions during failure. Children who are oriented towards learning goals (mastery) demonstrate a striving to continually increase their competence, relishing and striving to understand new and difficult situations. In the face of barriers these children persist, seeking the expertise and support of others in their view of a problem as solvable. On the other hand, children who seek approval from others tend to choose any easy option on offer, avoiding difficult tasks in order to maintain their appearance of competence by also avoiding negative judgements. Learning-oriented children maintain an even emotional keel when faced with difficulty, whereas performance-dependent children have few resources when they feel their performance is judged as lacking in some manner.

Te Whāriki (Ministry of Education, 1996a) provides ample evidence that the New Zealand early childhood sector has been encouraged to adopt an approach that supports the development of children's proclivity towards mastery learning. The principles of empowerment (*whakamana*), holistic development (*kotahitanga*), family and community (*whānau tangata*) and relationships (*ngā hononga*) demonstrate the document's sociocultural foundations; these are consistent with Dweck and her associates' concerns to support children in approaching learning with a disposition of mastery, rather than of performance. The strands, goals and learning outcomes developed from these principles are further indication of the expectations that learning for this age group (birth to 5) will be largely child-initiated and process-oriented and aimed at developing children who see themselves as capable learners (Jordan, 2003).

In furthering her work in developing *Te Whāriki* Carr (2000b) identified five domains of learning dispositions, all of which support children's mastery over performance orientations: taking an interest; being involved; persisting with difficulty or uncertainty; communicating with others; taking responsibility.

Research indicates that learning dispositions are strongly influenced by the cultural and social context of children's experiences (Carr, 2001a; Davies, 1990). Stipek and Byler (1997) discussed the influences on the development of children's learning orientations of contrasting teacher beliefs and teaching/learning programmes set up for children. Chak (2007) identified that preschool teachers and parents hold multidimensional views of the factors that contribute to curiosity and exploration in young children, which demonstrate their orientation to learning. In programmes based on the schooling, or transmission model, essentially a skills-based approach to programming, children learn through teacher-directed sequences of learning in didactic programmes, often reinforced with the completion of worksheets to practise skills. Bredekamp and Rosegrant (1992: 3) describe this model as the 'elementary error'. Subscription to such 'school-type' programmes in early childhood is based on the mistaken belief that the best preparation for children's later success in school is an early introduction to the formal activities characteristic of primary classrooms. Such programmes encourage the development of children's performance orientation towards learning; children are expected to follow instructions, thereby gaining the reward of praise and points for their efforts. In contrast, a teacher who believes in supporting children's mastery of learning will offer a programme of authentic activities based on children's interests and strengths. Teacher–child dialogues are central in all stages of the development of interest-based projects that honour both children's and teachers' interests and funds of knowledge (Gonzalez et al., 2005), at the same time supporting mastery learning.

Two terms that have been utilised in describing teacher–child dialogues and interactions are 'scaffolding' and 'co-construction'. The history of the research and theorising about learning for children and co-constructing understandings with them has led to some confusion in the literature, and teachers who exhibit a wide range of practices could all claim adherence to the scaffolding metaphor (Fleer, 1995; Rogoff, 1998).

Scaffolding learning

The role of the adult in supporting children's learning within their ZPDs is a crucial one. Wood et al. (1976) used the carpenter's metaphor of scaffolding to capture many aspects of adult support of children's efforts. In scaffolding the aim of the adult is to support the children in their efforts towards the level at which they are capable of working. In this process of graduated assistance (Greenfield, 1984) the adult or more expert peer gradually releases control to the child as she or he becomes more able to accept responsibility for task completion (Berk and Winsler, 1995; Bredekamp and Rosegrant, 1995).

The acceptance of Wood et al.'s (1976) conception of scaffolding as a metaphor for learning is itself contentious. Stone (1993) criticised scaffolding as being too mechanical a model, in that a scaffold is an inert support for a structure (the child) maintained by external forces (the adult) until further external forces (planning procedures, activities) are able to sufficiently build the structure that it is able to stand alone. Rogoff criticised the juxtapositioning of scaffolding and the zone of proximal development because of the weighting of control towards the adult in research on scaffolding: 'Scaffolding is a specific technique focusing on what experts provide for novices' (1998: 698).

Early research on scaffolding was characterised as a specific pattern of interaction that maintained the power and control with the adult as the tutor, providing challenges for children as the novices. These early studies in this area had a major focus on the mother–child dyad, investigating the mother's didactic performance in supporting her child's learning of a given task with a known outcome (Wood and Middleton, 1975; Wood et al., 1976). Given that these investigations usually also required the mother–child dyads to attend sessions in a clinical laboratory, the settings were contrived and outcomes therefore not necessarily generalisable. In most scaffolding research the adult had a specific end in mind, towards which the child was supported by an adult or by a more experienced peer.

Berk and Winsler (1995) developed a more generic list of the elements of scaffolding to include a focus on joint problem-solving and the development of inter-subjectivity. This conception of scaffolding included the 'engagement of children in an interesting and culturally meaningful, collaborative problem-solving activity [where] ... the two are jointly trying to reach a goal' (1995: 27).

> Inter-subjectivity creates a common ground for communication as each partner adjusts to the perspective of the other ... an essential element of scaffolding is that the participants in social interaction negotiate, or compromise, by constantly striving for a shared view of the situation – one that falls within the child's ZPD. (Berk and Winsler, 1995: 27–8)

Thus early childhood teachers have been introduced in print to the idea that scaffolding learning for children is an extension of Vygotsky's ideas of the ZPD as the zone in which learning occurs. However, Rogoff viewed scaffolding and working in the ZPD as serving different functions and being distinct in several ways:

> The zone of proximal development is not a characterisation of what the more expert does to the other. It is a way of describing an activity in which someone with greater expertise assists someone else (or participants in play stretch) to participate in socio-cultural activities in a way that exceeds what they could do otherwise. Sociocultural approaches to the study of experts assisting novices focus on examining how participants mutually contribute to learning, with attention to institutional, historical aspects of how the activity functions in the communities in question. (Rogolf, 1998: 699)

In this quote Rogoff's view of scaffolding is consistent with the original, teacher-directive one of Wood et al. (1976), in contrast with Berk and Winsler's (1995) elements that are more generic and do embrace a sociocultural perspective.

Co-constructing meanings

The term 'co-construction' emphasises the child as a powerful player in his/her own learning. The child as co-constructor provokes an image of the child as 'rich in potential, strong, powerful, competent, and, most of all, connected to adults and to other children' (Malaguzzi, 1993: 10). To co-construct is to construct with others. 'As a teaching strategy, co-construction refers to staff and children forming meaning and building knowledge about the world with each other. Staff and children co-construct their meanings and their knowledge' (MacNaughton and Williams, 1998: 177). Co-construction thus places emphasis on teachers and children together studying meanings in favour of acquiring facts. Studying meaning requires teachers and children to make sense of the world, interpreting and understanding activities and observations as they interact with each other.

In order to co-construct meaning and understanding, the teacher needs to become aware of what the child thinks and knows and understands, and to engage with the content of this body of knowledge. The child's own expertise is acknowledged as being as valid as the teacher's and is frequently more accurate and detailed when the topic under discussion is outside the adult's field of expertise but within the child's. Reciprocally, teachers need to learn to share and develop their own thinking about the topic under discussion with children, regardless of whether the adult or the child initiated the topic. Thus co-construction requires excellent skills of dialogue between teachers and children as well as a willingness to find out more content knowledge about the topic of the children's investigations.

Teacher–child dialogue empowering co-construction of meanings

While all types of teacher–child interaction, from child-initiated to teacher-directive, are relevant and appropriate at different times and for differing purposes, interest in this study was in a teacher's ability to operate at the most child-empowering level of co-constructed decision-making, when this is appropriate. If a teacher does not have the interactive skills to engage with children's understandings, or is unaware of the value to children's learning in doing so, then he or she is unlikely to be empowering children. It is during the child-empowering types of teacher–child interactions that differences between scaffolding and co-constructing learning become important. These differences emerged in the course of work with the teachers in the four case study centres.

Vignette 3.1: Scaffolding interactions

A teacher in a large community childcare centre in New Zealand is working around a table with 12 4-year-old children making muffins for their morning tea. Marion (the teacher) and the children have gathered together the one bowl and mixing utensils, a recipe and all the ingredients required, including eggs from their centre's own hen run. The bowl is passed around the circle giving each child a turn at contributing to the mixing of the various ingredients while Marion directs the mixing operations. Several of the children had accompanied Marion

(Continued)

(Continued)

to the local supermarket the previous day to purchase bran and brown sugar, an activity designed to extend the documented interests and strengths of 4-year-old Rachel. During the hour or so of the mixing several spontaneous interactions take place between pairs and small groups of the children, some of which Marion joins and many of which she misses. All within view are captured on the video camera, as requested by Marion herself.

Below is a transcription of a small section of the videotaped dialogue of Marion and 10–12 children as they engage in the joint activity of making muffins.

Marion: This is bran. Where do you think bran might come from, Rachel? Have a look at it.

Rachel: You have it on porridge.

Marion: Yeah, you can have it on porridge. Where do you think it might come from?

Jamie: Hey this is a mill? Seed.

Marion: Everybody have a wee look and see where it might come from. Does it look floury?

Peter: Yeh. I think it comes from flour.

Marion: Ah now you're getting onto it. And where does flour come from?

Philippa: Umm the beehive? [*confusion between flour and flower?*]

Marion: A beehive?

Philippa: The bee gets on the flowers and then the bee collects it.

Marion: Remember the story of the Little Red Hen?

Jamie: Oh, from the seed.

Marion: From the seed, from the wheat, that's right. They grind it and grind it and grind it. OK we need some bran in our muffins today. Now let's read what else we need. Some baking soda. What do we use baking soda for when we make something?

[...]

Marion: The eggs are from our chickens. So they are very special.

Jason: What's inside them?

Marion: What do you think might be inside them? Have you seen an egg inside?

Michelle: I have and it's a rusty bit in there.

Marion: A rusty bit. There's a clear bit, a white bit,

Jamie: ... and an orange bit.

Marion: That's right, an orange bit. A yolk. I'm going to let you guys have a crack at these today.

Throughout the dialogue Marion held the power. She read the recipe, which was in words and not pictures that would have supported the children's own interpretations; she controlled the measuring, the timing, each child's contribution, the topics of discussion, the baking, and even the eating of the product. Although this baking session was only one activity within an ongoing project, Marion was similarly in control of each activity.

On viewing the video of the muffin-making experience, the other teachers in Marion's team argued that she knew the children well, that she was developing intersubjectivity with the children, making links between current and previous activities and between their homes and the centre; the team believed that Marion was scaffolding children's learning. I agreed that this was the case, and yet I believed that there existed a level of shared understanding that Marion and the children had yet to reach.

In co-constructing meaning, issues of power and agency are important. Adults in our dominant society hold the power and agency; minority cultures and children can have them only if we allow it. It takes time to develop a community of learners (Konzal, 2001) in which the children know that they do really share the power and agency.

A model of intersubjectivity that makes sense for practitioners

It is likely that some degree of the intersubjectivity that is the core of co-construction will exist in even the most didactic of teaching situations, as well as in a free play situation, as teachers adjust their levels of explanation to the level of children's understandings. Co-construction depends on levels and amounts of shared understanding developed, and this depends on the metaphorical distance between participants and on the sharing of power between them. The following model of intersubjectivity (Figure 3.1) is a graphic representation of the qualitative difference between the minimal levels of shared understanding developed during either teacher-directed teaching or unassisted, child-directed play, and the much greater levels that develop when all parties are contributing to interactions through the sharing of power. The key features in this diagram are the sizes of the areas of intersubjectivity developed, representing the levels of shared understanding, and the distances from each participant to this area of understanding, representing the psychological distances between participants and the levels of power sharing. The perforated lines indicate that these are not solid boundaries and that they are open to input and influence from many sources.

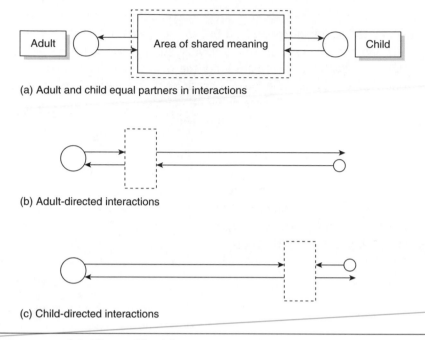

(a) Adult and child equal partners in interactions

(b) Adult-directed interactions

(c) Child-directed interactions

Figure 3.1   A model of intersubjectivity

(a) Adult and child equal partners in interactions

When full intersubjectivity is practised both contributors are considered to be experts in the topics of discussion. The child's understandings are as valid as the adult's and on many occasions the child will be acknowledged as more of an expert than the adult. Each participant listens to the other's ideas, contributes from their own and together they develop their unique 'shared meaning'. The child's voice is heard and valued and both participants make links between experiences, across time and distance. In this view learning outcomes would be described by Rogoff (1998) as a 'transformation of participation', as the learner takes new understandings from one context and is able to apply them into another context.

(b) Adult-directed interactions: scaffolding children's learning

The adult is in control of the activity and leads the discussions. While the topic of discussion and the planned activities may have arisen from the adult's observations of the child's interests, the child actually has little control and her/his thinking is heard only in the context of the adult's interest in extending it to meet the pre-set achievement objective. The adult is likely to be doing most of the organisation, with the child working hard to understand what is in the teacher's head and contributing wherever possible. There will be some links made between experiences, but the area of shared learning is less than it could be.

(c) Child-directed interactions

The child is in control of the activity and leads discussions and activity. In this situation the adult is observing the child, and supporting her/his activity and discussion with minimal input. The child's ideas might be heard by the adult, but the child is not being provided the opportunity of hearing what the adult thinks about this topic. The area of shared learning is again less than it could be.

Vignette 3.2: Co-constructed interactions

Having shared the transcript of her dialogues during the group muffin-making exercise with Marion, I introduced a draft of Figure 3.1 to her during her morning tea-break, immediately prior to her planned map-making exercise with her 4-year-old extension group. Marion's immediate response was to separate the group of 12 children into two groups. While one group of six children worked with another teacher to locate their homes on a map of their city, as had been planned for the whole group, Marion suggested to the other group that they draw a plan of the route from the centre to their home, so that she knew how to get there to 'Have a cup of tea with your Mum'. The children drew their maps independently, while Marion circulated to talk with them individually about their drawings.

Rachel: This is the dairy.
Marion: This is the dairy, so I go along the road here and straight along here, and is this another corner? Do I turn my car round there? What's this?
Rachel: My house.
Marion: Oh, that's your house. OK, so I go round the corner ... is this another corner here?
Rachel: Yes.
Marion: Whereabouts is your post box? Is it on the side of the road or is it ...?
Rachel: Here.
Marion: Oh, it's way up there. So Rachel's post box is way on the other side of her house.
Boy: You should have put your car park over there.
Rachel: That's not even on the right road.
[...]

(Continued)

(Continued)

Marion: I live at Farthing. Does anyone know how to get to Farthing?

Rachel: No because you haven't drawn a map!

Marion: Oh, OK. Have you been for a ride in the car with Mum and Dad out to Farthing, anybody?

Chorus: I have.

Marion: Oh yes, you and Jonah have been to the Farthing Show haven't you? Can you remember what you passed on the way?

Boy: We saw a plane with [*indecipherable*] ... And it was all rippling with smoke coming out.

Marion: So did you pass the airport?

Boy: And we saw the helicopter in the sky and it went up and down up and down up and down up and down.

Marion: What made it do that?

Boy: It just had to go up and down and it didn't crash. It just landed with its strike things on.

Marion: Did you stay and watch it?

Boy: When we went on the merry-go-round we saw it go up and down. ... We were in the front because we were in the boat. And I was the driver because there were two seats.

Marion: Oh, you were the driver because there were two seats.

During this dialogue with Marion the children's fingers and hands were busy describing the route to their home, beyond the words that were recorded. Marion developed shared meaning with each child through asking them to interpret what they had drawn and through being able to draw on her personal knowledge of the children's experiences and where they lived. The children interacted with each other, discussing their drawings and also influencing their neighbours' products. In this episode, the children were the experts in their knowledge of the route from the centre to their home and in interpreting their drawing, and Marion reinforced this in her interactions with them. Marion did not attempt to control the direction of the dialogue as it evolved from map drawing to car parking to going up and down in a helicopter and driving a boat on a merry-go-round. She listened to the children's ideas, responded contingently, and she utilised these ideas in the subsequent evolvement of a 'posting project'.

Marion changed her style of interacting with the children from one of what she called scaffolding, as demonstrated in her muffin-making episode in Vignette 3.1, to one of developing shared, or co-constructed meaning in Vignette 3.2. Even though Marion had instigated the topic of construction in the second vignette, the children engaged fully with her in co-constructing understandings and ideas. Together, Marion and I identified that the skills of scaffolding children's learning and of co-constructing learning with them are not mutually exclusive sets of skills. However, although there are skills that are common to both processes, there were also major differences between Marion's definitions of them. In scaffolding learning Marion's purpose of developing intersubjectivity seemed to be for her to know what the child understood about the topic chosen by her, so that she could support the child in learning more about the topic. The outcome of this learning was that the child understood some of what the teacher knew prior to the beginning of the exercise. In the muffin-making example Marion wanted the children to understand where flour came from and what was inside an egg, and she scaffolded children's talk to attempt to achieve these outcomes.

The skills of co-construction, on the other hand, were more relevant when the topic of discussion was open-ended, and the teacher and children were together establishing and extending their understandings of it. In their experience of making a map, it was the children who were the experts in knowing how to get to their homes and the features that were important to them on the way, and Marion supported them as they represented this understanding as a map.

Similarities and differences when scaffolding and co-constructing

Teachers in the four case study centres demonstrated the following interactions whether they were scaffolding learning *for*, or co-constructing learning *with* children:

- maintaining warm (trusting, reciprocal) relationships;
- questioning techniques (which are somewhat different under the scaffolding or the co-constructive model);
- using artefacts, such as photos of previous activities;
- encouraging children to work with each other;
- verbalising children's activities in support of their learning (reciprocal responding).

When scaffolding learning *for* children, teachers in the four case study centres demonstrated the following interactions:

- questioning techniques, with a particular knowledge outcome in the teacher's head;
- providing feedback on cognitive skills noticing children's small achievements and voicing this;
- demonstrating and modelling skills;
- identifying children's schema;
- supporting children's problem-solving and experimentation, with a predetermined outcome or task in the teacher's head;
- telling children specific knowledge facts, in the context of their interests, developing limited intersubjectivity with children.

When co-constructing learning *with* children, teachers in the four case study centres demonstrated the following interactions:

- co-constructing meanings, including hearing children and getting to know what they think;
- questioning techniques with no particular knowledge outcome in the teacher's head, aware of their interests, not interrupting them, allowing silences, following children's leads;
- making links in thinking across time and activities through revisiting children's ideas and interests, making links between many sources of ideas, knowing children really well;
- developing full, two-way intersubjectivity with children, through sharing their own ideas with children to extend their current interests, often as in-depth projects, entering the child's fantasy play, valuing and giving voice to children's activities, respectfully checking that a child would like the offered assistance.

Processes that support teachers in co-constructing understanding with children

At their centre level, teachers in the four case study centres identified key planning processes that contributed to the co-construction of learning in their centres. First, the teaching team articulated their planning processes, and in each centre in which a lasting change towards co-constructing understandings with children was made, this planning was a collaborative effort. Teachers shared their observations and planning with each other, with the parents and the children. A second requirement was support from their administrative group for professional development opportunities, including a commitment to and engagement in reflective dialogue. The third key to co-constructing with children was a willingness of their teachers to engage in their own research on topics of the children's interest. In their roles as senior semioticians or sense-makers (Vygotsky, 1929b) teachers need to learn about new subjects as children present with new special interests. At times such research can be done with the children, but the teachers found that they were themselves challenged to further understanding at their levels.

Transformation of participation for children of co-constructed projects

When children undergo what Rogoff called a 'transformation of participation' (1998: 690), their ways of behaving and thinking change. In this study children became full members of their communities of learning (Palinscar et al., 1993; Wenger, 1998) through accepting greater responsibility for their own learning. Their teachers reported that children experienced more involvement in collaborative inquiry with their peers and with their teachers as they were empowered to make decisions and to conduct their own experiments. A result was engagement in higher-order thinking through their authentic learning experiences, through ongoing projects and through being valued, with better links between their centre and home and better communication with both teachers and parents about topics of their interest. Teachers and children alike contributed from and extended their funds of knowledge and continuity of learning between centre and home.

In contrast to scaffolding, the language of co-construction of learning generally has no prescribed content outcomes (the teacher has no specific direction of the learning in mind); the focus is on developing shared meanings/intersubjectivity, and each participant contributing to the ongoing learning experiences from their own expertise and points of view. In early childhood programmes the development of evolving projects is considered an appropriate vehicle for supporting children's process skills of communicating their ideas, problem-solving and higher-order logical thinking and meaning-making (Dockett and Fleer, 1999; Forman, 1996), all of which contribute to their dispositions towards mastery learning. In practice, teachers who have access to the full range of skills move flexibly between those of scaffolding and those of co-constructing learning. The major issue here is one of the use of power (Lindfors, 1999). If children are to be empowered as equal contributors to learning situations, they need to be in an environment in which they learn that they have the power to make decisions about the direction of their learning.

Concluding comments

Is there a difference that matters between the scaffolding of learning for children and the co-construction of understandings with them? Given the definitions of 'scaffolding' and 'co-construction' developed in this chapter, the answer to this question is affirmative. When teachers consistently scaffold children's learning, they are supporting ongoing dependence on the teacher and children's dispositions towards performance and praise. Co-construction, encouraging children *and* teachers to contribute to developing understandings, is a strategy that develops children's mastery of learning. Teachers who are skilled in co-constructing with children are able to readily move between scaffolding and co-construction interactions, using strategies that support both their own and the children's funds of knowledge. Simmons et al. (2005) provided further evidence for the effectiveness of both co-construction and scaffolding learning in their three-year Centre of Innovation research. These researchers identified five 'teaching strategies that support complex and sustained learning', one of which they described as 'teachers mov[ing] intuitively between co-construction and scaffolding' (Simmons et al., 2005: 19). Research evidence has been provided in both Jordan's (2003) and Simmons et al.'s (2005) work that children engage in higher-order thinking through their involvement in authentic experiences that they valued because these are based on children's own interests and experiences in their communities of learning.

In Jordan's (2003) research, teachers were empowered to critique their philoso-phies of children's learning and their practices of implementing *Te Whāriki*, through their collaborative analysis of their own dialogues with children. As they embraced sociocultural theory teachers found they needed to listen to the children, developing intersubjectivity with them, and to develop their own content knowledge in the topics of children's special interests, as well as sharing and extending their own funds of knowledge. Planning and assessing collaboratively with children, their parents and with each other has implications for teachers' use of time, for resourcing and for ongo-ing professional development for teaching teams and for administrators at all levels.

CHAPTER 4

EXPLORING CRITICAL CONSTRUCTIVIST PERSPECTIVES ON CHILDREN'S LEARNING

Glenda MacNaughton

Introduction

Newborns enter a pre-existing world in which the objects, sounds, movements and smells that they meet have meaning. While they enter our world ignorant of these meanings, this rapidly changes and 'at birth the cultural past is, literally, thrust upon them' (Cole and Wertsch, 1996: 251). Yet, by as early as 4 years of age they have learnt the meanings of many of our cultural artefacts, to construct their own meanings in and through those artefacts and to manipulate meanings according to context.

In this chapter I will explore what Tom, a preschool child, had to say about a simple cultural artefact in his world and the gendered meanings embedded in it for him. Tom's stories arose in an 18-month Australian action research project in preschool services. In this project 12 Australian early childhood teachers and I documented preschool children's gendered play, talked with children about how they understood gender, and explored how gender equity is created in the classroom (see MacNaughton [2000a] for a detailed discussion of this project).

Tom by 4 years of age has learned that perfume bottles have cultural meaning and that those meanings are strongly linked to gender. What he has done with this knowledge is to construct different spaces in which he acts and thinks differently based on that knowledge. How did Tom achieve this complex space in which he could manage two meanings for his perfume bottle and in doing so create his own meanings for the cultural object that he held and talked with me about?

Introducing constructivists

For constructivists knowledge such as that which Tom has constructed is built through our experience of the world (Kincheloe, 2005). We can only imagine what might have happened when Tom first met a perfume bottle, touched it and interacted with it and what happened when he did the same with an aftershave bottle. But he has learnt through these interactions that perfume and aftershave bottles share enough in common for him to be able to 'fool' others through how he names a glass bottle that 'smells' nice.

Tom and the aftershave bottle

Tom is a 4-year-old Anglo-Australian boy who attends an early childhood programme in a predominantly Anglo-Australian middle-class suburban area of Melbourne. His mother is actively encouraging him to be non-sexist. His father is less certain about the need for this and about its impact on Tom.

Tom arrives at the centre clutching a small bottle with a gold top. He rushes over to where I am sitting and excitedly shows me his bottle. The conversation about the bottle unfolds like this:

Glenda: That looks interesting I wonder what it is?
 [Tom moves closer to me and he whispers to me]
Tom: It's a perfume bottle. Smell how lovely it is.
 [Tom offers me the bottle and I smell it]
 [Tom whispers to me]
Tom: Don't tell the other boys it's a perfume bottle. I'll tell them it's an aftershave bottle.
Glenda: Why would you do that?
 [Tom smiles at me]
Tom: You know.

I could certainly guess. Particularly when I combined this moment with a conversation we had had a couple of days previously. Then, Tom had told me that he didn't like being a boy because boys hurt other people and kill people lots. But, he didn't want anyone else to know.

Glenda: Whom can we tell about the perfume bottle?
Tom: Just us, I think.
Glenda: What about Carlie?
 [Carlie was Tom's teacher. She had an active gender equity programme and often encouraged Tom in his difference.]
Tom: Not today. Maybe, if ... *[fades]*. We might tell her later, then.

What did Tom experience that helped him to construct 'boy' as a person who 'hurts' and 'kills'? Piaget, father of the modern constructivists, might argue that it was through Tom's own direct experience of the world that this knowledge built. For Piaget, as for all constructivists, learning occurs as we as individuals interact with and adapt to our environment.

Children like Tom can do one of two things when they meet a boy who hits others. He can assimilate this experience into prior experiences of boys and if this has included boys hitting other people he can merely add it to his existing knowledge of boys. His knowledge is growing but in ways that do not disrupt or fundamentally alter his knowledge about boys. Or, if this is the first time Tom has seen a boy hit another person, he can accommodate (modify) his existing knowledge of boys and what they do in the light of his new experience. From this traditional Piagetian perspective on meaning construction we need the twin processes of assimilation and accommodation to generate knowledge.

As these processes occur within the individual, Piaget believed that we are capable of constructing our own knowledge (Piaget and Inhelder, 1969). Because Piaget believed that we construct our individual knowledge and meanings of the world through our explorations of it, he is often referred to as an individual constructivist.

Piaget would not be surprised to hear that Tom had given his own meanings to what it means to be a boy and that these meanings differed from those of other boys that Tom knew. For Tom, boys hit, like killing, don't like perfume bottles and do play with aftershave. This is not a common dictionary definition of what it means to be a boy. It is Tom's very own, individual meaning. It is not a classic dictionary definition of 'boy' nor is it a definition that you as an adult would be likely to produce.

However, Tom's definition of being a boy was problematic for Tom because he didn't fit within his own definition. He didn't hit, he didn't like killing and he did like perfume bottles. So, surely he couldn't be a boy? Rather than altering the meaning he created for being a boy, Tom had decided he didn't like being a boy. In doing so, he was beginning to construct a new meaning of who he was – a boy who was not really a boy. In Tom's world of individual meaning construction two sorts of boys existed – ones he didn't like and boys who weren't really boys.

So, if Tom is to build new meanings for being a boy that are more inclusive of himself and to engage in play using these, he will need to do this through his own activity. Tom's teacher would need to find materials that could interest and challenge Tom to rethink his sense of boys and what they do and he or she should allow Tom to solve the problem of different meanings for boys on his own. If the materials offered to him build on the twin processes of accommodation and assimilation then new knowledge will grow, new learning becomes possible and Tom will construct new meanings.

However, one of Piaget's closest theoretical 'relations', Lev Semenovich Vygotsky (1886–1934), would most likely disagree with this tactic. Vygotsky is often referred to as the father of the social constructivists because he gave much greater emphasis to the role of social contexts as drivers in our capacity to construct meaning, seeing 'development as participation in communities of practice' (Burman, 2008: 169).

For Vygotsky, social interactions and social experiences drive what children might learn and the processes through which they can learn (Crain, 2005). Specifically, cognitive development occurs as a result of collaboration between children and the more experienced others in their environment. Vygotsky believed that knowledge was constructed through 'collaborative cognitive activity' (Vygotsky, 1932: 16) and planned 'assisted discovery' (Berk and Winsler, 1995: 108) with more competent others.

Consequently, for Tom, the way to new meanings about being a boy and new possibilities in his learning as a boy would be in collaboration with others and through planned assisted discovery of new possibilities. Tom's teachers would need to work with Tom to challenge him to rethink his sense of boys and what they do. They could work with Tom to solve the problem of his different meanings for boys.

In contrast, Jürgen Habermas – a key thinker for critical constructivists – would argue that Tom will never be able to construct a 'true' sense of what it means to be a boy until the possibility of power in collaborative activity and assisted discovery is removed. Meaning construction for the critical constructivists is something that we do as individuals but it is always inseparable from our culture and the power relations embedded in our culture (Kincheloe, 2005; MacNaughton, 2005).

Critical constructivists

Hence, for critical constructivists, we have the capacity to construct meaning but those meanings are bounded by our culture and the meanings we construct most often reflect the meanings of those who have the most power within our culture to articulate and circulate meanings (Kincheloe, 2005).

Karl Marx captured the idea that individuals, culture, meaning and power are intimately connected and inseparable in his famous statement: 'Men make their own history but not under conditions of their own choosing'. To understand critical constructivism we can paraphrase this statement and say that: 'Children make their own meanings but not under conditions of their own choosing'. Instead, meanings are distorted, limited and silenced by the conditions in which meaning-making takes place. To illustrate, Tom can make his own meanings for being a boy but not under conditions in which he has chosen what is the normal and proper way to be a boy. Those conditions and understandings of boys were pre-existing at Tom's birth and he met them as he encountered the cultural artefacts and meanings of his particular culture – an Anglo-Australian, middle-class, late twentieth-century culture.

The conditions that most impact on children's learning they do not choose and I call them the conditions of power in what follows. I will now explore four conditions of power (ways of power) that impact on how children construct meaning and therefore on how children learn. I bring these four conditions of power to the fore using social and educational theory that has built from the critical 'isms' of feminism, feminist post-structuralism, postcolonialism and Marxism. The four conditions of power that the critical 'isms' emphasise in their analysis of the social world and the meanings we produce in it are these:

- Condition 1 – the power of pre-existing cultural imagery and cultural meanings
- Condition 2 – the power of expectations

- Condition 3 – the power of positions
- Condition 4 – the power of the marketplace.

Children enter a pre-existing world in which each of these conditions of power is already accomplished. They do not choose them and they do not choose to produce their learning within them. Yet children cannot escape producing meaning from within these conditions of power. It is for this reason that critical constructivists argue that we cannot produce any meaning we like. Our meanings are constrained and constructed in and through the dynamics of power.

Condition 1 – the power of pre-existing cultural imagery and cultural meanings

Children are born into a world with a history. For post-structuralists discourse (frameworks for giving meaning to the world) pre-exists each of us. We are born into an already discursive world in which cultural meanings are circulating and are constantly being sustained by cultural imagery and by cultural practices. In Foucault's terms these pre-existing discourses both normalise and regulate us (see MacNaughton, 2005). Through processes of normalisation and regulation we come to learn that certain ways of thinking and acting are natural, normal and preferred. These ways of thinking and acting arise at the intersections of gender, ethnicity, culture, language, social class and sexuality and our understandings and are always touched by these intersections (Ward and Robinson Wood, 2007; Reay 2007; Mellor and Epstein, 2007). We cannot be or think 'outside' of culture because its discourses and structures are pervasive.

For post-structuralists, children enter a pre-existing set of cultural meanings that are constantly reinforced through cultural imagery and cultural practices in ways that make some ways of thinking and being much more likely than others. Let's revisit Tom. Tom is constructing his meanings about being a boy. But they are intimately linked with and restricted to the conditions under which he has been able to access meanings and experiences about being a boy, especially by what is considered the normal way to be a boy.

Think about how possible it is for Tom to access a definition of being a boy that will enable him to include himself in it.

- How many images of boys loving perfume do you see?
- How many times will he be bought perfume as a gift?
- How often will his father wear perfume?
- How often will other boys around him come to kindergarten with a perfume bottle?
- How many times will he and other boys be bought guns/weapons as a gift?
- How often will other boys around him come to kindergarten with a gun?

What chance is there of Tom really constructing his own unique meaning of what it means to be a boy? How could Tom build a meaning for being a boy that ignores the dominant cultural images of boydom in his time? Could any child escape these images and remain untouched by them and the practices that are represented in and through them? Can any child construct meanings free from gender when gender never frees adults?

Tom didn't choose the particular cultural images and cultural practices about gender that are reinforced daily in his world. He didn't choose the conditions under which he learned about gender. But seeing and hearing from him how these conditions mediate his learning provokes me to ask:

- What are the pre-existing cultural images, meanings and practices that limit how young children learn?
- How might gender constrain the meanings circulating in our early childhood classrooms?
- What ways of being girls and boys are being normalised and regulated through the meanings circulating in our early childhood classrooms?

Condition 2 – the power of expectations

The second condition of power that touches young children's learning is the power of expectations that arises from the pre-existing social structures into which they are born. Social structures such as gender, 'race', class and ability prescribe and limit the possibilities for each of us from birth. Those of us who delimit our possibilities do so only by challenging the expectations of the structures into which we were born. Social structure refers to the 'underlying regularities, or patternings, in how people behave and in the relationships in which they stand with one another' (Giddens, 1989: 19), including the 'repetitions' (Giddens, 1989: 19) in how so many people relate to each other as male and female.

Social structures such as gender, class, 'race', ability and age are inescapable from birth (Burman, 2008; Macnaughton, 2008). The critical constructivists, drawing strongly on a lineage of Marxist thinking, argue that all of us, including children, construct meanings within these pre-existing social structures and that these structures place limits and expectations on how we should think and act (Darder, 2002; Livingstone, 2003).

Let's explore how gender structures work by revisiting Tom.

First some comments from 4-year-old girls in Tom's classroom. Their definitions of boys included the following:

- Boys they hurt you, they will kill you dead.
- Boys they knock your blocks down.
- Boys chase you and kill you.

Now listen to Sandra, another classmate of Tom's:

Glenda: I noticed in all the pictures I have taken of you playing in the sandpit you never seem to play with any of the boys. Why is that?

[*Sandra shrugs her shoulders, grimaces and then laughs. Her laughter indicated I should know why. She then said*:]

Sandra: 'Cos they are mean.
Glenda: How are they mean?
Sandra: They pinch your bottom, they pull your hair. [*Thinks for a bit*] ... they knock your blocks over.
Glenda: What do you think you can do about that?
Sandra: I don't like boys, they are not my friends.

Was it accidental that Tom's meanings about boys were shared by so many 4-year-old girls, or that the boys in the following moment of 'free play' with Barbie construct the meanings with her that they do?

Tom is pointing to the Olympic Barbie who is dressed in her tights and says to another boy, 'Take them off'. One of the boys starts stripping the Olympic Barbie. When the doll is naked Willie then grabs it and begins to kiss the Olympic Barbie. He then holds it up to Jamie's lips and makes loud kissing sounds. There are lots of giggles between the boys at this. One of the boys then says, 'Boobies, she's got boobies'. This is followed by lots of collective laughter from the boys. Willie then says to the research assistant, 'Heather look at this'. Heather is being invited by Willie to watch Tom press the naked Barbie's head to Jamie's lips. Jamie is being told by Willie to kiss the Barbie.

Can we reasonably believe that these meanings are merely discovered by Tom as a result of individual exploration?

Critical theorists would argue that Tom's meaning construction was not accidental, nor purely individual but fundamentally mediated in and through the social structures into which he was born. Feminists would emphasise that he was born into a culture where gender structures who we are, what we can reasonably do, and so how we should be. So Tom's meanings are mediated in and through these social structures of gender, class, 'race', age and ability. Cannella (2001), working from within postmodern and postcolonialist perspectives argues that adult/child categories create an ageism that privileges adults' meanings over those of children.

This will ensure that it is never Tom's definitions of being a boy that will enter the dictionary and be part of the pre-existing gender discourses that the next generation encounters. After all, his meaning is cute, amusing, mistaken – a child's meaning? How could we recast our meanings as adults about boys and subsume them to his?

The point of critical scholarship about meaning construction, whether it is postmodern, postcolonial or post-structuralist feminist, is to explore the effects of our position in the cultural structures we have created on the meanings and possibilities for ourselves we produce and reproduce (Cannella and Viruru, 2004) and to use this as a basis of social reform (Eckersley, 2004). In education, the point of critical constructivism is to explore the effects of cultural and structural positions on how and what children can and do know and learn (Darder, 2002) and to seek to challenge and to change those that work to oppress and discriminate (Kincheloe, 2005).

Moreover, the point is never to lose sight of how gender, 'race', class, etc. mediate learning. Indeed, the point is to ask how this meaning is made possible because of gender, 'race', class and the position of the child and the teacher within these structures. It is the feminists' concern with gender relations that reminds us to search for the effects of gender (MacNaughton, 2008). The Marxists' concern with class relations reminds us to search for the effects of class (Darder, 2002; Kincheloe, 2005). The postcolonialists' concern with 'race' relations reminds us to search for the effects of 'race' and ethnicity (Chambers and Curti, 1996) and to be alert to ongoing processes of colonisation and their effects in children's lives (Canella and Viruru, 2004). Without these reminders it is easy to ignore that where, when and into which family we were born fundamentally structures what knowledges we access, what experiences we have and therefore what meanings we give to our life.

The point for each of the critical 'isms' is to reflect on how they distort, privilege and silence meanings and to find ways to build teaching and learning relationships that make these distortions, silences and patterns of privilege less likely. For Habermas, as a critical Marxist, it is only once this occurs that we can find freedom and truth in our learning journey (Darder, 2002). For Foucault, as a post-structuralist, it is only once this occurs that we can understand why some meanings are produced and others are silenced and therefore begin work to bring the silenced and marginalised meanings to the centre (Foucault, 1982). For postcolonialists, this requires deep attention to what has been 'othered' and to the effects of the diaspora on what possibilities we can construct for ourselves (Ghandi, 1998). The effects of the diasporic are those effects of colonisation that caused and continue to cause the dispersal of people from their homelands. For feminists the centring of gender in all analysis of social possibilities, including learning, is essential if we are to avoid the gendered silences and patterns of privilege that have dominated the majority of Western theories of the child (Burman, 2008).

Drawing on the critical 'isms' to reflect on young children's learning raises the following questions about teaching and learning processes for early childhood educators:

- What relations of power have already been accomplished between teachers and children and between children and children that distort and silence some meanings and privilege others? What meanings compete in our classrooms for a privileged position?

- How do these impact on the meanings children construct in our classrooms?
- How do these impact on the meanings children choose to share or not in our classrooms?

Condition 3 – the power of positions

The basic premise of the third condition of power is that children construct meanings in situations in which power relations have already been accomplished and in which competing meanings vie for power. As you read the next story, consider what power teachers currently exercise because of their gender, 'race', socioeconomic and ability positions.

> In this story, Olivia, a persona doll that I sometimes work with in my research about how young children understand and construct gender, 'race' and class (MacNaughton, 2001), is given a blue badge for her birthday that has a '5' on it. She is so excited by the badge that she wears it to her preschool to show her friends. Her friends laugh at her and say it can't really be her badge because it's blue. We ask the children, 'Do you think that Olivia's friends are right?' The reply in unison from the eight children listening to the story is 'No'. Heather asks, 'Why?' 'Well, girls and boys can wear any colour they like' comes the response, once again in unison. It is clear that the children have been told this regularly by the staff. Heather then asks, 'Why do you think that Olivia's friends said what they did?' The response comes back, 'Because, well, pink's really for girls and blue is really for boys'.

This research moment reminds me how readily children learn to share those meanings with us we want to hear and raises many questions about how this third condition of power might be attended to by adults involved in young children's learning.

- To what extent do the power relationships that have already been accomplished between adults and children, and within that teachers and children, mediate what meanings children construct, and how and when they choose to share them with us?
- Have these children at 4 years of age already learned to silence some meanings and parrot others?
- To what extent do teacher–child relationships come between what a child might learn or share? How do the power relations embedded in teacher–child relationships mediate what a child in your classroom learns and what meanings they construct with you?

More interestingly, how did they come to construct an understanding that:

- you need to tell teachers what they want to hear;
- what the children really think and know about 'blue' and 'pink' is different from what the teachers know;
- their knowledge of blue and pink as children was so obviously right and therefore true.

As children learn to tame their ideas around adults they demonstrate how clearly they understand what adults have hidden. The power of position and the meanings are generated, accepted and therefore recirculated. Drawing on feminist post-structuralist perspectives, Walkerdine (2000) believed that as children learn to tame gendered discourses with adults we ignore the emotion and desire within children that are implicated in their ways of being gendered and their desires to maintain particular gender boundaries, such as those that Tom wants to maintain between his way of being a boy and that of other boys. Walkerdine argued that as we focus on learning in young children and how learning occurs we have established a 'cognitivism' (2000: 13) that ignores the place of emotion and sexuality in children's ways of being and thinking.

Can we make sense of young children's learning and what they choose to share with us as adults, as powerful people in their lives, if we ignore the irrational and emotional in their lives? Or if we ignore how we have placed ourselves in a privileged position over them as meaning-makers?

Condition 4 – the power of the marketplace

The fourth condition of power that it is impossible to escape is that children construct meanings within an increasingly globalised and commodified world in which increasingly narrow cultural meanings are being articulated and circulated. Building from the work of Karl Marx and the Frankfurt School in Germany, critical theorists (see Kincheloe, 2005) are interested in how capitalism in all its changing forms continues to produce 'domination, injustice and subjugation' (Gephart, 1999: 3) that distorts and restricts the knowledge that we construct. That influence begins when a newborn is thrust into a cultural present where globalised capital increasingly commodifies every aspect of social and cultural life. Children's entertainment and the toy industry is just one example of how global capital produces the material culture through which children construct their meanings.

Now, as in no time before, the cultural past is increasingly commodified and access to wealth buys you access to a very different set of cultural artefacts and cultural meanings from those you would access if you lived in poverty. Under these conditions, how can we believe that the knowledge children construct is separate from, innocent of and unmediated by global capital? Capitalism and the global marketplace are conditions of power children did not create but which fundamentally mediate their learning. Serious questions emerge that we should attend to when we are trying to make sense of young children's learning:

- What effect does the power of the marketplace have on the meanings that children can construct?
- Can children construct any meanings free from the effects of global capitalism and the commodification of the fashion, entertainment and lifestyle industries?
- What silences does the marketplace produce?

Furthermore, the ways in which the marketplace is shifting the possibilities for children's learning is intimately connected with the access that they have to new technologies (Hughes, 2005; Luke, 2000). For those children born into families where there is insufficient money to purchase what the marketplace offers, learning will be fundamentally different in content and processes from that of those children born into wealthy families.

Conclusion

If we are to understand knowledge production and what makes learning possible we must understand the conditions that limit it and how those conditions impact very specifically on the children that we work with. Critical theorists reject the idea that meaning, knowledge and, therefore, learning is a uniquely individual, value-free cognitive pursuit. Instead they believe that knowledge and thus learning is always social and always embodies ethics, values and politics (Foucault, 1982). It is always accomplished within a dynamic of power and the specific conditions that produce that dynamic will inevitably produce much of what is constructed and learned.

PART 2

THE NATURE OF KNOWLEDGE IN EARLY YEARS SETTINGS

CHAPTER 5

THE CO-CONSTRUCTION OF AN EARLY CHILDHOOD CURRICULUM

Angela Anning

Introduction

This chapter draws on a research and development project carried out by Angela Anning and Anne Edwards with early years practitioners working in education and care settings in the United Kingdom. The project aimed to create an informed community of practice among a group of practitioners through their involvement with action research. A significant outcome of the project was the enhanced professional knowledge embedded in the networks created between university-based researchers, local authority officers and practitioners. A second tangible outcome was a curriculum framework (with an emphasis on the starting points of literacy and numeracy) co-constructed by the project team and published within three local authority training/support systems as a set of materials called *Loving to Learn*. The chapter will focus on the processes by which the group confronted conflicts and combined professional knowledge developed from their cultural pasts and present communities of practice as educationalists, carers, local authority officers and researchers to create an innovative curriculum framework for birth-to-5-year-olds. Details of the methodology and curriculum model are to be found in *Promoting Children's Learning from Birth to Five: Developing the New Early Years Professional* (Second edition, Anning and Edwards, 2006).

Context

In Chapter 1 of this book there is an outline of the comprehensive reforms in early childhood services in the UK which have characterised social policy since New Labour assumed power in 1997. However, the historical baggage of the early childhood sector was carried forward into the new era. Traditionally in early childhood services the status of workers has been low, funding left to local authority discretion and market forces. Separate responsibility for care of under-5s was assigned to social services and education to education departments at both national and local levels. New Labour central government exhorted providers to 'join up' services and rationalise their delivery; but grassroots workers were given little time, training or financial support to operationalise the vision (Anning and Calder, 2008).

In the United States of America (Beatty, 1995) and the UK (Moss and Penn, 1996; Whitbread, 1972) preschool education and daycare have traditionally been dominated at grassroots level by women. The *Loving to Learn* project took place during a decade when female early years practitioners felt increasingly that their long-held beliefs, values and ways of being were under threat from male-dominated macro-level priorities. Male-dominated, 'disembedded', school/institutional forms of learning figured explicitly in policy documents on early childhood services emanating from the Department for Education and Employment (DfEE): the mind of the child was their focus. For example, the aim of nursery education was defined as 'that all children should begin school with a head start in literacy, numeracy and behaviour, ready to learn and make the most of primary education' (DfEE, 1997: 14–16).

During the 1980s and 1990s preschool educationalists in the UK were battling to preserve a broader view of the learning needs of the child with attention not only to the mind but to the body and emotions of children. Developmental psychology was the most influential paradigm in preschool education. In the discourse of practitioners the concept of 'developmental stages' was never far below the surface. Blenkin and Kelly (1994) have long argued for a 'developmentally appropriate' view of young children in designing systems for early education and care. Their argument is that we must take a holistic view of the child, catering for mind, body and emotions when determining how services, and in particular early education, should be designed. Their emphasis is on experiential learning and sensory-based activities, not on a pre-determined, disembedded body of 'school' knowledge to be taught to young children.

> Education is defined ... in terms of its processes rather than its content or its extrinsic aims and objectives ... Cognitive development is seen as dependent on, or interlinked with psychomotor and affective development. The social context of learning is identified as the most crucial element in human learning. Informal and interactive styles of instruction are ... advocated ... the importance of play in learning and development is emphasized. (Blenkin and Kelly, 1994: 28)

Such a view takes 'the developmental level of the individual child' as the starting point for determining practitioners' priorities and informs the construct of Developmentally Appropriate Practice dominant in the US discourse about early childhood education. Alongside 'catering for the whole child', the concept of 'catering for individual needs' is central to the discourse of early childhood teachers. This tenet is in direct conflict with policy imperatives based on 'universality', 'standardisation' and the measurement of 'quality' using schedules that finally reduce all judgements of both children and workers in preschool settings to crude numerical outcomes.

However, the tenet is also in conflict with the paradigm shift to the social (Vygotskyan) and situated nature of learning (Lave and Wenger, 1991; Resnick et al., 1991), and to the central importance of reciprocity in learning episodes between adults and young children (Schaffer, 1992). During the past decade the voices of professionals have been heard by the Department for Children, Schools and Family in England, and a new early years curriculum has been created. From September 2008 the Early Years Foundation Stage will be delivered to birth-to-5-year-olds in all education and care settings registered as providing preschool education. The guidance notes reflect principles underpinning many early years specialists' beliefs. There are four themes: a unique child, positive relationships, enabling environments and learning and development (DfES, 2007a). However, the 'standards agenda' lobby still has a powerful hold on government policy for early years education. A phonics scheme, *Letters and Sounds* (Primary National Strategy, 2007) must also be delivered; and a comprehensive Foundation Stage Profile must be completed for all children before they start the National Curriculum at Key Stage 1 at the age of 5. Northern Ireland, Wales and Scotland are each pursuing their own distinctive early years policies (www.deni.gov.uk; www.wales.gov.uk; www.scotland.gov.uk).

If practitioners from an educational background felt alienated from policy imperatives, those from the care sector in the UK were even further alienated. Education was given the lead role in working towards integrated services for under-8s. All settings claiming to offer an educational component (and therefore qualifying for government funding for preschool education) were under pressure to prioritise educational aspects of their work. But the beliefs of care workers, emanating from training and working practices within the culture of social services, emphasised the importance of responding to the emotions and nurturing the bodies of the children for whom they cared. An extract from a National Children's Bureau publication argued that the curriculum is:

> investigation and exploration, walks and puddles and cuddles, books and blankets and anything that is part of the child's day, play and routines. (Rouse, 1990)

Attempts to combine education and care in the Scandinavian construct of 'educare' in the UK have been slow to materialise (Anning and Calder, 2008) despite exhortations from central government. Now that more than 80% of daycare provision in England is delivered by the private sector, the task is even more daunting.

Theoretical frameworks

Constructs of childhood

There is a surge of interest in what Prout and James (1997) call 'a new paradigm for the sociology of childhood' in which children are seen as having power and agency in their own right, not simply in relation to the social constructions to which adults around them assign them. In searching for models of early childhood provision that might exemplify the concept of children as active co-constructors of knowledge and culture within their own identities as people and learners, the international community of early childhood educators has looked to the traditions of the preschool systems in Reggio Emilia in Northern Italy. The Reggio Emilia approach to early childhood is exemplified in this extract written by their founding father, Malaguzzi:

> Our image of children no longer considers them as isolated and egocentric, does not see them as only engaged with action with objects, does not emphasise only the cognitive aspects, does not belittle feelings or what is not logical and does not consider with ambiguity the role of the affective domain. Instead our image of the child is rich in potential, strong, powerful, competent, and most of all connected to adults and other children. (Malaguzzi, 1993: 10)

For Malaguzzi, childhood and children are accorded respect in their own right(s). The construction of childhood is oriented towards their present rather than our future. The significance of the final phrases of the Malaguzzi quotation, 'most of all connected to adults and other children', is also key. Children *are* seen as individuals, but what matters most is their place within the community of the preschool and its neighbourhood. The traces of the history of individuals feed into the traces of the history of the community.

Finally, of significance for the *Loving to Learn* project, in the Reggio approach there are no centralised curriculum guidelines. Planning for work with the children is based on recording and scrutinising evidence of what they are currently doing. Workers are expected to make extensive field notes based on the evidence of children's activities and their interactions with them. The documented evidence forms the basis of discussion at weekly staff meetings to shape the following week's planning and resourcing of activities.

Communities of practice

When designing the project, we drew on sociocultural psychology (Wertsch, 1991; Wertsch et al., 1995), focusing on: first, the meanings ascribed to activities and materials used by the practitioners; second, the language they used to discuss them; and third the features of the early childhood work contexts and cultures from which these meanings emanated. We wanted to develop a community of practice across a range of early childhood settings where common understandings, particularly about the development of literacy and mathematical understanding in very young children, would be developed. In particular we wanted to encourage the practitioners to see the educational potential in everyday, familiar activities and materials, rather than drawn from a pre-determined knowledge base encapsulated in a set curriculum.

A community of practice (Lave and Wenger, 1991; Wenger, 1998) is a place where knowledge is used in action and developed into forms that are acceptable within that community. Communities of practice have shared histories and values and as a result ascribe common meanings to objects and events. Knowledge, within a sociocultural framework, is developed and owned by the communities in which it is used. Knowledge is mediated to new members of the community through the objects (play materials, snacks) and activities (construction kits, preparing fruit) in the setting and the meanings ascribed to them (developing manipulative skills, spatial awareness and mathematical understanding, being inducted into healthy eating). Knowledge is often implicit in action, and practitioners may find it challenging to articulate it. It is likely that in communities where practitioners from different work cultures have come together in shared settings to work with children and parents, actions will have different meanings. For example, a practitioner from a daycare setting may see reading a story as a settling activity for a fractious child, while a teacher may see story reading as a way of inducting children into literacy behaviours. It was this kind of professional knowledge that we wanted to explore in the project.

Activity theory

Activity theory, exemplified in the work of Engestrom et al. (1999), is another source of theoretical framing to help us research into and try to understand the complexity of learning in early childhood settings. Engestrom's analyses of the processes underpinning work-based systems acknowledge their complexities and conflicts, rather than attempting to reduce them to simple, reductionist formulae designed to demonstrate 'what works'.

Like sociocultural theory, activity theory contests the focus of traditional research in psychology on individual behaviours and actions. Instead activity theory focuses on the study of the complexity of human behaviour in social groups and in specific contexts. The premise of the theory is that the contextual features of a task contribute to a subject/actor's (a child or an adult) performance on that task. Subjects/actors use tools (such as language, a particular action or a resource) to mediate their knowledge in interactions with each other in learning episodes. But the cultural features of the context in which they use these tools influence the way activities are performed and understood.

So, for example, a practitioner in a kindergarten setting may use a pencil with a child, using a didactic style of talk, while demonstrating how to write their name on a drawing the child has just completed. In the cultural context of an after-school club, a play worker may use a pencil with that same child, with a playful and reciprocal style of talk, to complete a dot-to-dot puzzle together. At home the child may pick up a pencil and doodle on the back of an envelope whilst her parent opens the morning post. The child's performance on the three pencil-based tasks may be quite different.

Within activity theory, tools have multiple layers of meaning. For example, in a nursery school context a book may be used to introduce children to literacy conventions – how a story is read, understood and re-represented in illustrations and print. In a home context a book may be used as a source of emotional comfort in a close one-to-one bedtime story ritual. In an early years setting where multi-agency teams operate together, professionals may use the tool of language in different ways depending on their training, personal histories and beliefs and the meanings embedded in their daily actions. A phrase written on a report card like 'Sarah is making progress' might mean something very different to a speech therapist, a classroom teacher and Sarah's parents. Activity theory gives us conceptual frameworks to explore these multiple layers of meaning.

Engestrom argues that a key process in sharing expertise is 'boundary crossing'. Crossing boundaries involves entering into territory with which we are unfamiliar and therefore in which to some extent we are unqualified. Groups may indulge in defensive posturing to counter the 'threats' of entering new territory. They may throw up obstacles to change. Obstacles are characterised as two opposing forces. One force is 'groupthink' where (often so-called high status) knowledge is defended as exclusive in a closed-minded way. The opposing force is 'fragmentation of viewpoints' where, because members of the group are not prepared to work towards a common language, it is impossible to make decisions. To overcome these two opposing types of obstacles to promoting change requires a major effort of cognitive retooling. Groups need to use 'boundary objects' such as whiteboards to brainstorm new ideas, or a focus on a particular action or case to explore their professional similarities and differences. They also need to use argumentation to confront conflicts and emerge into dialogue. Early years practitioners, mostly women, often find argumentation unfamiliar and testing, being cultured into passive and placatory behaviours from birth.

The complex features of activity systems provide both a rich resource and the potential for conflict. In workplaces parallel activity systems, such as those of the speech therapist and teacher and parent, have the potential to interact to create new meanings and understandings which transcend the limits of the three separate systems. The interactions between activity systems form the basis of expansive cycles of learning and the transformation of work activities. In expansive learning at work the notion is challenged that there is a stable and well-defined body of knowledge to be passed down by experts to novices within a community of practice. Engestrom argues that much learning in work organisations is not stable, not well defined or even understood ahead of time. In important transformations, in both our personal lives and working practices, we have to learn new forms of activity as we work.

Another important feature of Engestrom's work is his focus on knowledge exchange. Within a workplace such as a Sure Start children's centre, some knowledge will be tacit (demonstrated in actions) and some explicit (evidenced in documentation, dialogue or resources). Engestrom has explored the articulation of professional knowledge at individual and distributed levels by presenting teams of workers with evidence (documents, videos, photographs, tapes) of critical incidents in their workplaces. Prompts to stimulate dialogue about this evidence may focus on knowledge or expertise, contradictions between viewpoints, historical/cultural aspects of systems and activities, when new (expansive) learning has taken place (or not), and how this learning has changed (or not) activities in the workplace. This set of prompts might provide both the stimuli to 'lay out and assess what team members already know' and to challenge them about what new knowledge/expertise has been acquired and activated. This was the basis of the approach used with early years professionals from a range of settings in the project outlined in this chapter.

The project

The project team

The 20 preschool practitioners, based in three local authorities, brought to the project a wealth of background experiences, expertise and beliefs about childhood:

- eight worked in family centres or children's centres, mostly with training and traditions from social services daycare systems, though one was employed in an educational role;
- three worked in independent daycare nurseries, with nursery nurse training and health services experience;
- five worked in support services – family literacy, multicultural responsiveness, supporting childminders – with a range of training and background experiences in welfare and education;
- four worked in nursery schools or classes with teacher training and educational experience.

Professional knowledge and beliefs about children's learning

Though it was possible to characterise the 20 professionals as coming from a specific tradition or work culture – welfare, education, health – their personal lives and work histories gave each practitioner a unique set of values and beliefs. Likewise, the settings within which they worked, though categorised as, for example, daycare or educational provision, were products of the particular history of that setting and of the current chemistry and expertise of the practitioners, parents and children who made up its community. The idea of applying a 'universal' mindset to the workers or their workplaces was untenable. The influence of the local policy and charismatic 'leaders' within local authority systems also impacted on the beliefs and actions of the professionals in each of the settings. So, of course, did national policy initiatives.

Along with beliefs, each project member brought to the meetings their own storehouse of professional knowledge. All the project team were familiar with the centralised preschool curriculum, then called the Desirable Learning Outcomes (SCAA, 1996) and now the Foundation Stage curriculum (DfES, 2007a). Those with a background in education felt relatively comfortable with the curriculum framework, though suspicious of its emphasis on literacy and numeracy outcomes. However, those from daycare settings were uncomfortable with its emphasis on 'mind' and were intimidated by the prospect of Ofsted inspectors arriving with clipboards to monitor its implementation in their settings. They were worried that children who started school after leaving their settings with low baseline assessment scores in literacy and numeracy would reflect adversely on their provision. With the drift towards 4-year-olds enrolling in Reception classes in English primary schools (where they were offered so-called 'nursery education' on the cheap), they were caring for more babies and toddlers than 3- and 4-year-olds. Some daycare staff were overtly hostile to the concept of nursery settings being 'colonised' by education and clear that with under 3-year-olds and even with 4-year-olds their priorities should be different. One family centre nursery nurse said:

> Some of our 4-year-olds are here with us for a long day. They've got all their school years ahead of them. We're not teachers. None of us has been trained to teach a child to write their name, or read, or count. We did the basic things in training, but we are not teachers and we don't feel qualified to teach these kinds of things to the children. You hear horror stories about nurseries teaching the children the alphabet and then teachers have to re-teach them sounds – you know, they've been taught 'ay, bee, cee' and they want 'a, b, c' - and we're not teachers. But we can give them all the opportunities they need to prepare them for school.

Others felt deskilled in taking on the government's educational 'standards' agenda. One of the most knowledgeable and experienced managers of a family centre said, 'I felt I was entering an educational arena I was not fully equipped for'.

At the start of the project those with educational backgrounds appeared confident in catering for young children's minds; but as the project developed they became uncomfortably aware that their experience of working with very young children was limited. They began to express interest in learning from those in the care sector about working with under 3s, and particularly about how to respond to their physical and emotional needs. One way and another, over time all of us were able to admit that our professional identities were fragile in the national climate of creating 'joined-up services' across the traditional boundaries of education and care.

We knew that it was inappropriate to graft an educational framework or discourse onto designing a curriculum framework for young children in non-school settings. But the problem for practitioners in informal non-school settings, as many of these were, is that as yet there is no identifiable, alternative discourse about children's learning in their professional literature. As Munn (1994) pointed out, before children enter formal school settings their learning is often centred around 'everyday' practical activities such as learning how to get shoes on and off, or social skills such as sharing toys or taking turns in games. Such 'knowledge' embedded in the everyday actions of learners tends to be dismissed as 'trivial', or if attempts are made to codify it, educators work backwards from the discourse of schooling and retrospectively accord such activities the disembedded 'status' of educational language. Munn gives the following examples:

- Buttoning up coats involves one-to-one correspondence and therefore maps onto counting.
- Distinguishing colours and shapes involves perceptual discrimination and therefore maps onto letter recognition.

She points out that by such extrapolation, cognitive (educational) aspects of the pre-school curriculum are created artificially from everyday activities.

This reshaping of everyday learning activities into educational knowledge leaves early years practitioners from non-educational backgrounds feeling disempowered and alienated. So they tend to dismiss curriculum models as tangential to their own professional knowledge. When Blenkin and Kelly (1997) analysed the returns of practitioners from a wide range of preschool settings in the Principles into Practice in Early Childhood Education project (the PIPS Project), they found that many of them, including some formal school settings, made no response to the question, 'How would you describe a quality curriculum for young children?' Others simply stapled on local authority or National Curriculum guidelines. It was as if the documents had become a reason for them not to engage themselves with ideas about a curriculum.

Creating the community of practice

It was important for us to promote a dialogue among the 20 practitioners which would not dismiss their routine activities with young children as 'trivial' or simply recast them as 'preparation for schooling'. We wanted to build on the intuitive knowledge and expertise embedded in the realities of their workplace practices and support them in articulating their tacit knowledge and sharing it within the networks of the project.

We also wanted to confront the prejudices and misunderstandings those practitioners from the distinct traditions of health, welfare or education might have of each other's workplace practices and knowledge bases. This would mean breaking down defensive posturing about who had the 'right' approach and confronting mutual distrust. It was therefore essential that we based our exchanges around the authentic evidence of what was commonplace in each other's workplaces. The evidence we shared was based on documentation of our everyday work – logs, field notes, accounts of conversations with colleagues and parents, photographs, children's drawings/paintings/models – as in the Reggio Emilia model. We used Action Research Cycles to focus progressively on aspects of working with children and parents on promoting language development and mathematical understanding. We kept detailed research diaries monitoring our own journeys through the project processes, meetings and reflection in the workplace.

But building a community of practice required us all quite literally, though of course metaphorically too, to step out of each other's boundaries and visit as many of the settings as we could. In addition to attending the meetings, the researchers visited every setting represented in the project at least once. Our project meetings were sited in as many of the project settings as we could feasibly visit. Sometimes these meetings involved quite difficult and lengthy journeys and in a sense the journeys also were a metaphor for stepping out of our own comfort zones and opening up to 'otherness'. We also made a commitment to 'awaydays' during the 18 months (with the strangeness and challenges of overnights spent together on a university campus and in a hotel!) to focus intensively on the project.

Developing a professional discourse about curriculum

When we first met, practitioners seemed unaware of the professional knowledge they brought to the community of practice. This is not surprising when we consider the low status in which work with young children is held. Eraut (1999) distinguishes between two kinds of knowledge. He defines codified or 'C' knowledge in terms of propositional knowledge, codified and stored in publications, libraries and databases and so on – and given foundational status by incorporation into examinations and qualifications. Personal or 'P' knowledge is defined in terms of what people bring to practical situations that enables them to think and perform. The process of bringing evidence of events and interactions from their workplaces enabled the group to work from the specifics of their personal knowledge to the generalities of the communities' codified knowledge in confronting similarities and differences in their ways of working with young children and their parents. What is fascinating in the data recording our conversations is evidence of how the boundaries between different ways of thinking about young children's learning began to shift and open up new ways of conceptualizing a curriculum for young children. It was by working with the creative tensions generated by sharing the knowledge bases of the different members of our project team, rather than by denying and repressing them, that we were able to combine codified and personal knowledge into an innovative curriculum model.

The action research cycles

The practitioners in daycare settings

The practitioners in daycare settings chose as the focus of their action research cycles:

- involving parents in their children's everyday mathematics learning;
- mark-making to promote literacy in the construction play area;
- sharing books and nursery rhymes at home and in the nursery;
- young children learning mathematics through stories and rhymes in home and nursery settings;
- encouraging childminders to promote children's learning through everyday mathematics;
- the role of adults in enhancing children's learning through construction play;
- encouraging parents to 'tune into' babies' languages of gesture and sound;
- the importance of music in children's (and their parents') lives.

It is significant that parental involvement in children's learning figured prominently in their choices. In their accounts of their action research several stated explicitly where they were 'coming from'. Establishing an emotional rapport with the parents, as well as their children, was central to their ways of being. 'We consider our roles as family supporters and as educators of children' (manager, family centre); 'We look at the child as part of a family unit and community in which he or she lives' (nursery officer, children's centre); 'I want to develop the work with the mums from a social work perspective' (special needs support nursery officer, children's centre); 'Our role is to work to involve parents in their children's learning as a top priority' (nursery officer, family centre); 'Staff are always available to discuss children, issues, problems, advice, discussion on feeding, children's behaviour problems, benefits, etc.' (development officer, childminding networks).

The physicality of caring for young children was always acknowledged. Typical of the comments was:

> We realised we needed to discuss with our parents the actual physical handling of the babies when singing: one to one either with the child in the crook of the arm or facing. Held on the knee facing the adult appeared to get the best response. An important aim was to encourage parents to see the value of eye contact and turn-taking in learning how to communicate with their babies and for the babies to communicate with us. (Manager, family centre)

The practitioners in educational settings
The practitioners in educational settings chose as the focus for their action research cycles:

- mathematical development at home and in preschool through games and songs;
- enhancing the quality of the mathematical curriculum in the nursery school;
- literacy episodes with children and their grandparents.

Though they saw their role as educationalists as important, they also involved parents in their research foci. For example, in a nursery school in a community of many ethnic groups the teacher visited the families and exchanged tapes of songs from the world of school with those recorded at home in Arabic and Somali by parents and children. They also exchanged number games, and the children became the 'interpreters' of the rituals associated with these objects between the micro-systems of home and school. Despite their best intentions to broaden their approach to children's learning, the educationalists found it difficult not to emphasise learning to count, learning letter names and sounds and learning to write names as priorities. It seemed harder for them to rearrange their store of knowledge, which had the 'higher status' of concern with children's minds, and accommodate relatively 'low-status' knowledge related to 'bodies' and 'emotions'. In a sense they had been socialised by their training and working practices to believe they had, quite literally, a lot more to lose from opening up to the culture and practice of daycare traditions.

The practitioners from support services
The practitioners from support services were placed uncomfortably between the cultures of informal, community-based learning and formal, school learning. Their field notes reveal how taxing they found moving from the security of formal educational learning to the innovative territory of working with parents and under-3s together in informal settings.

In one project the focus was on mark-making. The practitioner had set up weekly activities on aspects of mark-making for the children at a mother and toddler group. She noted:

> I was enjoying the sessions and the children appeared to be also, but what about the parents? At first I thought I had created a cocoon around the children's learning and essentially left the parents outside. However, closer observations revealed that many of the

parents were listening to and observing the interactions that were taking place. I had collected many pieces of the children's work and decided it was time to display them. The
display became an amazing tool through which to discuss the children's drawing development. I would point out recurring patterns, movements or letters, representational
drawings and the inventions of letters. (Family literacy support worker)

Having once 'opened out', literally through the display of the children's work, she
encouraged parents to paste in and annotate examples of their own children's work
in scrapbooks. As she explained, 'The books provided many opportunities for parents
and children to review their progress'. The parents went on to set up a role-play area
based on a Post Office and to join in with confidence themselves with a range of mark-
making activities initiated by themselves or the children – filling out forms, taking
messages, doing lottery tickets, stamping letters.

Another project was based on encouraging parents to share books with their
babies. This practitioner had to work hard to learn to manage mothers and babies
learning together.

The occasional session was chaotic as I tried, unsuccessfully, to compete with 12
extremely mobile and vocal babies. However, we had a lot of fun in the sessions too.
Observing the literacy behaviours of both the parents and their babies was fascinating
and a very satisfying experience as I watched the changes in both. The really exciting
thing was that we, the parents and I, actually saw the babies taking a keen interest in and
responding to the books. As the parents became more confident, the parent/baby interactions blossomed and we saw a love of books being fostered in babies between 7 to 15
months old. (Babies Into Books project worker)

Discussion

As the members of the team brought their evidence to share with each other over the
18 months of the project, it came as quite a surprise to the group how much wisdom
resided within the group. Yet the hardest task was to put that implicit knowledge into
words. The team groaned at our insistence that we record in our research diaries or
after our meetings evidence of our thinking. But once having got into the habit of
writing, the team were clear when we met for our final weekend together that they
wanted to make their written work available to a wider audience.

The curriculum model that they co-constructed does not look like the watered-down
school versions of knowledge to be 'delivered' to children that characterise many guidelines for early years practitioners. Instead it has grown out of the analysis of episodes of
informal learning where knowledge has been co-constructed between real children,
parents and practitioners in a range of early childhood education and care contexts.
They value the 'everyday' as a source for learning rather than trivializing it. The guidelines recognise the importance of physicality in a curriculum for young children. They
acknowledge the importance of the need for intimacy and emotional engagement in
the quality of interactions between young learners and their 'teachers'. They exemplify
the importance of adults working diagnostically from the documented evidence of

what children do, rather than what policy-makers or politicians think they ought to do and know. They place playful interactions between children and children and adults (parents and professionals) and children at the heart of effective teaching and learning. They acknowledge the importance of the social and situated nature of learning. The construct of childhood underpinning the model is of active young learners connected to other children and to the adults in early childhood settings.

The account of the processes by which the curriculum was articulated and written down is as important in our project guidelines as the curriculum itself. The processes required the team members first to reflect on the meanings they ascribed to materials and activities in their everyday working lives. Second, they had to develop a language to share their reflections in spoken and written versions and sometimes to confront conflicts with other professionals in the project team. Third, they had to work together to create a community of practice where shared knowledge was used in action in ways that were acceptable to the community.

Our hope is that others will find the curriculum model of use, but more important for us is that the account of how it was created will encourage others to work together in this way.

CHAPTER 6

ADULTS CO-CONSTRUCTING PROFESSIONAL KNOWLEDGE

Joy Cullen

Introduction

An inclusive early intervention policy: the context

In this chapter I explore some of the professional issues that have challenged early childhood teachers and early intervention professionals during the implementation of Special Education 2000 (SE 2000) (now Special Education), the inclusive policy that regulates special education in New Zealand, including the early childhood sector. *Te Whāriki*, the early childhood curriculum (Ministry of Education, 1996a: 11), 'is designed to be inclusive and appropriate for all children and anticipates that special needs will be met as children learn together in all kinds of early childhood education settings'. As I have traced the professional debate and discourse that has accompanied the implementation of the inclusive policy, I have concluded that *Te Whāriki*'s sociocultural curriculum philosophy has not guaranteed inclusive practice and that early childhood educators and early interventionists alike are engaged in a complex journey towards inclusion. This chapter proposes that a critical component of this journey is the shared construction of professional knowledge that guides inclusive practices.

Te Whāriki has been acknowledged internationally for its strong focus on children and their learning (Drummond, 2000) and reflects the notion of 'the rich child' that has been promoted by the highly acclaimed Reggio Emilia early childhood institutions in Italy (Dahlberg et al., 1999). Within this ethos, young children with special educational needs are educated in early childhood settings that value children's interests and acknowledge the contexts and relationships within which young children learn.

Debate about *Te Whāriki* within New Zealand has highlighted its consistency with sociocultural perspectives on learning, a term used for the purposes of this chapter to encompass social constructivism, activity theory and related perspectives derived from Vygotsky, Leontiev, Luria and other theorists who stress cultural/historical perspectives on learning. Smith (1996a) published an influential analysis of the early childhood curriculum from a sociocultural perspective that has provided guidance to early childhood teacher education and professional development. This analysis, together with Fleer's writings in Australia (e.g. Fleer, 1995), has helped to move the sector from a focus on individualistic developmental programming to recognition of the socially constructed nature of learning and the desirability of teachers taking a more proactive role in children's learning. Against this background, professional debate has emerged about the place of subject knowledge and skills learning in a holistic curriculum, and the associated implications for teachers' professional knowledge base. With regard to the education of young children with special needs, this type of debate is most clearly evident in the contrasting focus on interests and skills in early childhood education and specialist provisions, respectively.

Currently, debate in New Zealand (see Jordan, Chapter 3; Podmore, Chapter 12), emphasises the co-constructive principle that guides the Reggio Emilia programmes (Dahlberg et al., 1999) and which is a key concept in interpretations of sociocultural theory that have influenced thinking in New Zealand (McNaughton, G., 1995). In terms of children's learning, co-construction highlights the active participation of learners and experts – peers or adult – in shared learning experiences as they engage in meaning-making. Jordan's doctoral research highlights the value of a co-constructive approach to professional development with early childhood teachers for their professional knowledge and for their pedagogical practices with children. In this chapter I argue that co-construction should also apply to the shared meaning-making of educators, early intervention (EI) professionals and other stakeholders involved in provisions for young children with special needs.

Early intervention services in New Zealand

Early intervention services in New Zealand cater for children aged from birth to 5 years, including the transition to school. Specialist services are provided through itinerant EI teams, with expertise drawn from health and education according to the needs of the child. Itinerant EI teachers support early childhood centre staff, and support workers' work with children with high needs in centres, usually in a part-time capacity. The majority of children are catered for in mainstream early childhood services with only a small minority of children who have high needs attending specialised facilities. These provisions place heavy responsibility on early childhood educators to implement individual plans (IPs) for children with high needs as well as taking the major responsibility for planning educational programmes for children with moderate or mild needs.

Early intervention professionals who are employed by the Ministry of Education work within an ecological systems framework, derived from Bronfenbrenner's (1979) ecological perspective. The ecological approach is family-focused, emphasising partnership with families, authentic assessment and learning in natural settings. This emphasis fits well with *Te Whāriki*'s holistic sociocultural philosophy. Its principles – empowerment, holistic development, family and community, and relationships – resonate with ecological theory and contribute to a coherent theoretical framework for the provision of EI services. Potentially, then, an inclusive EI policy should receive positive support from New Zealand's early childhood practitioners (Cullen and Carroll-Lind, 2005). However, research evidence indicates that there are difficulties in translating the vision of inclusive policy into practice. For example, data from two Ministry of Education-funded contracts that have monitored the new special education policy over a four-year period (Bourke et al., 2002; Cullen and Bevan-Brown, 1999) have provided evidence of dislocation in the knowledge bases of EI professionals, early childhood teachers and parents that impacts on the nature of children's educational experiences.

The first project (Cullen and Bevan-Brown, 1999) provided baseline data on early intervention services in 1998 and comprised a random sample of 122 children who had received EI services through Specialist Education Services, their parents and educators, and associated EI professionals. The second project (Bourke et al., 2002) involved a three-year national contract to monitor and evaluate the policy in early childhood services and schools, between 1999 and 2001. It included two national surveys of early childhood centres, randomly selected from the Ministry of Education's database, and two sets of interviews with educators in four regions covering urban areas, provincial towns, and rural and remote regions. Interviews with parents and EI professionals were conducted in the final phase. At the time of the research EI professionals were employed by Specialist Education Services, an organisation that has now been incorporated into the Ministry of Education as Group Special Education.

Professional issues for an inclusive early intervention policy

Working within the *Te Whāriki* philosophy and framework has challenged early childhood teachers and EI workers at two levels: through the philosophical and practical dilemmas they faced, and as they reconstructed their professional knowledge to meet the challenge of these dilemmas.

The nature of an early childhood curriculum: interests versus skills

Contrasting views about the implications of an inclusive early childhood curriculum for EI provisions were evident across the four years of the research. Differences reflected the professional knowledge bases that underpinned special education and early childhood education.

In the baseline study, the need for further investigation of issues to do with assessment and programming was highlighted by some educators and EI professionals.

Educators reported that assessment by EI professionals was often conducted in clinical settings rather than in the natural contexts of home or centre, and that inadequate information about the child's individual programme was communicated to centres. Such practices are, of course, inimical to ecological and sociocultural views about authentic assessment. On the other hand, EI professionals had suggested that the child's special needs could be missed if the holistic *Te Whāriki* framework was used exclusively for planning and monitoring. This specialist viewpoint is encapsulated in a claim from Twiss et al. (1997: 102) that the challenge for early interventionists in New Zealand is 'to insure that sophisticated needs-based teaching and therapies do reach the child'. The source of this tension between the views of educators and EI workers lies primarily in the conflict between the holistic model of learning that underpins *Te Whāriki* and the individualised needs-based programmes devised for children with special needs. This tension highlighted a need for an approach to assessment and programming that built upon the child's competencies and identified areas for additional support, at the same time as promoting the child's interests and learning within the interests-based programmes promoted by *Te Whāriki* (Cullen and Bevan-Brown, 1999).

Reconstructing professional knowledge with a sociocultural lens

In response to the challenges of a holistic curriculum, EI teams began to use the *Te Whāriki* strands to structure individual plans so that skills were embedded within the five strands: well-being/*mana atua*, belonging/*mana whenua*, contribution/*mana tangata*, communication/*mana reo* and exploration/*mana aoturoa*. For example, the use of large and small muscles could relate to the exploration strand. A limitation of this approach, however, is that while it may be valuable for linking skills-based goals to *Te Whāriki*, it does not necessarily highlight or build upon the child's interests. Accordingly, our data continued to reveal concerns from educators about an overfocus on the isolated teaching of skills in IPs.

This educator's statement highlights concerns about the objectives in an IP for a child with high physical and communication needs:

> His individual plan takes up all his time – there are goals for motor skills, for feeding and holding, but what about his interests?

Another educator, of Maori ethnicity, working in a centre with a high proportion of Maori children, stated:

> They [the EI specialists] should find out more about what the community wants for their children, not impose their views about what they need.

Given the significance of cultural contexts in a sociocultural theory of learning, this statement identifies a critical gap for children from culturally diverse backgrounds.

A way forward consistent with sociocultural theory was proposed by Margaret Carr, one of the authors of *Te Whāriki* and the researcher who has promoted learning story assessment in New Zealand (Carr, 2001a). Carr (1999) proposed two important characteristics of learning stories that hold important implications for early intervention. First, learning stories involve relationships and actions that are mediated by others, not simply the individual child's isolated skills. Second, learning stories focus on what makes sense to the child, rather than on external standards and expectations. Along these lines, Dunn (2002), a psychologist working in early intervention, has described the application of learning stories in early intervention as a way to promote inclusion. She outlines many advantages, including:

- data are collected in natural contexts;
- the environment in which learning takes place is described, including the roles of peers and caregivers;
- programmes derived from learning story assessment can work with the child's strengths and pinpoint where the child begins to have difficulty.

Learning stories therefore have the potential advantage that they may tell us a lot about what interests the child in the context of everyday routines and activities. In practice, learning stories may be overly individualistic if educators are still influenced by the strong developmental tradition in early childhood education. Fleer and Richardson's work on collective mediated assessment (see Chapter 10) illustrates how assessment stories may benefit from a focus on group experiences rather than on the individual. Maintaining this fuller sense of socially constructed learning in learning story assessment may depend on a deeper understanding of sociocultural principles, particularly when educators' understanding is constrained by the piecemeal and incomplete training that is still evident in the sector in New Zealand. In this regard, release of the Ministry-funded assessment booklets and associated professional development on sociocultural assessment and inclusive assessment (Ministry of Education, 2005) could strengthen teachers' understanding of sociocultural practices.

I have argued elsewhere (Cullen, 2001: 9) that 'teachers' knowledge of the child's skills and competencies, interests, cultural background and prior learning opportunities are critical if the learning story assessment approach is to meet the criterion of fairness'. It is in this area of professional knowledge that differences in the perspectives of early childhood teachers and EI professionals can most clearly be seen. Although they share a common philosophy of authentic assessment, the more specialised professional knowledge of the speech language therapist, physiotherapist or psychologist can be in conflict with the holistic interests-based planning of the early childhood programme. The continuing academic debate about such tensions in the New Zealand literature suggests there is an urgent need for professional development that promotes communication across the interests–skills divide. From a sociocultural perspective, a shared language would form the essence of such initiatives, building on the concept of intersubjectivity (discussed by Jordan in Chapter 3; Rogoff, 1998). Accordingly, intersubjectivity refers to shared meanings that are co-constructed as participants engage in collaborative activity.

Whose responsibility? Exclusive practices through a sociocultural lens

In its most extreme form a lack of shared meanings about inclusion is evident in the existence of exclusive practices. The concept of exclusion was highlighted by the research of Purdue et al. (2001), which suggests that parents of children with special needs may experience difficulties finding an early childhood centre to accept their child's enrolment. Inappropriate facilities and inadequate resourcing were cited by educators as justifications for such practices. The SE 2000 data confirmed perceptions that resources were sometimes inadequate, particularly in health funding regions that did not provide specialised equipment for early childhood settings, or there was no budget for environmental changes such as installing a ramp for a wheelchair. Some EI professionals reported accessing private trust funds, while some kindergarten associations developed equipment pools for use in kindergartens. Such innovations were uneven across the country, and for community-based centres with small budgets that depended on fund-raising to cover additional expenses, inadequate resourcing could create real barriers to inclusion. Nevertheless, within such constraints many teachers were actively supporting inclusive goals. How did these teachers differ? It is now becoming apparent that indirect effects on inclusion also arise from an inadequate understanding of a sociocultural curriculum theory, which, in turn, limits professional growth (Cullen, 2002). Another perspective on exclusive practices therefore is to consider the professional knowledge of educators and EI workers through a sociocultural lens.

Indirectly, barriers to children's inclusion can occur when children are excluded from curriculum activities with peers and via the stultification of professional growth that could occur when teachers fail to face the challenges of inclusion. It is evident from our data that exclusive practices may arise inadvertently from inadequate understanding of what a sociocultural curriculum means in a play-based early childhood setting. For example, two phenomena – the child who is 'Velcroed' to the support worker and, at the other extreme, the child who is 'on the fringes' of activities – suggest a form of exclusion described by EI professionals as not 'taking responsibility' or 'ownership' of the child. Our observations of children in the baseline project indicated that both these forms of exclusion were occurring even though overall the majority of teachers, and parents, reported that the children were integrated in curriculum activities and were accepted by peers.

The 'Velcro' effect: a child with severe behaviour, communication and learning challenges

The support worker takes C's hand and leads to collage table. Directs C to choose paper and models language. C takes felt pen, then dips brush in paint, paints curve on paper, making lines with felt pen at same time, 'oo' to support worker, who points to paper saying 'row' and 'two'. [*Other children at table leave to go outside. C continues with paint activity for 15 minutes with supervision from the support worker.*]

On the fringes: a child with moderate hearing and communication needs

M picks up dried noodles off floor, places into container. Starts eating noodles, watching other children. Sits down on ground beside another child who is playing with Lego. Moves to next room, finds a large cylinder and climbs inside. Starts rolling cylinder to other end of room. Returns to Lego area, lies on floor using blocks as cars. Moves to activity table and watches two other children cutting paper. Returns to floor and starts using Lego pieces as cars again. [*Fifteen minute observation in which no interaction with child or adult recorded.*]

Several interpretations of sociocultural/social constructivist principles are helpful for the analysis of such exclusive practices. During the 1990s a small number of early interventionists in the United Kingdom and United States of America proposed that social constructivist theories of learning could provide a theoretical rationale for early intervention (Bishop et al., 1999; Mallory, 1998; Mallory and New, 1994). Mallory and New, for instance, argue that social constructivist principles could form the basis of inclusive early childhood programmes. They suggest four principles that highlight several sociocultural challenges for inclusive early intervention:

- the inclusive classroom functions as a community of learners;
- social relations are the catalyst for learning in the inclusive curriculum;
- content and context are linked through inclusive curriculum;
- processes for feedback and assessment are authentic and emotionally supportive.

From a human rights perspective on inclusion, I have suggested (Cullen, 1999) that three sets of rights can be identified in a programme that reflects sociocultural principles:

- the child's right to belong;
- the child's right to share interests;
- the child's right for differences to be acknowledged and respected.

To these rights, Dunn (2002) has added a fourth:

- the right to be seen in the same way as everyone else.

Several practical implications follow from these perspectives. Belonging could involve practical steps such as altering the environment to facilitate the mobility of a child with a physical disability or it could involve acknowledging cultural perspectives on special needs. Sharing interests with peers could involve assisting a child with communication challenges to take a role in socio-dramatic play or it could involve learning story assessment to identify the child's special interests. Content and context are linked when adults and children share interests and talk about meaningful every-day events. In this approach, direct assistance from a support worker or the establishment of specific needs-based goals would not isolate the learning of skills but embed these in meaningful activities. Likewise, assessment is authentic and supportive if learning story narratives identify and support children's interests as well as prerequisite skills, and focus not just on the learner but on qualities of the learning environment and the extent to which it creates a supportive, responsive context for learning.

In a community of learners, a valid role is available to the learner with special needs even though it may not be identical to the contributions of other children. Further, in a community of learners the adult's role may involve assisting peers to interact supportively as much as it involves helping the child with special needs, so that processes such as self-exclusion or being ignored do not restrict the learning opportunities available to the child. Such principles emphasise the co-constructive nature of learning that is pivotal in a sociocultural curriculum and applies to both child–child and adult–child interactions. Failure to understand the co-construction principle is likely to result in the forms of exclusion illustrated above, that is, the 'Velcroed' child and the child who is 'on the fringes'.

Interviews with EI professionals in the final year of the SE 2000 project indicated that exclusive practices were still occurring in centres, despite the availability of a professional development resource package and associated professional development on the inclusive policy. In the national survey only a small majority of educators (52%) considered that the resource package, *Including Everyone: Te Reo Tataki* (Ministry of Education, 2000a) had increased their competence. Do these findings indicate a need to shift from an expert model to a collaborative model in professional development (McWilliam et al., 2001)? From this perspective, a deeper understanding of sociocultural principles of learning is not solely the responsibility of the teacher; it applies also to support workers, EI teachers and other professional members of the EI team. Teachers would be less likely to abdicate responsibility for a child if EI workers valued children's interests as well as their skills.

Co-constructing professional knowledge – the next step

I have argued that challenges to an inclusive policy can arise from lack of understanding of a sociocultural curriculum even when the philosophies of early intervention policy and early childhood curriculum are compatible. When combined with the tradition of individualistic developmental philosophies in early childhood education and the specialised needs-based expertise of early intervention, it is not surprising that tensions have occurred in the implementation of the inclusive policy. More positively, there is an emergent trend in the early intervention field that suggests a community of practice (COP) approach to professional development may help to resolve such tensions and move the early childhood sector towards a stronger interpretation of inclusion.

The concept of community of practice (Wenger, 1998) refers to shared under-standings and practices within a professional community. The concept has entered the field of early childhood education (see Anning in Chapter 5; Anning and Edwards, 1999) and early intervention (Bussye et al., 2001), with encouraging signs that cross-disciplinary professional growth can occur when a collective inquiry approach to pro-fessional development is adopted. Bussye et al. (2001: 182) note that, 'In education, the emphasis has shifted from describing various communities of practice to creating communities for the purpose of *improving* practice as a model of professional devel-opment'. They argue that barriers to high-quality inclusion include lack of quality in early childhood practice as well as a lack of consensus about best practice among the diverse professional groups involved in early intervention. They suggest further that family–professional partnerships as the cornerstone of work in early intervention can also be fostered through a COP approach. A key challenge 'lies in transforming exist-ing professional development approaches from emphasizing the transmission of knowledge to promoting the construction of knowledge' (Bussye et al., 2001: 196). Through processes such as shared reflection and collaborative inquiry, a COP approach can involve parents, practitioners and other professional and community-based stake-holders to 'build a knowledge base and improve services for children and families' (Bussye et al., 2001: 198). Arguably, a COP approach to early intervention differs from multidisciplinary and transdisciplinary approaches to service delivery in its explicit commitment to the co-construction of a shared knowledge and discourse about the education of young children with special educational needs.

Collaborative professional development: 'Losing my jargon'

A professional development programme that aimed to acknowledge the different per-spectives that parents, teachers, support workers and EI professionals bring to the interpretation of learning stories illustrates the value of developing shared meanings in EI teams (Williamson et al., 2006). Team members surrounding two young children with high and complex needs, including parents, teachers, support workers and health and education professionals, received professional development on the use of learning story assessment and shared their stories at IP meetings. The project aimed to develop more effective collaborative assessment and planning that acknowledged the importance of children's interests-based learning within their social and cultural contexts, as well as their skills-based learning. Goals for the children were developed collaboratively, drawing upon the different perspectives that team members brought to the interpretation of learning stories. The approach accommodated the many per-spectives held by individuals within the teams and successfully harmonised the skills and interests-based assessment models. Further, the project highlighted the empow-erment of parents and educators in the planning process and the strengthening of collaborative relationships. An important focus in this project was tracking the participants' progression towards understanding how their individual perspectives contributed to a shared perspective on children's learning, and the co-construction of a common discourse that facilitated growth of a community of practice. The challenges this collaborative approach can create for participants is epitomised in the response of a hospital-based EI professional when asked about the possible disadvantages of using learning stories in the early stages of the project – 'Losing my jargon'. Willingness to take this step could be the foundation for the shared understandings that would move EI services away from reliance on the expert view of service provision towards a collaborative COP approach. Significantly, such a goal also accords with a core goal of the Ministry's Strategic Plan for Early Childhood, namely, to promote collaborative relationships (see Chapter 1).

Concluding comments

In the final phase of the SE 2000 project EI professionals reported innovative preventative approaches that reflected their strengthening focus on diversity and working with community meanings (Bourke et al., 2002). Work with teenage parents in community settings, supporting playgroups and family/*whanau* training, and Maori and Pacific Nations initiatives to strengthen EI team approaches in Maori and Pacific communities, are evidence of this trend. These community-based and participatory collaborative trends offer encouraging signs that the partnership model that underpins a community of practice approach is viable in the early intervention field and holds potential for improving outcomes for children.

Dunn's (2006) interview study of four participant groups – parents, teachers, EI specialists and support workers – co-operating in EI services at their local early childhood centre, highlighted different perceptions of three key dimensions of a community of practice proposed by Wenger et al. (2002): its domain, its community and its practice. This suggests that the creation of a new COP for EI service teams requires willingness by all participating groups to reconsider the beliefs and practices they bring to the new community. When all participants in EI provision understand the co-construction principle that underpins the inclusion vision, change should be effected at three levels. First, shared professional knowledge should articulate with systems and policies to support coherent service delivery. For example, the recent integration of Early Childhood Development, a government body responsible for co-ordinating and supporting parent playgroups and parenting programmes, into the Ministry of Education created an opportunity for closer relationships between parenting services and EI provisions that should facilitate the process of co-constructing knowledge about inclusive educational practices. Second, a co-constructive philosophy also leads participants to view their contribution collaboratively rather than through an expert lens in which one form of knowledge, the expert's, is privileged over another. This is not to say that specialist or educational expertise is not valued, but rather that it may take new forms and meanings when multiple perspectives are shared and contribute to decision-making. Third, at the implementation level, when children's contributions are acknowledged as a primary source of curriculum, the interests–skills divide can be seen in clearer perspective. Skills are something to be taken into account, even targeted, but not at the expense of the child's opportunities to share interests with peers or to contribute to ongoing curriculum activities as a member of a community of learners.

Adequate resourcing of EI provisions is, of course, a critical component of effective inclusive services (Bailey et al., 1998). In this regard the Ministry of Education has implemented an Equity Funding Policy which provides supplementary funding for eligible centres with the aim of reducing educational disparities. The policy seems likely to facilitate access to centres for children with additional needs; it is argued here, however, that for inclusion in its strongest sense to evolve, teachers and specialists need to understand sociocultural principles and practices and to re-evaluate some of their traditional routines and practices on this basis.

To conclude, the sociocultural lens is a powerful means of viewing the journey towards inclusion. In Rogoff's (1998) terms, the sociocultural activities that constitute this journey can be analysed as three interwoven planes (or lenses): the institutional, the interpersonal and the personal. At the institutional and systemic plane, philosophies and policies channel participants' perspectives, actions and environments; at the interpersonal plane, co-construction of professional knowledge can guide and strengthen inclusive practices; while on the personal plane, the empowerment of children, parents and families that arises from a partnership approach to EI can lead to positive outcomes for all participants.

Acknowledgements

The two research contracts discussed in this chapter were commissioned and funded by the New Zealand Ministry of Education. Sincere thanks are extended to all participants and to Joy Cullen's co-researchers, Jill Bevan-Brown and Janis Carroll-Lind from Massey University.

CHAPTER 7

BUILDING BRIDGES BETWEEN LITERACIES

Denise Williams-Kennedy

The pattern of Indigenous achievement generally mirrors that of non-Indigenous students; however, in every case, there are large gaps between the achievement of Indigenous and non-Indigenous students (DEST, 2006: xxiv)

Improving the educational opportunities and achievements of Indigenous Australians is an urgent national priority. (Kemp, 2000: 4)

The Building Bridges Project

The Building Bridges project evolved as a response by the Australian Early Childhood Association to find ways to bridge the educational chasm that exists between many Indigenous students and Western education in Australia.

If 'education is essentially a social process', as stated by Dewey (1933: 65–66), then the Australian Early Childhood Association (AECA) realised, that, in order to learn about the cultural knowledge that young Indigenous children acquire and develop in their home environments, they would need to find a way to study the social processes involved in the transmission of this knowledge from families to their children. In effect, they had to find a way to study a child's culture in action. In particular, the project would have to focus on developing insights into the manner in which young Indigenous children acquire and develop literacy skills and knowledge in their own cultures. The methods used to do so were to give high-quality video cameras to six extended Indigenous families and their communities and ask them to record aspects of their children's daily lives which they valued as passing on important cultural skills and knowledge. The video recordings were shared across the communities and with researchers at a week-long workshop.

It was important that authentic and culturally sensitive methods for gathering cross-cultural data would be from the perspective of a child's family. This was one of the most important strategies underpinning the Building Bridges project. We took the position that in order to learn about another culture we have to look from 'inside to outside'. Essentially we have to learn to see our environment (including institutions such as Western education-based schools and the processes that influence and drive them) from another cultural group's worldview.

In effect our research was based on the premise that we could not discover how young Indigenous children acquire and develop literacy skills and knowledge by studying them in isolation from their families, communities and cultures. Rogoff et al. (1995) highlight the significance and importance of this understanding in their study of cookie sales by the Girl Scouts of America:

> We regard individual development as inseparable from interpersonal and community processes; individuals' changing roles are mutually defined with those of other people and with dynamic cultural processes. (1995: 45)

Rogoff (1994: 209) further argues that 'learning and development occur as people participate in the sociocultural activities of their community'.

This strategy of looking at education and learning from an Indigenous perspective positioned the families as the central agents in the project. For many family members this experience with Western education was a complete role reversal. Their experience had been that the knowledge, skills and culture of many Indigenous families and communities were overlooked, excluded or even denigrated at various times throughout the history of education for Indigenous children in Australia.

The mutual sharing of cultural knowledge between the Indigenous families and the Western academics in this project is a process that was adapted by Fleer and Williams-Kennedy (2001: 108) from Jordan's (1999) model of a co-construction of cultural knowledge. (See Chapter 3 for a full discussion of this model.) Figure 7.1 represents this process. Where mutual sharing occurs between families and teachers, a broader understanding of important Indigenous knowledges for learning occurs – as is shown by the shaded box.

Co-construction of knowledge has not historically been an integral part of the education process for Indigenous children. Fleer points out that:

> Too often schooling for Indigenous children has concentrated on the school culture only, with Indigenous children having to learn the rules of school. Very little cultural knowledge is shared or used to build teaching and learning programs. (2001: 24)

Figure 7.2 represents this inequality in sharing of cultural knowledge. The shaded box, skewed to the school area, shows that only school knowledge is shared, and limited Indigenous knowledges are mutually understood. In this model, it is the responsibility of the child to learn the school's ways of doing things (Crozier and Davies, 2007).

AECA undertook the Building Bridges project because it believed that within Indigenous families and communities there is an often unrecognised and untapped reservoir of skill and knowledge. Hill et al. (1998: 17), cited in Fleer and Williams-Kennedy (2001),

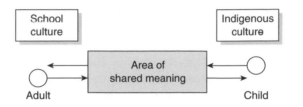

Figure 7.1   The explicit sharing of cultural knowledge

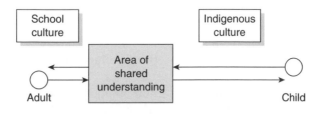

Figure 7.2   Western knowledge is assumed as the norm

support this view that cultural and minority groups possess their own systems of literacy practices which may differ from the dominant culture's practices. They argue that the literature clearly shows (2001: 2):

- there is enormous diversity in home literacy practices among and within cultural groups;
- rather than being literacy-impoverished, the home environments of poor, under-educated and language-minority children are rich with literacy practices and artefacts;
- although beliefs about literacy, and its payoffs vary, marginalised families generally not only value literacy, but also see it as the single most powerful hope for their children;
- parents who themselves have limited literacy proficiency support their children's literacy acquisition in many ways.

Indigenous families understand that gaining Western education is important for their children. They want their children to have access to the same range of educational and economic opportunities and choices as are available to other Australian children (DEST 2006; Indigenous Higher Education Advisory Council, 2006).

What did we learn from the family stories?

The family stories derived from the video data and related dialogues did reveal a number of interrelated key features and issues that often impinge upon the way in which many young Indigenous children develop, interact and learn within their home and school environments. These features focused on:

- the active deconstruction of school structures and culture;
- the need for a holistic Indigenous educational framework for learning;
- the need to recognise and build on the diversity of Indigenous cultures across Australia;
- the importance of family, roles, obligations and interdependence;
- Indigenous families' cultural understandings and practices in relation to the concepts of autonomy, time and space;
- the power of the dominant language and culture in relation to other languages and cultures co-existing in Western schooling;
- the need for acceptance of an Indigenous child's home language;
- defining and understanding the concept of literacy from both Indigenous and Western perspectives;
- the multiple literacies that many Indigenous children experience within the context of their home cultures (Fleer and Williams-Kennedy, 2001: 74–89).

These features will form a framework for discussion of what we learned from the Building Bridges project.

Indigenous culture and dissonances with Western versions of schooling

Deconstructing Western school structure and culture

The basic structure of schooling provided by the federal government in Australia has many similarities with schooling in the USA. Rogoff et al. (2001: 3) describe the culture of schooling as:

- being compulsory for all children;
- segregating children from the daily activities of the adults in their communities;
- isolating several dozen children with a single adult charged with their instruction;
- grouping children according to their birth dates to provide large numbers with standard instruction in a step-by-step fashion;
- isolating skills from their integrated use in productive activities;
- attempting to motivate children by grading their performance.

Within Australia these aspects of schooling are accepted as the norm for many families.

The basic characteristics of Western schooling/education differ markedly from those of Indigenous Australian cultures. Indigenous families have their own systems of education within their home environments and communities. This process of education is broadly characterised by the following features:

- children learning while participating in daily activities with elders and family members;
- children learning from a range of educators within the extended family;
- children learning from educators who have a kinship obligation to care for and teach members of their family;
- children learning within an environment where they are at ease and comfortable;
- children learning within a process of education that is known and predictable;
- children learning within a system where mistakes are accepted as part of the learning process;
- children learning in an environment where they are provided with time and space to make their own decisions, follow their interests, explore and learn within this process;
- the promotion of interdependence, obligation and collaboration as core cultural values;
- children taking on positions of responsibility for younger siblings at an early age;
- children understanding the importance and purpose behind learning skills.

When both systems of education are compared, we can see that within Indigenous culture learning is built on collaboration in ongoing activities, and the purpose of the daily activities and reasons for learning are obvious to the children. Rather than step-by-step increments that do not require children to understand the purpose of the learning experiences, children contribute to real-life family activities where the purpose and significance of such activities are clearly understood. Essentially, the children are not just being prepared to participate in their communities at a later date; instead, they learn while they are participating in and contributing to their families and their communities (Rogoff, 2003).

Holistic Indigenous framework for learning

From the families' perspectives, any discussion about their families and their culture has to be considered from a holistic point of view, because families, cultures and religion are all interconnected. To help explain an Indigenous worldview, a visual aid in the form of a holistic educational framework was drawn up by the families with the support of a couple of Indigenous academics (see Figure 7.3). This framework enabled the families to explain and demonstrate their way of thinking about and relating to each other and their surrounding environment.

Diversity of Indigenous Australian cultures

Within Australia the lives and cultures of Indigenous people have been and continue to be influenced by two main factors. These are length of exposure to Western culture through historical, political, social (including educational) and economic policies, and isolation (both geographic and social) from traditional homelands, family, Indigenous languages and cultures.

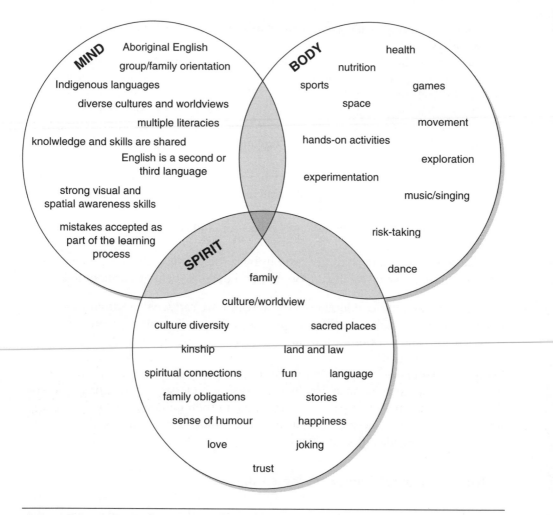

Figure 7.3 A holistic framework for learning

The experiences of a family from Sydney, as well as the members of the other families in the project, highlight some issues relating to the perceptions of many Anglo-Australians and immigrants that Australia's Indigenous people belong to one cultural group who all look the same, practise the same customs and traditions and speak the same language.

> Teachers need to acknowledge the children for who they are and not put stereotypes on them. Aboriginal people are a very diverse group … across Australia. (Fleer and Williams-Kennedy, 2001: 48)

These misconceptions about Indigenous cultures can have and have had a detrimental impact on the lives of Indigenous children. Learning becomes secondary or even irrelevant when children feel that they are not understood or accepted as a member of their cultural group.

Family roles, obligations and interdependence

Many times throughout the workshop process the family members stressed the importance of caring for families as being a core value and an integral part of Aboriginal culture. Each family member has specific roles and obligations to fulfil in order to support the family and, as has been previously noted, Indigenous children do not see themselves as individuals but rather as members within their extended family.

> The children are taught by their families to value working together, to be self-sacrificing for the common good and to carry out tasks as part of their obligation to their families. Social cohesion and a sense of social responsibility are traits which are highly valued – particularly in communities where survival means working together. (Fleer and Williams-Kennedy, 2001: 32)

This strong allegiance to family is not usually understood or catered for in schools. Rather than accommodate this view of family, schools tend to expect families to organise themselves around or to fit into traditional Western school cultures. For example, schools often foster an individualistic worldview and they promote independence, whereas Indigenous families value interdependence and encourage their children to share with and support each other. One of the mothers in the project gave the example that her children felt obliged to share their homework to help each other. She explained, 'My Gail does the words and her brother does the illustrations'. We concluded:

> If you look at competition it is an individual thing, you are really competing against others …; with sharing, you are sharing with everybody; it is a different way of doing things. (Fleer and Williams-Kennedy, 2001: 28, 31)

In effect, when Indigenous children adhere to their cultural values at school they may clash with school values and rules and may be criticised or punished for their actions. However:

> Working as an individual – for learning and for assessment – [is merely one] … cultural construction. Historically and globally we see many other cultures which view themselves as team players, e.g. in some countries, such as Italy, where in the Reggio area preschool programs feature easels set up to support group rather than individual painting. (Fleer and Williams-Kennedy, 2001: 32)

Autonomy, time and space

Within the Australian mainstream culture children are generally expected to listen to and obey their parents' verbal instructions. However, Indigenous children are often given more freedom and independence from a young age to make their own decisions and choose their own activities. They are expected to learn through observation, participation in daily extended family activities and non-verbal systems of communication. Like:

> the Navajo ... individual freedom of action is seen as the only source of co-operation ... Navajo [and Indigenous Australian] people place immense value on co-operation while simultaneously holding great respect for individual autonomy. (Chisholm, 1996: 178, as cited in Mosier and Rogoff, 2000: 4)

The family video footage depicted lifestyles that were very relaxed. The children were free to move about, were actively encouraged to share and to use their Indigenous language and were surrounded by their extended families. The children were provided with the space and time to engage for long periods, by Western measures of time, in family activities. There was no obvious beginning or end to events, but rather a timeless movement of activities (Fleer and Williams-Kennedy, 2001: 68).

> Most Australian schools are the antithesis of Indigenous homes in that they work to rigid timetables. It is not surprising that some Indigenous children experience culture shock when they first start school. We argue that educators need to devise strategies to re-conceptualise time and space in ways which take into account the children's home culture and provide latitude for moving about in a relaxed manner. (Fleer and Williams-Kennedy, 2001: 68–9)

Implications for learning literacies

The power of language

Standard Australian English (SAE) is not only the main form of communication and literacy in Australia, it is also the literacy with the most power. Proficiency in SAE is highly valued in schools. Educators need to consider the power structures that maintain and position SAE above other forms of literacy and the implications of this domination for children who speak other languages or dialects of English (including Indigenous languages and Aboriginal English). Hill et al. (1998) argue that:

1 Issues of power are enacted in classrooms.
2 There are codes or rules for participating in power (i.e. there is a culture of power).
3 The rules of the culture of power are a reflection of the rules of the culture of those that have power.
4 If you are not already a participant in the culture of power, being told explicitly the rules of that culture makes acquiring power easier.
5 Those with power are frequently the least aware of or least willing to acknowledge its existence, while those with less power are often most aware of its existence. (Hill et al., 1998: 29)

It is not that educators deliberately sanction one form of speaking above another; rather it is the acceptance of the dominant modes of communication that hinders their capacity to see the power structures inherent in language acquisition. Educators from middle-class families are less likely to see the power they hold because Standard Australian English is their first language and they are proficient in it (Fleer and Williams-Kennedy, 2001: 12).

Acceptance of a child's home language

Although contemporary educators on the whole do not sanction one form of speaking over another, the historical experience of many Indigenous families has been characterised by past government policies that either prohibited, criticised or neglected the use of Indigenous languages and Aboriginal English in schools.

In Australia today a number of Indigenous languages are being taught and built on, particularly in the areas where these languages are commonly spoken in the children's home communities. However, in other more densely populated parts of Australia, Aboriginal English is the common language spoken by many Indigenous families (see *Preschool Profile*, DETYA, 2001).

Families from these backgrounds felt strongly about the issue of acceptance of Aboriginal English in schools. The importance of Aboriginal English to Indigenous families is highlighted by Eades (1993), when she explains that:

> Aboriginal English is spoken throughout Australia as either the first or second language of a great majority of Aboriginal people ... Aboriginal English plays an important role in the maintenance and assertion of Aboriginal identity ... Aboriginal people have long used language and speech as markers of group identity ... Aboriginal ways of communicating remain strong, and Aboriginal English signals Aboriginality in many subtle ways.
>
> The accent, vocabulary and grammatical patterns of Aboriginal English enable Aboriginal people from all over the country to recognize other Aboriginal people, even in contexts where visible markers of identity are not present ... (Eades, 1993: 30–1)

The cultural construction of literacy: what is Indigenous literacy?

In order to understand what Indigenous Australian literacy might entail, we first need to consider the accumulated experience we call Indigenous culture and the belief that literacy development is essentially a collaborative social process rather than an individual activity. As with Western religions, Indigenous spiritual beliefs explain how the natural world was created. For many Indigenous cultures their lore explains how the land was shaped by the *creation beings* as these creatures traversed the land. The stories of these feats have been orally handed down continuously to each successive generation for more than 40,000 years.

The natural features within the homelands of each indigenous cultural group are therefore the symbols that contain important information. Indigenous people have drawn on this information to explain their origins, to make sense of their world and

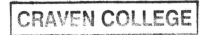

to practise and maintain their cultures. Reading the land is therefore only possible within the context of the stories, lores and ways of relating to each other and to their homelands. Most of the family stories we co-constructed with the Indigenous communities in the project contained examples of reading the land (Fleer and Williams-Kennedy, 2001: 34, 96).

Generally speaking, a traditional Indigenous view of Indigenous literacy would be the ability to communicate appropriately within kinship systems, as well as being able to read and interpret local symbols of nature, in order to sustain and maintain family and culture. The various modes of interaction within the family stories demonstrate a range of communication methods.

In contemporary Australia, language and culturally recognised symbols (e.g. kinship relationships, terms and symbols, hand signs, gestures, symbols in paintings and stories) are the media used by many Indigenous people to communicate with each other. These modes of communication are also used to record, express and pass on information to others within local kinship systems. One of the parents on the project defined literacy as follows:

> Literacy is language.
> Literacy is how we communicate.
> Literacy is in dancing, singing … and culture.
> Literacy is how to pass on a message to younger children and to everyone else.
> Literacy is how we communicate, not just reading and writing.
> Literacy is everything else. (Fleer and Williams-Kennedy, 2001: 98, 100)

Multiple literacies

Indigenous literacy therefore involves speaking, listening, reading natural and man-made symbols, recording language in lore, stories, songs, dance, rituals and traditions, and observing body and sign language, combined with intuitive and critical thinking. Religious and spiritual beliefs, values, customs and traditions are embedded within all of these elements.

Both spoken and symbolic language are used by Indigenous people in many different forms. Included within these forms are speaking, reading, writing (using Indigenous symbols and languages as well as English), painting, making music, singing, dancing and story-telling. Versions of representation vary according to context, purpose and audience.

Language is also contained within intangibles such as feelings (made obvious through body language and actions), thought pictures (images and visions) and word pictures or metaphors. Thought pictures, pictures and word pictures are multidimensional and at times intuitive representations that can be interpreted from many different perspectives. Words, however, are usually more prescriptive symbols with a specific range of meanings that change only if placed and used in different contexts (Fleer and Williams-Kennedy, 2001: 98).

When many Indigenous children first commence preschool or school, they already know how to listen and how to speak in their mother tongue, in English or in both languages. They can also read many symbols of significance to their various cultures. Within Indigenous literacy, meaning is expressed through the people themselves. Even though Indigenous peoples differ in their contemporary use of literacy, for many their skills and knowledge are still linked to a traditional view of the world. Therefore when many Indigenous children enter schools or preschools, they are second literacy learners. It is not surprising, then, that they may experience confusion and difficulty when learning a partially or completely new system of literacy – Western school literacy (Fleer and Williams-Kennedy, 2001: 97).

Western school literacy

What is literacy? The *Preschool Profile* notes (DETYA, 2001) state that:

> In preschool, children need to begin to understand the purposes and function of written language (the details and the 'how' will come later in school) and how, as we do with oral language, to vary it to suit audience and context. Children are assisted in this process if their preschool environment reflects and more closely matches the environment of the home and community. The children then become more rapidly aware of the range of purposes and functions of print in the lives of literate people in real-life, authentic contexts. (p. 13)

The National Literacy Plan developed by the Department of Education, Training and Youth Affairs (DETYA, 2000) defines literacy as:

> Language in use – speaking, listening, reading, viewing, writing and drawing. What is involved in each of these language modes varies according to context, purpose and audience.

Context, purpose and communication are common threads between the definitions. These dimensions are also evident in Chapter 13 by Hill and Nichols. In contrast to Tymms and Merrell (Chapter 9 this volume), Hill and Nicols illustrate the significance of purpose and context through case examples where home and school linkages are made visible when making judgements about how and what children know in literacy. Reading the land, spiritual connections and communicating through dance and music are generally areas that are not included in Western school forms of literacy (Fleer and Williams-Kennedy, 2001: 100). These areas did not appear to be evident in Tymms and Merrell's assessment of literacy for children in Western Australia, a state with significantly large numbers of Indigenous children.

Indigenous and non-Indigenous children read the world all the time. Young children are continually trying to make sense of their environment by interpreting the visual cues that particular groups have framed for them and expect them to know. For example, young children soon learn to interpret hand gestures, facial expressions, tone of voice, body language, relationships with family members, artefacts (e.g. pictures, toys, books, digging sticks) and environmental features (significant landmarks).

> Although different cultural groups will have different emphases and place greater importance on some elements (such as family relationships), what is important is the recognition that children learn to interpret these symbols in their prior-to-school environments,

and that these be valued as the child's early forms of reading. They are examples of how to acquire reading process skills. Understanding that young children already possess reading process competence is the first step in developing reading programs which build upon the children's developing literacy skills. For educators, the second step is learning about the symbols that young children have already learned to read in their home environments. (Fleer and Williams-Kennedy, 2001: 23, 24)

The family stories briefly opened a window into the lives of six Indigenous children from different areas of Australia whose everyday, lived experiences were at the core of the project. These stories provide researchers and educators with a series of real contexts to begin the process of demystifying Indigenous worldviews, school learning and literacy outcomes for young Aboriginal children growing up in Australia today. However, it must be acknowledged that only a portion of the complex and tightly woven set of connected cultural practices can ever be revealed and shared by the families within the workshop process and the time available for this project. The family stories can provide only a starting point or snapshot and not a full picture of literacy learning for young Indigenous children, but we can learn much from them about the nature of knowledge in communities within informal (home) and formal (school) communities.

PART 3

ASSESSMENT IN EARLY YEARS SETTINGS

CHAPTER 8

THE CONSEQUENCES OF SOCIOCULTURAL ASSESSMENT

Bronwen Cowie and Margaret Carr

Introduction

Assessments are a tool for social thinking and action. We suggest that in an early child-hood or school setting this social thinking and action is of a particular kind and has a particular purpose: mutual feedback and dialogue about learning. Although assessment for this purpose is part of pedagogy and therefore can be ongoing and undocumented, this chapter is about documented assessment.

We take the view that learning and development, rather than being primarily about individual achievement, is distributed over, stretched across, people, places and things (Perkins, 1993; Salomon, 1993). This is a situated or sociocultural viewpoint about learning and development, one in which the early childhood centre or the classroom is seen as a 'community of learners' (Brown et al., 1993; Rogoff, 1990; Wenger, 1998), and in which teaching will target the learner-plus-the-surround. In James Wertsch's words, teaching and learning is about individual(s)-acting-with-mediational-means (Wertsch, 1991: 12) rather than individuals on their own, and so there is an emphasis on development as the transformation of participation in a range of contexts (Bronfenbrenner, 1979; Rogoff, 1997). To be consistent with this view of learning and development *assessment* needs to be distributed across people, places and things.

People refers to peers, teachers, families in the widest sense: their relationships with the learner, expectations, goals, prior knowledge and experience, and intuitions. *Places* refers to features of the classroom or early childhood setting, the centre or classroom atmosphere and organisational structures. *Things* refers to artefacts and materials. Given these general assumptions about learning, development and assessment we have found that the consequences of documented assessments in early childhood can play out in three ways:

- Assessments act as a 'conscription device' (a recruitment) for participants, establishing the membership of a social *community* of learners and teachers: children, families and the staff team.
- Assessments are a means by which *competence* and competent learners are constructed.
- Assessments illustrate and support *continuity* in learning. They provide a venue for the negotiation and navigation of individual and collective learning trajectories. They invite participants to discuss what is being learned and to decide what might come next. This storying and restorying constructs multiple pathways of learning as 'work in progress'.

This chapter explains and illustrates each of these three clusters of consequence, using examples from New Zealand early childhood settings.

Community

Writing about classrooms, Roth and Roychoudhury (1994: 439) have suggested that concept maps act as a 'conscription device' that 'brings together individuals in a common task' and 'serves as a social glue between them'. Assessments can do this too. In terms of 'bringing individuals together in a common task' they can illustrate and influence the curriculum for participating children, teachers and families. In a study by Cowie (2000), Year 7–10 students (age 10–14) were emphatic that what would be 'in the test' guided what they did and learned. While this is a kind of 'hard conscription', a softer alternative is for participants to come to share and value similar goals. If we return to the French medieval meaning of conscription, as 'writing together', then conscription can refer to the co-construction of stories about learning and what is to be learned, jointly authored by learners and teachers. In the following example, Quin and her teacher write an assessment together, and Quin's conclusion refers to the learning that both teacher and learner might have gained.

Example

Quin draws a picture of her house and letterbox with a large 4 on it. She dictates an accompanying story to her childcare teacher who has difficulty with the street name, getting it wrong several times. The teacher finally looks it up and writes it correctly. The teacher's errors are written into the assessment record and a comment on the learning in this episode is also dictated by Quin: 'Everyone makes mistakes'.

Narrative assessments (written by teachers or families, dictated by children), particularly those accompanied by photographs, are especially good conscription devices. In New Zealand a number of early childhood centres are using 'learning stories' as a framework for assessment interactions (Carr, 2001a and b). This framework has been developed as a response to a socioculturally oriented national curriculum, as outlined in Chapter 1, in which the strands of outcome are well-being, belonging, communication, contribution and exploration: an emphasis on participation. 'Learning stories' are structured narratives that track children's strengths and interests: they emphasise the aim of early childhood as the development of children's identities as competent learners in a range of different arenas. They include an analysis of the learning (a 'short-term review') and a 'what next?' section. The narratives frequently include the interactions between teacher and learner, or between peers; often the episode is dictated by the learner as a 'child's voice'. The portfolios or folders in which they are housed invite families to contribute their own stories and comments.

The national curriculum document, *Te Whariki*, leaves considerable opportunity for local 'weaving' (*Te Whariki* means, in Maori, a woven mat) so the curriculum can be locally responsive (Carr and May, 1994) and achievement can be locally legitimated (Bishop and Glynn, 1999). The community may have a strong voice in the interpretation of such aims as 'belonging', 'contribution' and 'communication'. The following example illustrates a parent's role in shaping the curriculum through her contribution to the assessments.

Example

Andrew's mother wrote a contribution to his assessment portfolio describing a family day at an adventure park during the weekend. She described how he had the courage to have a go on the 'flying fox'. She then added, 'So I would like to see Andrew sharing his stories with his friends at the kindergarten mat time'. She interprets as part of the 'communication' strand of the curriculum an ability to stand up in front of peers and relate a story or an experience.

Andrew showed the teacher his mother's story and she then wrote the follow-up: 'We had a great discussion about the fun he had had on the flying fox and his visit to the park. I then suggested that he might like to draw or paint a picture about his great weekend and then we could write his story too. Andrew decided to draw a picture and went and collected paper and pens. As he created his picture he explained how the flying fox worked and I recorded his words. After I had finished writing Andrew said he would write his name. Andrew requested to share his story and his mum's story at mat time. He very proudly stood up the front with his file and picture. He told the children about his flying fox adventure and I read his story from his file.' A copy of the drawing and a photograph of Andrew telling the story was added to the portfolio as well.

Learning stories are designed to reflect and enhance reciprocal and responsive interactions and to develop and support atmospheres of trust and respect. They encourage children to be prepared to think about and to display their learning at appropriate times (a disposition associated with early literacy achievement emphasised by Susan Hill and colleagues (1998: 165) and Bronwen Cowie's research with students aged 10–14), and they encourage families to share their expectations and concerns. These documented, narrative and credit-based assessments crystallise the long-standing early childhood practice of describing and discussing what a child has done and achieved during the day – and of children taking home their paintings and models. Etienne Wenger (1998) describes this process of documentation as an example of 'reification': informal practice has been 'concretised' or reified.

A curriculum reified in written assessments that are accessible and detailed enables children and families to suggest developments and alternatives, to bring ideas and knowledge from home, and to clarify teachers' interpretations. In this way the assessment both enlists participation and is jointly constructed as an artefact of the community of practice. In the following example, a parent adds an analysis to a learning story.

Example

Vini, aged 4, tells the teachers that his mother needs new slippers. He makes a pair for her (with much measuring and gluing and decorating), and when the teachers write this up their assessment emphasises Vini's developing identity as a 'caring' and thoughtful person. His mother contributes a comment to the assessment folder that adds a reference to the technical expertise that this work illustrated: she writes that the slippers Vini made were 'unbelievable in terms of thoughtfulness and technical perfection for a little child'.

Research indicates the power of family expectations on learning achievement and on what could and should be achieved (Frome and Eccles, 1998). Documented assessment makes learning visible in ways that can provide opportunities for negotiation and families may revise their 'folk' (Olson and Bruner, 1996) assumptions. Radford (2001) described a parent making a contribution to her son's kindergarten portfolio. One of the stories the parent chose to write about was of Tom making a card for his Nan in which he wanted to draw a 'gust of wind' and persevered until he was satisfied. The parent commented that writing stories for the portfolio led her to 'stop and really look' at her view of valued learning in early childhood:

> 'Cause you just get on with ordinary everyday life, and you start taking things for granted about them, whereas this sort of thing [being invited to contribute to the assessment folder] makes you stop and really look, and think about "oh … yes that's really interesting". Or that's quite a big learning step for them, by doing what they did, or what they said.'

The same parent commented about her response to the early childhood centre's learning stories: 'It's really made me realise, and I'm so glad, 'cause now I'm quite happy to do more fun things with Tom, and don't care if we don't do what I used to call "learning".' She had revised her views of what is involved in school readiness. Documentation or data collection can also prompt teachers to revise their assumptions about children in their classrooms or early childhood centres (Timperley and Robinson, 2001).

Competence

Etienne Wenger has this to say about competence within a community (1998: 152):

> When we are with a community of practice of which we are a full member, we are in familiar territory. We can handle ourselves competently. We experience competence and we are recognised as competent.

From the perspective of the early childhood centre as a community of learners or a community of practice, the major goals and outcomes of learning are not primarily the collection of skills and knowledge but are 'successful participation in socially organized activity and the development of students' identities as learners' (Greeno, 1997: 9). Gipps (2002), writing about sociocultural approaches to assessment, comments that 'assessment plays a key role in identity formation, in particular because of its public nature'. Writers on assessment remind us that students bring models of learning and of the self as a learner which may be an obstacle to their own learning (Purdie and Hattie, 1996). Black and Wiliam comment that 'There is evidence from many studies that learners' beliefs about their capacity as learners can affect their achievement' (1998: 24).

What might developing 'identities as learners' mean? We suggest that there are three possible facets to this popular idea: identifying with a range of sociocultural roles, developing learning dispositions towards participation, and becoming a self-assessor.

Identifying with a wide range of sociocultural roles

In a learning community children will have the opportunity to take up a range of sociocultural roles and acquire their associated skills, knowledges and attitudes: teacher, student, friend, measurer, jam-maker, tower-builder, painter, observer of insects, reader. In the following example, Tyler-Jackson is a teacher for Tenaya. Some time later, Tenaya takes on the same sort of teacher role for Sean.

In a setting where the curriculum is woven locally or 'permeable' (Comber, 2000), children set curriculum goals for each other. In the following example, Tyler-Jackson has taught Tenaya that peers help each other here, in the same way as teachers assist children. The documentation reifies this as a valued curriculum goal.

Example

On 23 August an entry in Tyler-Jackson's assessment folder records his assistance to Tenaya. Tyler-Jackson is 27 months old. 'Tenaya [20 months] is sitting in a high-chair with her lunch box on the table beside her. Tyler-Jackson opens Tenaya's lunch box and offers her raisins. She shakes her head. He offers her yoghurt. She nods and reaches out with both hands. Tyler-Jackson struggles but takes off the foil top and puts it on the high-chair tray. He then walks towards the cupboard saying "Soon, soon [spoon, spoon]". "Tyler-Jackson, do you want a spoon?" He nods and points to Tenaya. I give Tyler-Jackson the spoon and say "Did you give Tenaya her yoghurt and open it for her?" He nods – walks towards Tenaya and says "No fig as [fingers]", takes the yoghurt off the tray, gives the spoon to Tenaya then puts the yoghurt back on the tray and says "Soon, soon".' [The teacher's analysis of the learning lists the following: took responsibility for others, met the needs of another before his own, followed a sequence of events: opened lunch box, offered choices, opened yoghurt and got spoon.] On 12 September an entry in Tenaya's folder records the following: 'Tenaya walks over to Sean in the high chair, gives him his lunch box, opens it and takes out the raisins. Sean holds out his hands. Tenaya asks, "Raisins?" Tenaya opens the box and takes out some of the raisins and puts them on the tray in front of Sean. (There is some difficulty but she succeeds.) When Sean has taken three raisins she gives him more, puts the box of raisins back in Sean's lunch box and pulls out the sandwiches wrapped in glad wrap ... She separates one sandwich and gives it to him.'

Tyler-Jackson is also teaching Tenaya that at lunchtime the rule with yoghurt is 'spoons, no fingers'. Assessments recognise role models from the community outside the classroom as well:

Example

In a group learning story, written for each child who participated in a tapa-making project at a centre, the children are reminded of the work of a Pacific nations artist by the inclusion of a photo of the artist and his work, together with some background information of interest to families. The teacher wrote: 'The children were very interested in discussing how tapa was traditionally made as well as what motivated the artists in making their designs.' [Tapa is a cloth made from fibre, traditionally decorated in geometric blocks.]

Through interactions with peers children also construct their own communities and explore a range of social identities (being a 'good girl' for instance – Carr, 2001a, 2001b). Adults, however, will want to offer alternatives, assuming that education is about 'suggesting new directions in which lives may go' (Donaldson, 1992: 259).

Developing learning dispositions towards participation

In a learning community children will have the opportunity to explore and to take up a range of learning dispositions. The learning story assessment format is framed around learning dispositions or participation repertoires: being ready, willing and able to, for instance, take an interest and be involved, tackle difficulty and persist when the outcome is uncertain, share ideas with others and take responsibility. Portfolios can track such learning dispositions. The following is a comment from a parent about deep involvement and persistence.

Example

Neeve has been focused and involved at her childcare centre in making dinosaurs in a range of media over some time. Just before she goes to school, her mother commented in her portfolio on 'How intensely she applied herself to the task and how quickly she learnt'. In another context she wrote: 'Robyn [one of the teachers], I think I understand what you said the other day about Neeve using her learning strategies in other areas of learning! Neeve wanted to tie up her shoelace and I showed her how. She practised and practised and practised and in the morning she said, "Look, Mummy I can do up my shoe lace!" And she could.'

In this way assessment serves to strengthen children's identifications as learners across a range of contexts in ways that benefit and avoid harm to learning dispositions or habits of mind (Crooks, 1993).

Becoming a self-assessor

James and Prout (1997: ix), writing about constructing and reconstructing childhood, comment that 'it is now more common to find acknowledgement that childhood should be regarded as a part of society and culture than a precursor to it; and that children should be seen as already social actors not beings in the process of becoming such'. Young children are very capable of self-assessment. Confident self-assessment of what constitutes a valid and valued learning contribution or question is crucial if students are to participate spontaneously as members of a community of learners.

> ## Example
>
> A 4-year-old is hula-hooping and says to the teacher: 'Write about my moves. I keep wriggling to keep it moving. When it goes low I have to go faster, see?' [The teacher does write about the hula-hooping moves and the child's analysis of these. She also takes photographs illustrating the hoop both high and low.]

In early childhood settings where learning and assessment are distributed across and legitimated by *things*, activities and materials, the criteria for successful learning are embedded in the actions. Completing jigsaws is a classic example of an activity that provides feedback about success; so is an activity like making a hat that fits the maker (Carr, 2000a), or a toddler learning to climb into a swing. Activities with this autotelic quality are often accessible and engaging for children and they play a key role in fostering children's agency by maintaining their independence from teacher judgement.

Claxton (1995: 340) points out that many goals in education are developed by learners as they go along, and many of them are hidden from the adult observer. This is especially the case in early childhood:

> It is striking that the focus here [in a paper in a journal] is predominantly on evaluation of the work with respect to criteria that are largely external, explicit, predetermined and generalized. What is excluded here is all the situations in which learners are developing their sense of what counts as 'good work' for themselves – where it is some inner sense of satisfaction which is the touchstone of 'quality'; where the sense of 'quality' is an holistic matter of taste, 'nose' or intuition, rather than the application of rules; where the sense of what it is that one is trying to achieve develops and changes in the course of the learning itself – where the goal is at least partly revealed as you go along, rather than being clearly specified in advance; where the criteria are specific to a piece of work. (Claxton, 1995: 340)

In the following example, the teacher records an occasion in which Lauren appears to be developing her sense of what counts as 'good work' where the goal was not clearly specified in advance.

> ## Example
>
> Lauren is screen-printing, and the teacher records her comments throughout the process. 'As she was drawing she said almost to herself, "I'll have to concentrate" and she did.' When she aligned a second template (a basket) over an earlier print (a cat) and made a second print: 'She looked at it and said "Oh no! That's not right! The cat needs to be in the basket, not up there!" She tried again, and when she aligned basket and cat to her satisfaction, and added a few more items to the picture, she commented "I like that".'

Documented assessments can also contribute to children's appreciation of what is valued and what they have accomplished.

> ### Example
>
> A parent's contribution to Charlotte's assessments comments: 'Charlotte is very proud of her folder ... she took it home and couldn't wait to show her sister as soon as she got out of school and then all our family who came to visit at the weekend. She wanted to talk us through every aspect!'

The process of documenting assessment through jointly authored storying highlights for teachers and parents the scope of children's appreciation and analysis of their own learning.

Continuity

The literature on formative assessment concerns itself mostly with an assessment's capacity to shape learning pathways. Often that pathway is defined by reference to levels or standards. For Sadler (1989), for instance, the formative 'shaping and improving the student's competence' means closing a 'gap' between an actual level of competence and a reference level. As teachers and students learn to recognise a fine performance, 'feedback' provides a means for bridging the gap between this and the student's current performance. However, where pathways are developed with reference to 'developing identities as competent learners' – expertise in a range of available sociocultural models, increasingly complex and wide-ranging participation repertoires, and the pursuit of personal and locally collective goals – then such pathways will be multidirectional, locally contextualised and emergent. It is unlikely that many of them will be available with universal, national or completely prescribed reference levels and standards.

With this proviso, documented learning pathways can provide platforms for further learning. In New Zealand early childhood settings, for instance, many portfolios or folders record continuity in children's participation in the community as children become more 'at home': their developing sense of belonging. One parent noted on her baby's record the day she came that the baby was absorbed in a music activity and didn't 'drop everything and cry if Mum doesn't pick me up immediately'. Support for continuity is important as children explore what it means to build relationships, develop and express ideas and seek to make sense of their environment. Maria, in the next example, is reviewing her art portfolio for the previous months.

Example

Maria's folder includes the following: 'I showed Maria her folio, which contained all of her *kowhaiwhai* designs [completed over a number of months]. She was very excited to see all of her work displayed and looked through her work, examining it closely.' Comments from Maria included: recall about the process, the context (one of her sketches was drawn during a *marae* visit), the similarity in designs over time, and a criticism of one of her paintings (a small section of the design had not been painted). The collection included background information on *kowhaiwhai* patterns and Maria identified the '*kaperua*' pattern that another child had painted. The teacher commented that Maria finds patterns throughout the environment, and a written contribution from Maria's mother recounted a story about Maria's recognition of *kowhaiwhai* patterns at the mother's workplace. [*Kowhaiwhai* patterns are a type of frieze that appears in maori architecture.]

Here is an example in which the teacher remembers previous learning stories in which Harry has made elaborate frames for his drawings and paintings. She calls on this prior experience to suggest some continuity.

Example

A learning story in Harry's portfolio starts in this way: 'Harry has done three small pastel drawings and Jo and I were admiring them with Harry. "Perhaps you could frame them?", I suggest to Harry (thinking about his previous learning stories)? "Yeah!" says Harry.' [He does so, with much decision-making and measuring.]

Frequently a parent will provide some of the continuity. In the next example, a parent contributes to an accumulation of evidence of rich and intertwined individual and collective learning.

Example

Parent contribution to Tane's folder: 'Tane has had an ongoing enthusiasm for sewing projects following a session at kindy [kindergarten] where he used a needle and thread for the first time. With his Mum-mum [grandmother] he made a bag with button decorations and pictured above is the apron he made last week ... The biggest challenge was coming to grips with having to finish each seam with some kind of knot to keep it all together.' Tane's folder records the development of this enthusiasm and these skills at the early childhood centre over time, together with the involvement

> of other children: his mastery of a sewing machine, his drawing of patterns, his discussion with Sarah about the best fabric for the job, his sewing of an outfit, a motorcycle helmet, and, together with two other children, a decorated jacket.

In the learning story framework, a 'what next?' section prompts consideration of the possibilities for further learning. It is designed to refer to the past and the present to encourage consideration of where to go next by providing a space for this to be discussed between children and teachers (and, perhaps, families). In the following example, the teacher contributes a tentative note to the goals for the next step.

Example

Isaac and a group of children have been reading a book about space with the teacher. Isaac decides to make an 'alien' out of green card 'cos aliens are green'. In the 'What next?' section of the assessment the teacher has written the following: 'Keep supporting and extending his interest in Space, which is encouraging him to try new things (using the art area resources) and practise exploring his imagination and communicating his ideas. We have downloaded pictures of planets off the Internet for him, bought new books, and been playing the "Planet" CD for the children to listen to. The term break may have some effect on the interest, so we will have to wait and see if this is still topical when he comes back. A little "provocation" (alien footprints in the family area perhaps, or a trip to the Star Dome), may help trigger something ... who knows?'

Learning trajectories documented in this way are not 'deeply coded' (Sadler, 1989) in the way grades or marks might be. Sadler adds that if feedback information is too deeply coded (i.e. as summative grades), it can be difficult for learners to monitor their learning pathway. Rather, they are designed to be accessible to learners and their families. They represent teachers' professional understandings but couched as they are in tentative terms they encourage dialogue and support a view of learning as ongoing. Although in early childhood grading is unusual, baseline assessments at school entry may use grading, and these assessments have the potential to powerfully influence the opportunities to learn in the year before school entry. When one of the aims for early childhood education and, we could argue, education for life-long learning (Carr and Claxton, 2002) is learning dispositions and participation repertoires, then assessment that itself encourages the learner's desire to learn by documenting interest, involvement, persistence, communication and responsibility will contribute to the emergence of a disposition towards 'learning goals' rather than 'performance goals' (Ames, 1992; Smiley and Dweck, 1994). Assessments that call on reference levels or standards that children and families have not understood or legitimated are likely to shift this orientation towards *performance* goals: an interest in 'being right', not being discovered to be unable, a reluctance to risk making an error.

Conclusion

In early childhood settings that take a 'distributed' view of curriculum and assessment, assessments will call on criteria that will be emergent, situated, student- or child-referenced and negotiated. The assessment process will acknowledge those occasions when children have their own sense of satisfaction in a task well done, using their own (frequently hidden) criteria. They will reflect the balances that have been struck between discussion and documentation, between participation and reification, in providing feedback to learners and their families and in suggesting what the next step might look like. And they will provide avenues for all participants to achieve a considerable measure of access, ownership and legitimation. This level of active engagement poses a challenge for teachers who are more used to top-down curriculum and assessment processes. In New Zealand, curriculum policy initiatives in the school sector have set up an alignment between five key competencies in the school curriculum (Ministry of Education, 2007) and the five strands of *Te Whāriki*, the early childhood curriculum. This provides new possibilities for the documentation of learning trajectories from early childhood to school and therefore for collaborative discussions on children's learning and assessment that use a common language. This recognition of the continuity of learning experience is important when the vision is the development of dispositions for life-long learning. Learning stories as a sociocultural assessment practice are being explored in international projects where learning dispositions are of interest (for example, Leau et al., 2007).

Sociocultural assessment practices are complex and dynamic and are therefore a challenge for teachers. In recent years, the authors of this chapter have been involved in the development of assessment exemplars for the early childhood sector that illustrate the practice of sociocultural assessment (Carr et al., 2004). Three of the exemplar books illustrate and provide theoretical underpinning for the three clusters of consequences in this chapter. These exemplars have been designed to act as a conscription device to establish a *community* of early childhood teachers who want to talk about learning and assessment. They aim to be permeable: providing social spaces for new *competencies* in assessment. Finally, they invite teachers to think about *continuity* in their own learning around assessment: to set up dialogue opportunities within their own settings as they adapt formats and try out new ideas. Sociocultural assessment practices distribute responsibility for assessment across the early years community, local and national.

Acknowledgements

This chapter is adapted from a Position Paper prepared by the authors for the New Zealand Ministry of Education Early Childhood Learning and Assessment Exemplar Project. The authors acknowledge funding assistance from the New Zealand Ministry of Education. We thank the families and teachers for their permissions, through the ECLA Exemplar Project, to include their quotes and assessments.

CHAPTER 9

ON-ENTRY BASELINE ASSESSMENT ACROSS CULTURES

Peter Tymms and Christine Merrell

Introduction

This chapter describes the development of an on-entry baseline assessment that has been used extensively in England for several years and has also been translated and modified for use internationally. The baseline was originally devised to provide a fixed point from which progress could be assessed. Its purpose has, however, evolved and it is now seen as providing practitioners with a detailed profile of their pupils from which to plan an appropriate curriculum and against which progress can be measured. Additionally, collecting data internationally from a single assessment gives an opportunity for the investigation of the developmental pathways, levels and skills of children from different countries and cultures from the point when they start full-time education.

The PIPS on-entry baseline assessment

Development of the assessment

The original assessment was created for use in England to provide teachers with information about what children could do when they started school so that there would be reliable data from which later assessments in schools could be put into context. More specifically, the idea was to look at the relative progress of children in their own situation compared with the relative progress of children with similar baseline profiles in other, similar contexts. This 'value-added' approach has been widely adopted within England and, increasingly, in the rest of the world (see, for example, Fitz-Gibbon, 1996; Fitz-Gibbon and Tymms, 2002; Sanders and Horn, 1995; Tymms, 1999a). The work described in this chapter was carried out within the Curriculum, Evaluation and Management (CEM) Centre at Durham University and forms part of the broad family of professional monitoring projects run from the Centre. It is distinctive in that it involved working directly with the profession (teachers, heads and advisers) as well as building upon theoretical research findings in order to construct a monitoring system that would be of use to the profession. This is in stark contrast to the government-run testing system of England, which was created in order to hold teachers and schools to account. The statutory End of Key Stage assessments currently used in England are part of this official system designed to drive up standards (see, for example, Shorrocks-Taylor, 1999) though their use in primary schools is currently under revision.

The baseline assessment, which is part of the Performance Indicators in Primary Schools (PIPS) project (see, for example, Tymms and Albone, 2002), was created in 1994 with the support of the National Association of Head Teachers and two local education authorities with working parties advising on the development work. It was refined over subsequent years in response to the statistical analysis of the data collected and comments from teachers largely concerning the practical issues of administration. Most changes were made in the first couple of years and, as time has passed, fewer and fewer changes have been made. This makes it possible to monitor trends over time with a stable assessment. The basis of the assessment was a structure that took the stance that children start at school having come from a very great variety of different backgrounds but, regardless of that, the assessment should establish what they know and can do at the point of entry. The choice of material for the assessment focused on information that would best inform us about how children would be likely to progress in school. In other words, the idea was to create a baseline that would allow for fair comparisons of progress later. The literature was consulted to see what were good predictors of later success or difficulty of young children. There is extensive literature on which to draw, particularly for progress in literacy, to a lesser extent for progress in mathematics and to a much smaller extent for progress in other areas. Later we were able to confirm that the subunits of the baseline, chosen by reading the literature, were acting well as predictors (Tymms, 1999b), although, as expected, there was variation in their efficacy. Teachers have traditionally carried out a baseline assessment, either of their own making or published, with new pupils when they started school but using that information for value-added purposes was rare at the time when the PIPS baseline assessment was first developed (see, for example, Wolfendale, 1993), and existing published baseline assessments were not designed for that purpose. There was no published baseline that included phonological awareness as well as vocabulary and digit identification, all of which have been shown to be good predictors of later achievement. Nor was there any computer-adaptive baseline.

The PIPS on-entry baseline assessment is now used in several thousand schools. These are largely in England but it is widely used in Scotland, Australia and New Zealand, with growing use in the Netherlands, Germany, Hong Kong and South Africa as well as several international schools around the world. It is conducted on an individual basis and takes approximately 20 minutes per child.

Although the initial purpose of the assessment was to act as a base for value-added, its use has evolved in practice and teachers routinely use it to get to know the pupils when they first arrive at the school and to help to inform their practice. Further, many teachers have found the action of assessing to be useful in itself. They often comment that spending 20 minutes with each child helps build a good relationship and that it is not just the child's reaction to assessment items that matters but the way in which the child responds which gives valuable information. In response to requests from teachers, the assessment has now been extended to include personal, social and emotional development. There has been an additional extension of it down into the nursery years, where motor development is also monitored, in a project known as the Assessment Profile on Entry for Children and Toddlers (ASPECTS).

The manner in which the assessment was constructed has already been noted but there were other basic principles employed during the development phase and they were that it should be something that children enjoy doing, that teachers see as valuable and that it involves as little work and time as possible. Further, it would not simply record what the teachers knew already but it would develop new knowledge and would be as objective as possible, so that whoever carried out the assessment would get a similar result. Taken together, these requirements define an exacting task, especially with young children who are very variable in their attention spans and are often slow to respond. Getting a reliable assessment typically requires responses to many different items and this presented a problem. By careful work and refinement over the years, however, and crucially by constructing an assessment that was adaptive to the pupil's responses, the major problems have been overcome (further details can be found in Tymms, 2001).

How it works in practice

The assessment now comes in two formats – text and computer-delivered, although only the latter will be discussed here. Data from both formats of the assessment are returned to the CEM (Curriculum, Evaluation and Management) Centre for processing. Schools receive feedback in the form of standardised scores for each pupil and, at the same time, the CEM Centre has built up a large dataset over several years.

The following areas are assessed:

- handwriting – the child is asked to write his/her own name;
- vocabulary – the child is asked to identify objects embedded within a complex picture;
- ideas about reading – assesses concepts about print;
- phonological awareness – rhymes and repeats;
- letter identification – a fixed order of mixed upper and lower case letters;
- word recognition and reading;

- ideas about mathematics – assessment of understanding of mathematical concepts;
- counting;
- sums – addition and subtraction problems presented without symbols;
- shape identification;
- digit identification;
- maths problems – including sums with symbols.

The teacher works with individual pupils. The computer program presents the child with questions (orally) and, depending on the nature of the question, the child responds either by pointing to the answer from the choice of options on the screen or by saying the answer. The teacher records the child's response on-screen and the program selects the next question.

The way that the assessment works can be well illustrated by referring to the section relating to vocabulary. A child is shown a picture and asked to point out where a certain item is on the picture. The picture is of a kitchen and the first item for the English version is 'carrots'. We now know that practically every child starting school at the age of 4 in England whose first language is English can point to carrots on the picture, and this is, incidentally, also true in New Zealand, Scotland and Australia. The program then moves on to another item and another. Each time the item becomes harder.

There are three pictures to assess vocabulary, each with progressively more difficult items until finally it becomes too difficult for almost all children at the start of school, with items such as yacht and microscope. However, being adaptive, children are not faced with items that are inappropriately difficult. The computer continues until the child has got a few wrong and then moves to a different section. In each section the plan is the same: to start at an easy point and move through to harder items.

When we reassess pupils after the teachers have assessed them, with the pupils picked at random around England, we find almost coincident results. The latest exercise produced an exceptionally high reliability figure of 0.98. We also find that this assessment does exactly what it is intended to do: it predicts later success or difficulties well and the correlation up to reading three years later is about 0.7, and for mathematics about 0.7. The correlation with general academic success at the end of primary education seven years later when the children are 11 years old is also almost 0.7 (Tymms et al., 2007). In psychometric terms this is an exceptional assessment.

Adoption of the baseline assessment in England

The PIPS baseline assessment was used in England for several years before there was any statutory requirement for assessment in the Foundation Stage. It started off in a small way but expanded rapidly. Just three years after its introduction approximately 42,000 children were assessed. Its use in English schools has continued to become more widespread despite the introduction of statutory assessments, including the Foundation Stage Profile, with 2500 schools using it in the 2006–7 academic year.

International experiences of PIPS

The content, adaptive nature of administration and high correlation with later achievement of the PIPS baseline assessment has attracted the attention of researchers in other countries and it is now used in the ways described earlier and also as an instrument to evaluate the impact of particular educational initiatives.

In Scotland (Curriculum, Evaluation and Management (CEM) Centre, 2007) there has been quite a rapid growth of the project and a third of education authorities are now using the PIPS on-entry assessment. In New Zealand (CEM Centre, 2007) it is used in about 80 schools and in Australia (CEM Centre, 2007), in about 800. The adoption of the assessment in each of these three countries has followed a different pattern, although the foresight of individuals has been important each time and it has been individual schools or districts that have decided to implement the assessment. It has not been something that schools have been required to do in the same way as the statutory requirements, such as the Foundation Stage Profile in England. The administration of the PIPS baseline was modified for use in Scotland, New Zealand and Australia by using a voice with a local accent for the sound files. Although the majority of items have remained the same, some small changes have been inevitable. For example, the picture of a traditional English windmill was thought to be inappropriate in Australia and the picture was changed.

PIPS has been adapted for use with deaf pupils who use British Sign Language and also for first language speakers of Bengali, Cantonese and Urdu in England. Additionally there are versions in Dutch, French, German, South African, Chinese, Slovenian and Thai. Researchers who understood the assessment and the area of development that each question was probing carried out each translation/adaptation. Any alterations to the nature and difficulty of the questions were kept to an absolute minimum.

International comparisons of assessment data

The data generated from the assessment administered in different countries allow a number of different questions to be explored. The starting points of young children in different countries might be expected to reflect the impact of home, culture, nutrition, preschool provision and the mother's health during pregnancy, among other factors (see, for example, Bellamy, 2001). Detailed information about children's development before the formal state school system allows hypotheses about preschool developmental influences to be more clearly formulated. It also sets down markers, which can be used to assess the impact of schooling in different countries. Some of the most valuable educational research comes from longitudinal data and, by setting up an international project that looks at the starting point of children, the groundwork can be laid for follow-up studies in the years to come. The purpose of international comparative data must ultimately be to assist policy-making and key issues about the impact of schooling across countries that can be addressed only by knowing more about the starting points of young children.

But is it feasible to use the same assessment across different countries? Of course, Scotland, Australia and New Zealand have a very similar heritage to England when

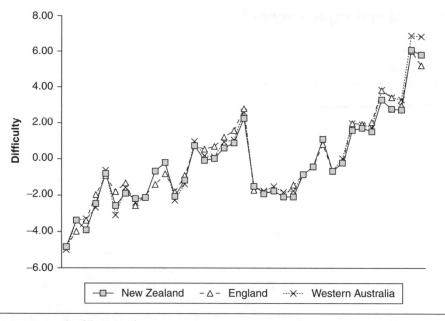

Figure 9.1   Maths (first part)

compared with most Asian, African, European or American countries. They are however, different in important ways in terms of their culture. The next logical step is to find out whether the questions in the assessment retain the same characteristics in different cultures. One way to explore this is to ask whether the relative difficulties of the items in those different countries remain stable.

Cross-cultural differences explored

Cultural influences are likely to be greater in some parts of the assessment. For example, while we might expect that the development in early mathematics (arithmetic) might be fairly consistent across different cultures, and indeed there is now evidence for a universal starting point of newborn infants in arithmetic (Wynn, 1992), nevertheless it might be that different cultures follow different developmental pathways after birth. It is clear, for example, that different counting systems have evolved in different cultures (Butterworth, 1999).

Figure 9.1 relates to the first part of the early maths section of the PIPS baseline and shows the relative difficulties of the items from England, Western Australia and New Zealand. An almost identical picture appears in each case. The data were based on a representative sample of 1000 cases from England and all of the data available in 2001 from New Zealand (1680 cases) and Western Australia (3390 cases). From each sample a Rasch model (see, for example, Bond and Fox, 2001) was used to estimate the difficulty levels of the items. The correlations between the difficulties were extremely high, as shown in Table 9.1.

At the other extreme, language clearly depends on the culture into which one is born. One would not expect a strong relationship between the difficulties of different

Table 9.1   Correlations between maths item difficulties

	New Zeland	England
England	0.987	
Australia	0.997	0.984

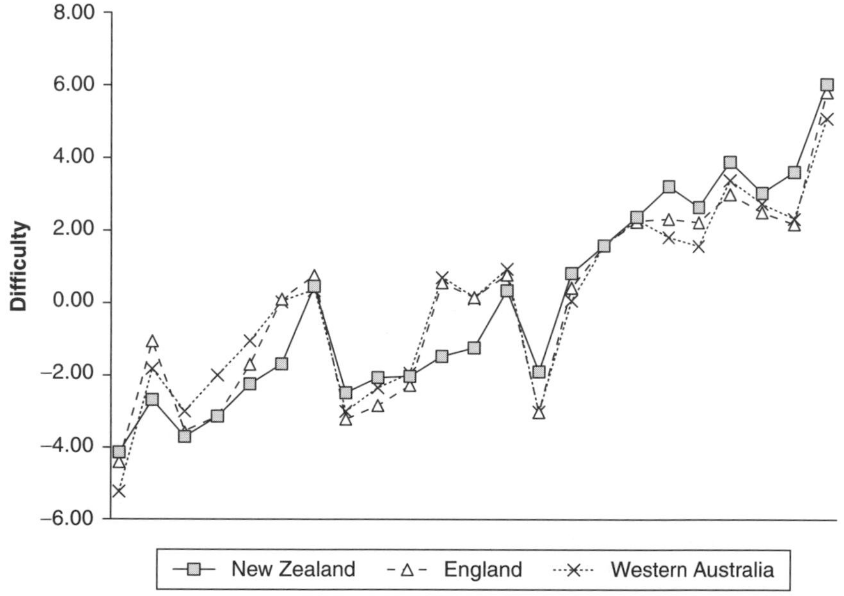

Figure 9.2   Vocabulary

words such as 'carrots' in different languages. Nevertheless there was a very strong relationship between the results from New Zealand, England and Australia as Figure 9.2 and the correlations in Table 9.2 show.

Lower correlations might be expected once the assessment is translated into another language, and that is indeed the case. The correlation between the English and Dutch maths item difficulties was 0.899. The correlation between the difficulties of vocabulary items (the Dutch items were simple direct translations of the English items) was 0.797. Despite being lower, the figures were still high.

Pursuing the theme of differences across cultures, it is instructive to ask if the assessment's predictive power lies in any one particular part of the assessment. Before this issue can be properly addressed, it is important to see how the assessment coped when predicting first reading and then mathematics of English pupils. This was done with a series of multiple regression analyses.

The results of these analyses are shown in Figure 9.3, which looks at the prediction of a maths assessment carried out three years later. The proportion of variance explained is plotted as each new variable is added into the equation. The line called 'full' shows that

Table 9.2   Correlations between vocabulary item difficulties

	New Zealand	England
England	0.934	
Australia	0.983	0.946

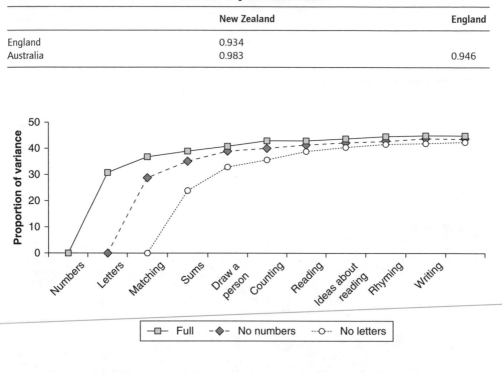

Figure 9.3   Prediction of maths assessment

30% is 'explained' by the best single predictor variable, called 'numbers' (a.k.a. digit identification). In fact digit identification remains the best single predictor of reading and mathematics achievement at age 11 years (Tymms et al., 2007). As each successive variable is added to the equation more variance is 'explained' but by less and less each time. The chart suggests the line asymptotically approaches about 45%. The second line was constructed by omitting the best predictor (numbers) entirely. Now the second best predictor comes into play immediately. This is 'Letters' (letter identification). Again the line continues to approach 45%. The third line omits both letter identification and numbers and the pattern repeats itself.

Is a Universal baseline assessment possible?

The analysis encouraged the view that it would be possible to construct a universal baseline that could act as an efficient predictor of later performance whatever the country and whatever the culture. This is because even if the most predictive parts of the assessment turned out to be heavily culturally related it would still be possible to rely on the more culturally independent sections of the assessment, of being able to do simple sums, count, understand basic concepts of print and write their own name.

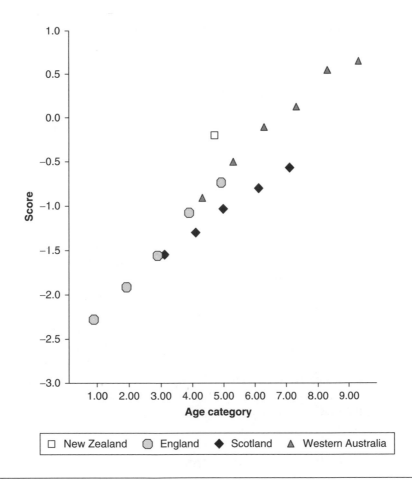

Figure 9.4   Reading scores of children starting school in England, New Zealand, Scotland and Western Australia

This should give a clear idea of the developmental level of children free of culture-dominated aspects. This is a strong claim and needs further investigation. But as more data have been collected the view has been strengthened. For example, when we compare the relative difficulties of the items from Indigenous populations in Australia against the non-Indigenous group we find very close similarities – the correlation between item difficulties for the whole assessment on entry to school for the two groups was 0.97 (but see page 101 for a different perspective). Within England we have found that the prediction of success in reading and mathematics follows almost identical patterns for children with various levels of hearing loss including those children with a severe level of impairment (Tymms et al., 2003). Data from children of different cultural backgrounds within the Netherlands show very similar patterns. So far, when comparing the assessment data of children from different cultures and very different situations, we have found very similar results for the pupils that have been assessed. Figure 9.4 compares the starting points of children in England, New Zealand, Scotland

and Western Australia. The age range of children on entry to school in these countries is different, although there is some overlap. The ages have been categorised on the bottom axis of the figure, with category 1 being the youngest at 4–4.25 years. The categories increase in quarter-year increments. Age for age, the reading scores of children in England and Western Australia are the same. The scores of the children in New Zealand, who all start school close to their fifth birthday, are slightly higher. The scores of children in Scotland show an interesting pattern, with the younger children being in line with those in England and Western Australia, but the older children starting school with relatively lower scores. It may be that the groups of older children include a significant proportion of children whose entry to school has been delayed because of special educational needs. The mathematics scores were very similar to those for reading. For a full description of the analysis, see Merrell and Tymms (2007).

One of the major areas of difference between countries is the writing system that is employed. Few difficulties arise when translating PIPS into European languages such as Dutch or German; they are essentially the same as English so far as the writing system is concerned and it is quite possible to include a section of letter identification for different countries. Similarly, a Thai translation can include a section assessing letter recognition since Thai writing is alphabetic. However, if one wants to translate the same section into Cantonese, there are considerable difficulties. Within the Cantonese system one is not dealing with an alphabetic system, which changes the entire nature of the section. It also, of course, has major implications for the child's education and the culture in the child lives. PIPS has been translated into Cantonese and is being refined but we have yet to test the hypothesis that prediction of later success at school will follow similar patterns to those in England.

The assessment climate in different countries

There are many uses for an international baseline assessment, some of which have been described in the previous section. It has also been shown that the format and content of the PIPS baseline assessment are appropriate for use in different countries and that the data collected are reliable with good predictive validity. However, an assessment cannot be successfully implemented without support from the teaching profession and possibly the government of a country. The assessment climate varies enormously from country to country and over time within countries, and in terms of both the methods of assessment and the uses of assessment data.

Significant changes in England during recent years provide a case in point. When the National Curriculum was starting, the PIPS project was also starting. The first author visited a primary school in the North-East of England and administered a half-hour test of mathematics with children aged 11. In doing the test, the author asked the children not to talk while they worked. The teacher was astounded and thought that the children would not be able to sit quietly for half an hour and that the test simply would not operate as was intended. She was genuinely surprised to see that the children managed to get on with what was required for 30 minutes. That was before the National Curriculum appeared and national testing got under way on a large scale. Since then the atmosphere has changed significantly. Government policy relating to the increased accountability of schools led to testing becoming a major feature across English state primary schools. Within the early years there are groups of psychologists and other researchers who would regard objective testing of young children as absolutely essential in order to make progress. Conversely, there are others who would regard objective assessments to be unreliable and inappropriate with young children, partly because of behavioural fluctuations, and propose observational data as the best way forward. The differing views are strongly held and are backed by heart-felt arguments. The influence of opinion has led the English government to make the latest statutory assessment for 5-year-olds (the Foundation Stage Profile) observational (see Chapter 1). With this assessment there are concerns about moderation and its reliability. If an assessment is unreliable, this inevitably means that the uses of the data are severely limited.

Outside England, there is also a diversity of practices and views, and the take-up of PIPS within the Anglophone countries shows that the assessment has made sense to and has been seen to be useful by many professionals. For example, Cowie (2002) described how the PIPS on-entry baseline assessment was introduced into the city of Aberdeen very successfully without a period of consultation and at a time of uncertainty over assessment in Scotland. He concluded that the successful introduction was dependent on 'the quality of the material; the ongoing tension between managerial and professional accountability and on the integrity and commitment of staff in schools and the education authority'. In Australia Wildy et al. (2001) reported that a strong assessment culture had not developed in primary schools but that 'there is evidence of support among practitioners for the use of an entry-level assessment program in both government and non-government primary schools'. By building on that feeling, respecting, consulting and responding to practitioners as well as creating an efficient administrative arrangement, the project has grown throughout Australia. There is evidence that classroom teachers are beginning to use the PIPS data to plan their teaching programmes and to group students. School leaders are also using the data to allocate resources, particularly to support those with potential learning difficulties. Moving to Germany, the situation is different again. As with Australia the system is structured along state lines. There is a strong research tradition in the early years and in assessment but no universally available on-entry assessment such as PIPS. For this reason Wylde (2002), while working at the German School in London, saw the need for an assessment like PIPS and set about translating and adapting it for German children. This resulted in FIPS (Frühindikatoren zur Leistungsfähigkeit in der Primarstufe).

Harries (2002) conducted a small-scale trial of the PIPS baseline with young children in Lesotho, which is a country that currently suffers from a severe shortage of trained teachers. There were typically at least 50 pupils of a mixed age-range per class. He suggested that 'the country would benefit from a training programme for potential teachers which was clearly focused on the early learning foundation needed by pupils in order to give them the best opportunity of progressing and developing'.

One aspect of that early learning foundation is a baseline assessment and awareness of PIPS could be a useful addition in such a training programme.

Van der Hoeven-van Doornum (2002) conducted a longitudinal research project in 11 schools in the Netherlands using a translated version of the PIPS baseline assessment (OBIS – Onderbouw Informatiesysteem) to investigate 'the effects of regular assessment on pupils' progress and teachers' professionalism'. Teachers conducted OBIS and were then given feedback about the baseline assessment scores of their pupils from which they set individual learning targets. This intervention was found to have a positive impact and has been reported nationally and internationally. Since then, OBIS has been used for other research projects. Meanwhile, in the Netherlands, the government's attitude towards baseline assessment has undergone a period of change. From the mid-1980s the funds allocated to Dutch schools were partially based on the socioeconomic and ethnic composition of their pupil population. The underlying theory for the policy was that those children were considered to be educationally disadvantaged and the government hoped to combat the perceived disadvantages by providing extra funding. More recently, the Dutch government has proposed that rather than relying on background factors alone to determine additional funding, a baseline assessment for 4-year-old children should be compulsory and is exploring different possibilities.

Within Hong Kong the climate is different again. The idea that there might be an assessment from which the results were not made generally available and discussed, and pressure put on children to get higher scores, is anathema. In fact, it seems to be almost impossible to have an assessment within schools without creating pressure on the children, which would be seen as quite inappropriate in the West. A similar situation is found across much of South-East Asia.

Summary and conclusion

There is a vast literature which marks the key variables that can indicate the likely success of children as they advance through primary school. This literature has been used to create a computerised adaptive multimedia assessment known as the PIPS on-entry baseline. This assessment has proved to be attractive to teachers and is used widely within the UK and increasingly in other countries. It is used to help teachers in their professional roles and to start the vital process of monitoring children's progress.

With the wider use of the assessment, issues concerning its cultural appropriateness in different contexts have had to be addressed. The evidence so far is that with small adjustments the baseline is entirely appropriate in Anglophone countries. It is also encouraging to note that data from the Netherlands and statistical analysis of English data indicate that it can be usefully adapted to other European cultures and perhaps more widely. In other words the assessment can be translated and adapted for use in different countries, and yet maintain the nature and difficulty of the content, thus enabling reliable and meaningful international comparisons to be made of the cognitive development of children when they start school. This opens up the possibility of broader work looking at the development of children across many different contexts with a threefold purpose. First, there is its established use by teachers. Second, there is the possibility of relating the starting points of children to the preschool facilities in various countries. Third, there is the possibility of interpreting later school-based data from international studies such as the Trends in International Mathematics and Science Study (TIMSS) (see, for example, Howie, 2002) in the light of PIPS data.

CHAPTER 10

CULTURAL-HISTORICAL ASSESSMENT: MAPPING THE TRANSFORMATION OF UNDERSTANDING

Marilyn Fleer and Carmel Richardson

Introduction

Approaches to teaching in early childhood education have moved towards a sociocultural approach (Berk and Winsler, 1995; Cullen, 1994, 1996; Fleer, 1992; MacNaughton, 1995; Smith, 1993, 1996a) or cultural historical approach (Chaiklin, 2001; Fleer and Richardson, 2004), while assessment and evaluation have generally stayed within a Piagetian framework or, at best, as a 'social influence approach' (Rogoff, 2003). However, how practical is it to work within a cultural-historical perspective when considering evaluation and assessment? What sorts of tools would be needed to gather data, and how might practitioners frame their observations when following a sociocultural or cultural-historical approach (Fleer and Raban, 2007)?

The study reported in this chapter sought to determine ways of documenting how young children participate in cultural-historical activity and to record how their participation changes from being relatively peripheral participants to assuming responsible roles in the management or transformation of such activities. Teacher observations framed from a sociocultural perspective (Rogoff, 2003) are presented alongside diary records documenting the transition from a traditional to a cultural-historical approach. These data demonstrate both the theoretical and practical implications of following a sociocultural approach to assessment and evaluation.

A cultural-historical perspective on learning

> Child development is represented as a process subject to natural laws and taking place as a kind of maturation, whereas education is seen as some purely external use of the capacities that emerge during the process of development ... education is the tail behind child development, guided not by tomorrow, but by yesterday, by the child's weakness, not his [sic] strength. (Vygotsky, 1982–84, vol. 2: 225, cited in Davydov and Zinchenko, 1993: 100; emphasis added)

Vygotsky wrote about the need to develop pedagogy that looked forward (toward tomorrow) in child development rather than being situated always in the past. In these arguments he spoke of working with children within their zone of proximal development (ZPD). Although this term and the learning processes of inter-psychological and intra-psychological functioning have been fully addressed in the literature (see Berk and Winsler, 1995; Chaiklin, 2003) and need not be reproduced here, the implications for assessment are enormous.

Western assessment has predominantly focused on the individual, usually in contexts in which the child is unsupported. Vygotsky (1987, 1997) argued that this approach to assessment only ever tapped into a child's present and unsupported development and understanding. An individualistic orientation does not allow the assessor to determine children's potential capabilities. It has been argued elsewhere (Fleer, 2002a; Fleer and Richardson, 2004) that mapping a child's potential is far more valuable for programme planning. Figure 10.1 models the assessment of both unsupported and supported learning. Although all children can be viewed as achieving at the same level, assessment within the ZPD measures more accurately the potential capacity of the children (Vygotsky, 1987, 1997):

> To gain a complete picture of assessment, it is necessary to assess the child at the second level, i.e. the zone of proximal development. Such assessment by definition involves a dynamic interaction and focuses on the child's processes of learning or ability to interact with a more competent adult. (Lunt, 1993: 160)

Western approaches to assessment are less likely to examine what children do when supported by others, and therefore are unlikely to map the potential capabilities of children. The assessment for tomorrow (the ZPD) examines the children's strengths rather than their weaknesses. Measuring the children's potential level of development allows early childhood teachers to plan more thoughtfully. Sociocultural or cultural-historical assessment moves the focus from a deficit view of assessment to a much more powerful and useful assessment practice for informing teaching and learning practices. Carr has used the term 'credit' to describe this orientation to assessment (Carr, 1998a, 1998b). Yet a cultural-historical view of assessment has generally not been taken up in assessment practices.

A sociocultural or cultural-historical approach to assessment is also influenced by the image we have of the child. Although educators' views are diverse and constantly changing, there is at any one time a predominant view which dictates our understanding of how children learn and develop and also how we assess this development.

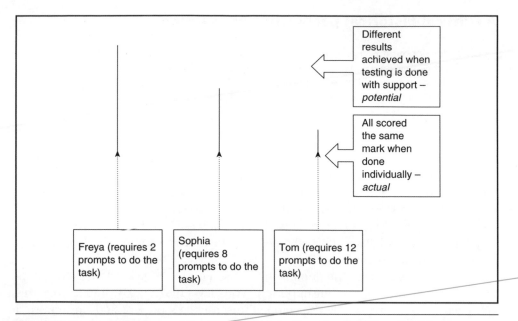

Figure 10.1   Assessing beyond the *actual* and into the *potential* (Fleer, 2002)

Our assessment practice in the field of early childhood education has been influenced by developmental psychologists, whose image of the child can be expressed as 'the scientific child of biological stages'. In this construction:

> the focus is on the individual child who, irrespective of context, follows a standard of biological stages. Despite frequent talk about a holistic perspective ... the child is frequently reduced to separate and measurable categories, such as social development, intellectual development, motor development. Consequently, processes which are very complex and interrelated in everyday life are isolated from one another and viewed dichotomously, instead of viewing them as intrinsically interrelated functions that all work together in the production of change. (Dahlberg et al., 1999: 46)

Assessment following this developmental approach can be seen to be fragmented. Observational data are collected and then separated into discrete areas of attainment. A desire to be 'objective' in the collection of this information necessarily denies recording details of the observer or others who may influence the behaviour of the child being observed.

However, Loris Malaguzzi, founder of the innovative early childhood educational programme in Reggio Emilia, has presented us with an alternative image which foregrounds the competence and complexity of children and also the deep embeddedness they have in the community to which they belong. In Chapter 5 Anning quoted the seminal paragraph in which Malaguzzi defined the Reggio Emilia version of children as:

> rich in potential, strong, powerful, competent and, most of all, connected to adults and other children. (Malaguzzi, 1993, cited in Dahlberg et al., 1999: 50)

This image of the 'rich' child is reflected in the work undertaken in the Reggio Emilia centres. While this work and the relationship that exists between the centres and the communities they serve is unique to the cultural context of the Reggio Emilia region in Italy there are elements that are equally transmutable to the Australian and other national contexts. Foremost of these is the notion of the 'rich' child. If we adopt this construction of children and childhood, then we equally adopt the notion of 'rich' teachers, 'rich' families, 'rich' learning experiences and consequently 'rich' assessment that recognises 'that the young child as learner is an active *co*-constructor' (Dahlberg et al., 1999: 50). Dahlberg et al. argue that 'constructions of childhood are *productive* of practice; in other words, pedagogical work is the product of who we think the child is' (1999: 52).

This 'pedagogical work' necessarily includes assessment. A cultural-historical approach to assessment within this framework moves beyond being objective and exclusive to being subjective and inclusive. Documentation of interactions becomes the focus of study and the collection of rich observational data is made possible. 'What we document represents a choice … in which pedagogues themselves are participating' (Dahlberg et al., 1999: 147).

In addition, this pedagogical work reminds us of the importance of really listening to children. A 'pedagogy of listening' entails being open to the possibility of learning more about children and the complexity of their thoughts and lives, when we engage in thoughtful reflection on not only what we do with children but on why we do it. Moving beyond and resisting normalising practices, such as those assessment practices prescribed within developmental approaches, offers the possibility of bringing new and multiple understandings to children's learning. This can be considered to be both a more ethical and a more responsible way of working with them (Dahlberg and Moss, 2005).

Assessment approaches have developed from the traditional practice of norm-referenced, criterion-referenced and curriculum-based assessment (see Losardo and Notari-Syverson, 2001), with some researchers beginning to embrace approaches that link more closely with sociocultural theory. Research by Margaret Carr and her colleagues in New Zealand (Carr, 2001a, 2001b), although concentrating upon individuals, provides a richer image of the child as a result of mapping children's learning journeys which includes recording evidence of other children's behaviours and cultural artefacts valued by the community. Similarly, alternative assessment as proposed by Losardo and Notari-Syverson (2001) begins to articulate the ways in which assessment practices can be embedded, authentic or mediated. Further, work undertaken by Feurestein and his colleagues (see Kozulin, 1998) documents the intentionality/reciprocity of interactions, the transcendence of learning and interactions that are transfused with meaning.

In cultural-historical approaches to teaching and learning we foreground the notion that learning is more than an individual construction. Meaning occurs in the context of participation in the real world. Ideas are socially mediated and reside not in individuals but are constituted in collectives, such as a particular community of practice (Wenger, 1998). Since meaning and therefore understanding are enacted in social contexts, assessment of this understanding must be viewed as transient and fluid (see Rogoff, 1998; Wenger, 1998). Using this approach assessment does not simply focus on the 'end product' but rather documents the whole learning journey (see Carr, 2001a and b) of the groups of children, rather than individuals, in order to document achievements of the whole community of practice (Wenger, 1998). That is:

> cognitive development [must be seen] as a process, as people move *through* under- standing rather than to understanding. (Rogoff, 1998: 690; emphasis is original)

Consequently, assessment practices that follow a sociocultural perspective are framed to map the transformation of understanding and not some end point. Rogoff (1998) explains this idea within the field of research:

> What is key is transformation in the process of participation in community activities, not acquisition of competences defined independently of the sociocultural activities in which people participate. (Rogoff, 1998: 691)

Rogoff (1998) articulates this perspective further through her thoughtful question- ing of how this transformation can be adequately mapped:

> How do people participate in sociocultural activity and how does their participation change from being relatively peripheral participants (cf. Lave and Wenger, 1991), observ- ing and carrying out secondary roles, to assuming various responsible roles in the man- agement or transformation of such activities? (Rogoff, 1998: 695)

Yet very little research has been undertaken to investigate and record the benefits of a cultural-historical approach to the assessment of young children in early childhood education. The study reported below is an attempt to do so.

The study

The study sought to determine whether early childhood teachers in a centre could docu- ment how young children participate in cultural-historical activity and how their participa- tion changed from being relatively peripheral participants to assuming responsible roles in the management or transformation of such activities. The centre, in Australia, was a University Childcare Centre with 30 children between the ages of 2.5 years and 5.4 years. Teacher observations framed from a sociocultural perspective (Rogoff, 1998) were gath- ered over 12 months alongside the diary records that documented the teachers' transition from a traditional to a cultural-historical approach. While over 200 child observations were initially recorded by the staff it is interesting to note that the effects of this initial phase of the research continue to inform evolving assessment strategies in the centre.

A total of 25 diary entries were made between February and November 2001. Six staff members were involved in the study. Only the preschool teacher kept a diary. Five of the six staff were student teachers in the third year of their Bachelor of Early Childhood Education.

The analysis of the diary entries was undertaken using Rogoff's (1998) three planes of analysis. Rogoff (1998) has identified these lenses at three planes, closely mirroring

Figure 10.2   Using a personal plane of analysis (Rogoff, 2003: 57)

the Vygotskian idea of inter-psychological and intra-psychological functioning (Vygotsky, 1987, 1997) (see Figures 10.2–10.4):

> Using personal, interpersonal and community/institutional planes of analysis involves focusing on one plane, but still using background information from the other planes, as if with different lenses. (Rogoff, 1998: 688)

In Figure 10.2 the traditional focus on the individual in research contexts is shown. In this study the individual perspective present in the diary entries was examined for patterns or changes over time.

In Figure 10.3 the lens is on the interaction between the individual, the teacher and other children. The diary entries were examined for evidence of comments on interactions between teacher and child, and teacher and teacher. The social context was featured.

Finally, in Figure 10.4 we note that the focus is on the whole cultural or institutional context. This is symbolically represented by the artefacts being used in the context. However, the discourse of schooling, the codes of behaviour and ways of learning are all part of this third lens. For instance, the taken-for-granted practices of the staff, the centre, as well as the policies, are all considered when the third lens is applied to the context. The habits or habitus (see Bourdieu on habitus, discussed in Grenfell et al., 1998) assumed as normal practice are critically examined in order to provide a broader and richer analysis of the early childhood context.

What is interesting about this approach to assessment is that the adult's participation in the lived teaching-learning, and the cultural tools that are being used, are

Figure 10.3   Using an interpersonal plane of analysis (Rogoff, 2003: 59)

Figure 10.4   Using a community/institutional plane of analysis (Rogoff, 2003: 60)

considered as part of assessment. The diary entries were analysed for references to documentation, charts, techniques for gathering data and other cultural or institutional tools.

The findings

A predominant theme that emerged over the course of the journal entries was an expression of discomfort in the way that the sociocultural or cultural-historical observations were to be recorded and collected. Staff at the centre had previously assessed children by collecting observational data based on a developmental approach. Over several years the technology for collecting these observations had varied and the success of different methods questioned. At the outset of the research project, observations – still largely based on a developmental approach – were recorded on small sticky Post-it labels and then affixed to an observation chart later to be transferred to an observation folder. In addition, staff members were asked to consider whether children's participation in any activity recorded could be described as *modelled*, *shared* or *independent*. Staff members were encouraged to record observations with this in mind and to affix these new 'sociocultural observations' to a new chart, called the Interactions Chart.

Staff members had difficulty with the terms *modelled*, *shared* and *independent*: how could observations, still firmly entrenched in a traditional individualistic developmental approach, fit within this continuum? Observational records were focused primarily on the child and the child's individual achievements and there was rarely any additional content about interactions between children or between child and adult. Context was rarely included. Staff were having difficulties recording observations that included this additional material. A note in the research diary recorded:

> We are observing children and their sociocultural interactions constantly and yet we seem to be reluctant? resistant? to recording them. Why? Is it the time and effort involved or the fact that it's difficult to capture in words some of the rather intangible things that we see or are part of?... difficult to record? (7 June 2001)

There was a feeling that staff members did not really know or understand what was meant by the term 'sociocultural interaction'. Could it be the obvious event witnessed or a rather more intangible event that demanded a greater depth of understanding than is otherwise required? Or was it the fact that recording an interaction required more time and effort than just recording a brief 'objective' observation of what happened? Early childhood educators have long held the belief that observations are to be made from an objective 'distance' that did not include themselves or their subjective interpretations of what they were witnessing. Again a research diary entry records the dilemma:

> Recording interactions is problematic because they are often done after the event/ learning experience/interaction and can become vague post-event recollections. (18 June 2001)

This initial reluctance to record sociocultural or cultural-historical interactions has continued to challenge staff members working at the centre. The initial concern about how to record detailed, context-rich interactions that included teacher input and scaffolding strategies remains a persistent concern. How do teachers create a record of events that represents the complex array of circumstances necessary to create the possibility for those events to happen in the ways in which they do? And what should teachers focus on when they record learning and teaching events? Furthermore, what do stakeholders want to see recorded? In other words, what learning is most valued in any particular community of learners and how can this be best illustrated? The following diary entry, recorded during the initial project, illustrates some of these ongoing tensions:

> One of the student teachers said to me today that she was happy to do observations but really didn't know what to record. Later she informed me that she had recorded an observation of a child writing [see Figure 10.5]. (21 July 2001)

Why was she comfortable recording this observation? Was it because she had observed a child involved in an activity that was valued and easily identified? How else could this have been recorded? What other information would have informed this observation?

This next journal entry typifies the general concerns expressed by staff with regard to any observation that is made and then recorded. How do you determine just what to record? Why do we choose to record some things while choosing not to record others?

> As I look on this journal I realize that I have asked these same questions many times. Perhaps the answer lies in the fact that we need to record more about each day – What happened? What did children say and do? What did I say and do? (7 August 2001)

Our observations are always subjective and reflect those things that we value. Dahlberg argued: 'When we document we are co-constructors of children's lives, and we also embody our implied thoughts of what we think are valuable actions in a pedagogical practice' (Dahlberg et al., 1999: 147). For instance, the observation recorded in Figure 10.6, taken much later in the project, documents evidence of staff and children co-constructing meaning. It highlights how difficult it is to isolate learning simply to an individual.

Observations recorded in Figures 10.5 and 10.6 reflect the value that is placed on early literacy attempts at the centre. The first example is deeply influenced by a developmental approach to assessment. The observer makes no reference to any scaffolding that may have been offered to the child. The child is seen to be acting in isolation. The information provided is important but lacks sociocultural context. Yet in the second observation staff begin to document the sociocultural context in which literacy

---

Bronte: attempted to write name: Wrote B R O – then asked how to do the E. (R) handed – good pencil grip. Using invented letter forms to write her name. (21 July 2001).

Figure 10.5   Domains-based observation

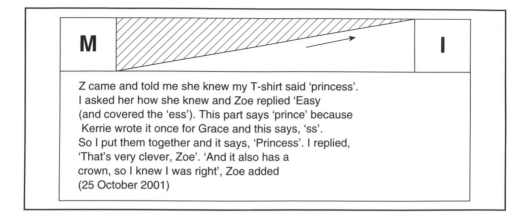

Z came and told me she knew my T-shirt said 'princess'.
I asked her how she knew and Zoe replied 'Easy
(and covered the 'ess'). This part says 'prince' because
Kerrie wrote it once for Grace and this says, 'ss'.
So I put them together and it says, 'Princess'. I replied,
'That's very clever, Zoe'. 'And it also has a
crown, so I knew I was right', Zoe added
(25 October 2001)

Figure 10.6   Sociocultural or cultural-historical observation (M: modelled; I: independent; the diagonal line represents shared interaction. The shaded area represents scaffolded assistance)

understanding is being co-constructed between teachers and children. Jordan discusses such interactions in Chapter 3.

In an attempt to better understand the sociocultural context of an interaction it was decided that more information needed to be recorded about each day's activities. This occurred within the context of the journal. The journal entries themselves provided a context for daily activities that added another dimension to the brief observations collected by staff members. However, this was problematic because only the preschool teacher accessed the journal. A further problem was that the journal was not addressed on a daily basis: '*Another busy day! Too busy to write lengthy observations*' (7 August 2001). Although acknowledging the importance of the journal and the contributions it could offer to a sociocultural approach to assessment it seemed obvious, based on previous experience, that anything that required lengthy observations was destined to be unsuccessful. Another way of recording observations that would provide this contextual information in a succinct, yet meaningful, way was needed.

> Noticed more observations on the daily Obs. Chart but no new observations on the Interactions Chart. Perhaps a different method of recording should be employed? Perhaps a sticker system to identify whether interactions are modelled/shared/independent would be useful? (8 August 2001)

At this point in the year staff were recording more observations that contained sociocultural information. The voice of the observer was occasionally heard and the interactions were more fully explored. However, there was still a tendency to place these on the observational chart rather than on the interactions chart. The preschool teacher felt that perhaps another method of identifying whether an interaction was modelled, shared or independent could be employed. Perhaps a sticker or colour-coded system indicating whether children were working independently, in partnership with a teacher or peer, or with the assistance of someone else could be useful. Observations could then be moved from the chart to the observation folder with this piece of information intact. However, there was still the problem of identifying the degree of interaction, especially the degree of scaffolded support offered to the child either by the adult or more capable peer. The staff still expressed a reluctance to use the terms *modelled*, *shared* or *independent* when describing an interaction.

> Recording daily in journal but not transferring this to Interactions Chart. Still not entirely sure how to do this. (22 September 2001)
>
> This afternoon I attempted to place some of the observations on the Interactions Chart. The chart has many limitations. It doesn't really have enough breadth in the shared area. Some of the children are barely in this zone while others have reached far beyond this, only needing occasional support. How can this be illustrated so that it is meaningful? (23 September 2001)

Towards the end of September a two-week unit of work was undertaken in the centre that had a distinct literacy theme. Work revolved around a book that had been written for this express purpose. The children had collaborated in some of the design elements of the book and they were exposed to all stages of its production. The preschool teacher and the student teacher staff members believed it was an ideal time to concentrate on the sociocultural assessment project. Perhaps a concentrated effort to collect assessment data related to this one specific unit of work would reveal more about the possibilities of sociocultural assessment and also expose a better way of recording the gathered assessment data.

Daily entries were made in the journal and these provided a great deal of contextual detail about the activities that were taking place in the centre. At the same time, brief observational notes were collected on a small group of children with the intention of placing these on the interactions chart. At the conclusion of the two-week period these collected observations were placed on the original interactions chart and it was at this time that it became obvious that the chart had many limitations that had not been previously noted.

Most significant of these was the fact that most interactions fell in the area identified as *shared interaction* and yet identifying an interaction as *shared* did not fully allow an expression of the degree of participation being observed. Rogoff (1998) talks about specialised as well as asymmetrical roles in collaboration:

> Collaboration also includes interactions in which participants' roles are complementary or with some leading and others following, supporting or actively observing. Under varying circumstances, different partners may be more responsible for initiating and managing shared endeavours. (Rogoff, 1998: 723)

The staff felt that these shared interactions were of great significance because they often contained evidence of scaffolded assistance. An understanding of 'scaffolding' as being 'qualitatively different from "help" was important in that it is aimed at supporting students to tackle *future* tasks in new contexts'.

We were attempting to map interactions and wanted to see if it was possible to record movement from one designated area to another. Using the terms *modelled*,

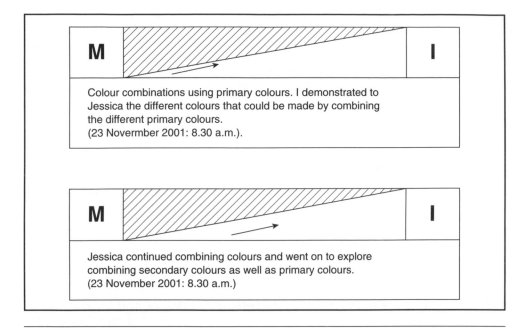

Colour combinations using primary colours. I demonstrated to Jessica the different colours that could be made by combining the different primary colours.
(23 Novermber 2001: 8.30 a.m.).

Jessica continued combining colours and went on to explore combining secondary colours as well as primary colours.
(23 November 2001: 8.30 a.m.)

Figure 10.7   Mediated assessment (two linked observations – M: modelled; I: independent)

shared and *independent* increasingly appeared to be too simplistic, as there seemed to be a wide range of possibilities for interactions within the '*shared*' zone. For example, a child's shared behaviour recorded on one day may influence behaviour witnessed on a subsequent occasion that may still fall within the '*shared*' zone. What may change is the child's degree of participation in the interaction or the degree of scaffolding required to support the child. This movement from an area of significant support to an area of less support could not be demonstrated by using dots or stickers. This was also true of the differences to be seen in a group of children participating in a shared activity. In other words, children could take on different roles in a shared interaction or need differing degrees of scaffolding to reach a desired endpoint but this could not be easily shown. If we were to adopt Rogoff 's definition of learning and development as '*transformation in participation* in sociocultural activity' (Rogoff, 1998: 687), then we needed some way to document these dynamic processes and this included movement within the area of *shared* interaction.

Although staff members felt frustrated by the constraints imposed by the interactions chart they believed that a minor change to the current method of recording interactions could overcome these shortcomings. The value of sociocultural assessment had become more evident and it was felt that recording these interactions, including the scaffolding efforts of the more capable other *and* any movement that may occur within the shared zone, was valuable. Information gathered not only indicated what was said or done in the interaction that could be used to inform future action, but the information also suggested a competence in the scaffolded child that may not have been otherwise appreciated. Figure 10.7 provides an example that

Once the children were settled in the writing centre (after hearing a story about the Aussie Postie) they began to work on the problem of writing the word 'motorbike'. The children worked together to identify the main phonemes and sounded out and wrote the letters MTOBIC. I suggested that they attempt to write 'postie' and once again the children worked together to write POSD, I asked the children to decide what they should write next and the suggestion was made to attempt the word 'mailbox'.

In the writing sample (not included here) it can seen that while two children (C, G) wrote MALBC the other (F) sounded out and wrote the letters LBC to represent the word letterbox. The children's work was further embellished with their own names and other known names, such as 'Mama', 'Silvia' and 'Zoe'. Drawings of mailboxes completed these impressive pieces of group work (not included here).

E had not participated in the initial discussion that had so engaged the first three children but she was interested in the writing activity in which they were presently occupied. While C, G and F worked on a joint project, E was on the periphery. E's work (not shown here) shows a collection of known and invented letters. While there is evidence to show that she is working at a different level to that demonstrated by the others, she can still be seen to be acting in collaboration with them. E's peripheral participation was not passive. Everything she observed was preparing her for future participation in related enterprises.

Figure 10.8   Collective mediated assessment (writing postbox/mailbox)

demonstrates one way in which the staff attempted to record the movement (note the arrows) within a zone alongside of the adult input.

Although the majority of the observations made of children tended to focus on individual children, it was possible to see some examples early in the study, as shown in Figure 10.6, of interactions between children and staff being documented. Towards the end of the study period, observations were made and work samples gathered, along with their corresponding assessment, and it was evident that the teachers had begun to demonstrate a 'collective' mediated orientation, as shown in Figure 10.8.

It should be noted that moving from an individualistic orientation to a collective perspective was one of the most difficult aspects of the teachers' work during the study. Although the staff felt comfortable noting informally what collectively was taking place, they found it much more difficult to document formally 'collective activity' – preferring to focus more on what an individual was doing and gaining from the experience. However, as they gathered more evidence of learning through work samples and observations of what was taking place as groups of children worked together, they found at these times it was very difficult to 'pull the children apart' in order to make individual assessments. In fact, by focusing their assessment on the performance of an individual they found that their judgements were no longer accurate – since what the child could do alone would be very different from what the child could do when working with more capable peers or with adult support or mediation (depending upon the context). Figure 10.8 demonstrates the collective nature of the children's learning. An assessment of each child independent of the teacher or the other children would render the assessment inappropriate for this approach. The complexity arises in documenting collective mediated assessment. In much the same way as teachers identify the 'teachable moment', the staff needed to determine the 'assessable moment' (Fleer 2006) in order to document and assess children's learning collectively.

Conclusion

Over the 12 months the staff at the centre moved from being relatively peripheral participants of sociocultural assessment through to assuming responsibility for documenting sociocultural observations. In particular, the staff began to consider the whole sociocultural context when they made their assessments. The voice of the teacher in the observations emerged over time, as demonstrated in Figure 10.6. The teachers had positioned themselves, rather than rendering themselves 'invisible', in the observations. They also began recording the scaffolding and other deliberate or intentional interactions in learning episodes, as demonstrated in Figure 10.7. Similarly, the teachers included records of reciprocity between the child and themselves, but also began to include peer interactions. Towards the end of the year the observations were of collective mediated interaction, as in Figure 10.8. Teacher observations depicted interactions that were infused with meaning and contexts. The dynamics in thinking during the interactional sequences were recorded through the use of arrows and notes – thus mapping movement in cognition. Finally, observations made by staff also identified and recorded evidence of teacher modelling. Prior to the commencement of the study, modelled interactions were never recorded in child-observations.

However, as Vygotsky notes, assessment must record not only those cognitive processes of the child that are fully developed, but also those that are in a state of being developed at the time of assessment, and that:

> This development, according to Vygotsky, depends on a co-operative interaction between the child and the adult, who represents the culture and assists the child in acquiring the necessary symbolic tools of learning. (Kozulin, 1998: 69)

As such, what the adult does is a highly significant component of mapping children's cognitive competence. Yet this is rarely done in observations made by most early childhood teachers. The findings of this study indicate that when staff take a sociocultural approach to assessment, they record their intentional interactions, their modelling and use of cultural tools, and child–teacher and child–child (depicted as reciprocity) interactions in their observational notes. In the process of moving from an individualistic orientation to a sociocultural perspective, assessment practices shift from being an analysis of observations that 'carve up the individual child' into domains of competence, such as physical, social and cognitive attainments, to viewing assessment practice as part of a mediated process residing within the collective rather than the individual. This orientation to assessment represents a significant paradigm shift in early childhood practice. In taking a sociocultural approach to assessment, early childhood educators will be able to record broader, richer and culturally embedded data on the groups of children they interact with each day in their centres. This will allow for more meaningful assessments to be made about learning and teaching. Teachers will find the 'assessable moments' (Fleer 2006) when the majority of observations should take place.

Teaching staff at the centre continue to refine their approaches to documenting children's learning. More recently they have begun to record teaching and learning using a more narrative approach. These observations are necessarily longer than those initially kept at the outset of the research project. But they are rich in context and most often focus on group learning processes (see Fleer and Richardson, 2004). This means that one carefully observed and recorded observation can be copied and presented in several portfolios simultaneously. These observations continue to be qualitatively different from developmental observations. Context, including a history of the event and the learners' emotional engagement, is valued. Teacher actions and even occasionally their thoughts and intentions are included to provide a continuum of contextual meaning. Community members share in these achievements because they are not only displayed in portfolios but also displayed in the Day Book and on the walls. In this way learning, both individual and collective, is honoured and shared within the community.

But it should be noted that the initial period of transformation in participation by the staff detailed in this chapter took place over a 12-month period. The time needed for staff to move from an individualistic approach to a sociocultural approach was extensive. It demonstrates the challenge that lies ahead for early childhood professionals as we reflect upon and begin to move away from decades of training in observational techniques and related individualistic and reductionist assessment practices.

Acknowledgements

We would like to thank the staff, children and families from the Wiradjuri Preschool Childhood Care Centre, University of Canberra, who participated in this study. We would also like to acknowledge the Department of Education, Science and Training for their facilitation of the developmental work described in this chapter. Without the prior work done on the development of the Preschool Profile, important conceptual questions would not have been asked about assessment. In particular, we would like to acknowledge the scholarly contribution made by Bridie Raban through her insightful questioning and generous support for the directions taken.

PART 4

EVALUATION AND QUALITY IN EARLY YEARS SETTINGS

CHAPTER 11

QUALITY TEACHING IN THE EARLY YEARS

Iram Siraj-Blatchford

Introduction

Many readers may find the title of this chapter something of a problem in itself. In many Western societies a consensus has emerged that early childhood provision should be individualised and play-based, and that adults should be non-directive and 'facilitate' learning rather than 'teach' (Siraj-Blatchford, 1999: 21). This general belief underpins notions of quality in early childhood education. But in the following pages I will be arguing that teaching should be as much the concern of those working in early childhood settings as it is any other educational sector. I will argue that teaching is implicit in pedagogy and therefore of great importance when analysing quality provision in early years education. I will also argue, along with Freire (1995: 379) and others, that those who restrict their work to facilitation are neglecting their civil duty to teach in a society where there is social injustice and inequality.

Quality as early childhood pedagogy

One of the key variables in determining outcomes for young children that we find detailed in many reports, studies and discussion papers is the effect of the teacher on the nature and quality of education (Sammons et al., 2002a, 2002b; Siraj-Blatchford, Sylva, Muttock et al., 2002; Siraj-Blatchford, Sylva, Taggart et al., 2002). In examining quality provision in the early years, the role of the teacher should be viewed as central to any critique. As such, the pedagogy adopted by the teacher should be considered closely. The term 'pedagogy' has often been defined quite broadly in continental Europe and the term has sometimes been applied in a similar way in early childhood contexts in the United Kingdom. At times this has resulted in accounts where the use of the terms 'pedagogy' and 'curriculum' appear indistinguishable. But the approach taken in the study of the sociology of education has been quite different, where 'pedagogy' has been understood as analytically distinct and complementary to the term 'curriculum'. While curriculum may therefore be understood as denoting all of the knowledge, skills and values that children are meant to learn in educational establishments, pedagogy is referred to as the practice (or the art, the science or the craft) of teaching. To be a pedagogue is therefore essentially, and by definition, to be a teacher. The provision (or 'facilitation') of 'instructive' environments for play and exploration may therefore have been seen as just one of the pedagogical strategies that may be legitimately applied by the early years teacher alongside others, such as modelling and demonstration, questioning and direct instruction.

Pedagogy refers to the interactive process between teacher and learner and the learning environment (which includes family and community). A wide range of authorities (including Bowman et al., 2001; Leach and Moon, 1999; Mortimore, 1999) have applied essentially the same model where, in their day-to-day interactions with children and parents, capable educators are seen to draw upon a repertoire of pedagogical techniques that have been in some way tested and/or stood the test of time and experience. From this perspective much of my recent reseach may be seen as an ongoing endeavour to identify more fully the range of techniques most effectively applied in teaching children in the early years (Siraj-Blatchford, 1999; Siraj-Blatchford, Sylva, Muttock et al., 2002; Siraj-Blatchford, Sylva, Taggart et al., 2002).

Models of early childhood education

An assumption that I made in the introductory arguments has been that there are some particular cultural skills, attitudes and dispositions that we should be teaching children in their early years. For some readers this may be questionable. They might consider, for example, that it would be enough to support children in developing their individuality and self-expression, or that whatever curriculum there is should be determined by the children's individual choice of activity (Bennett et al., 1997). Such a view may even be seen as supported by popular notions of the 'kindergarten' where children may be seen as developing naturally and requiring minimal nurture. But if there is no legitimate curriculum to be taught in the early years; then there is clearly no need for teachers/educators.

A typology of the most commonly applied models of early childhood education has been provided by Weikart (2000) and is shown in Figure 11.1. The categories that are applied are broadly consistent with others developed by Kohlberg and Mayer (1972) and Baumrind (1971). Recent research carried out in the UK by the Effective Provision of Preschool Education (EPPE) project[1] suggests that as 'ideal types' they are applied just as much in the UK early childhood context as in the US context where they were first developed (Sylva et al., 1999).

The analytical difficulty with the typology is in the definition of curriculum that is applied and the way the term 'initiative' is used. According to Weikart the major

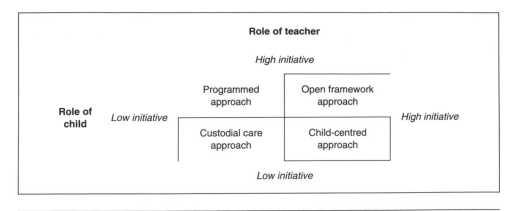

Figure 11.1   Role of the teacher and role of the child

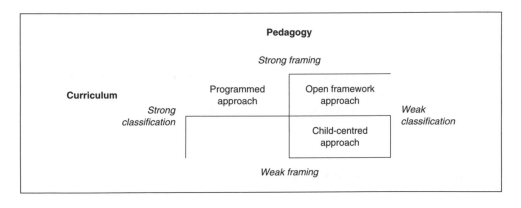

Figure 11.2   Pedagogy framing and curriculum classification

organising principle to be considered is the role of either high or low curriculum 'initiation' on the part of the teacher/adult and the child (Weikart, 2000: 58), with later work elaborating a highly structured pedagogy and high child initiative in terms of their control over the curriculum.

The major organising principle might therefore be better conceived in terms of pedagogy and curriculum (Figure 11.2). This would also be consistent with Bernstein's (1981) elaborate analysis of pedagogic codes and their modalities of practice.

Classification refers to the degree of boundary maintenance between curriculum subject contents. Where the curriculum content is clearly defined in terms of subjects, we can therefore refer to that as strong classification. Framing is about who controls what – who selects, sequences, paces, etc. the learning. When framing is weak the child (or parent) has more apparent control; when strong, it is the educator/professional who is most clearly in control.

The custodial (or basic care) approach described by Weikart (2000) has been omitted in Figure 11.2 and will also be omitted in the following account of the major educational approaches because no specified curriculum has traditionally been intended in these programmes. There is an increasing emphasis on combining education and care, so that this distinction in combined education and care settings is becoming blurred (OECD, 2004).

The programmed approach is highly teacher-directed, providing for little initiative on the part of the child. This pedagogy is usually applied where curriculum objectives may be clearly (and objectively) classified and is likely to be most effective where learning involves the development of simple skills or memorisation. The curriculum content is often highly structured.

The open-framework approach provides the teacher with a strong pedagogic structure (or framework) that supports the child in his or her explorations and interactions with, and reflections upon, the learning environment. In this model, the curriculum classification is weaker as the child has a good deal of freedom to make choices between the various learning environments that are on offer.

In the most extreme applications of the child-centred approach the teacher responds entirely to the individual child's interests and activities. More often, topic or project themes are adopted that have been chosen especially to appeal to the children's interests.

Of course each of these approaches remains an 'ideal type' and the practices in many settings will still involve a combination of all three. In the following pages I will argue my case for adopting stronger classification and framing principles in early childhood education from three directions: (1) exemplary practices; (2) learning theory; (3) social justice.

A case for teaching in early childhood

Exemplary practices

While there are wide differences of opinion and variation in understanding regarding the degree of influence that adults should have over the curriculum, one area in which there has been widespread agreement in Western societies is that 'early years education should be play-based'. Wood makes a strong case for this in Chapter 2.

A range of pedagogical practices related to the development of positive learning dispositions and 'emergent' learning is also suggested as popularised in the emergent literacy approach (Bowman et al., 2001: 186). These include practitioner modelling (pp. 22, 29) and the provision of socio-dramatic role-play (p. 31). We are also advised that assessment should be used to provide individual children with challenging but 'achievable' experiences that 'do not frustrate or demoralise children' (p. 30).

A systematic analysis of the original English Curriculum Guidance for the Foundation Stage (CGFS) (DfEE/QCA, 2000) was carried out to identify the general principles underlying the statements of 'What the practitioner needs to do' in each area of learning (Siraj-Blatchford and Siraj-Blatchford, 2001). A total of 185 unambiguous pedagogic recommendations were identified. The largest group of these (88 statements) relate to practitioner 'modelling' through demonstrating appropriate language, values and practices. The 21 statements that refer to 'direct teaching' are concerned entirely with the development of particular skills and/or safe practices. Twenty-seven refer to practitioners providing 'praise, encouragement and reinforcement', 14 to 'questioning' and 24 to other forms of 'verbal intervention, interaction and discussion'. Eleven statements relate to the importance of practitioners 'observing, listening and assessing'. References to peer collaboration and visits made outside the centre are also included. A revised Early Years Foundation Stage (EYFS) curriculum (www.everychildmatters.gov.uk) will be applied by all registered early years providers and schools in England from September 2008. The Guidance Notes refer explicitly to developing 'language for thinking' and to the importance of promoting episodes between adults and children, and children and their peers of 'sustained shared thinking' (Siraj-Blatchford, 2007).

In a chapter written for an edited cross-phase text on the subject of pedagogy (Siraj-Blatchford, 1999) I provided a pedagogic analysis of 'Developmentally Appropriate Practice' (DAP) along with five other popular models of early childhood education: High/Scope (USA), Reggio Emilia (Italy), *Movimento da Escola Moderna* (MEM) (Portugal), *Te Whāriki* (New Zealand) and Quality in Diversity (UK) (Early Childhood Education Forum, 1998).

These popular models of exemplary practice were seen to have a great deal in common. Three particular areas of pedagogy were identified that are seen as of equal importance to learning in the early years: the use of pedagogic instructional techniques, the encouragement of affective involvement and the encouragement of cognitive engagement or co-construction.

Teachers may act as role models, expressing their own interest and enthusiasm for the subject (as in High/Scope). They can also respond to the child's own interests (as in MEM), encourage parents and community involvement (as in *Te Whāriki*) and encourage the children to recognise the 'validity' of what they are doing by communicating it beyond the classroom (as in both MEM and Reggio Emilia in particular). Whatever strategy is employed, the aim must be to achieve a high degree of intrinsic motivation and involvement in the activity in the short term and improved learning dispositions such as perseverance in the long term.

High/Scope takes the emphasis on continuous planning and review that is found in Reggio Emilia a stage further, providing a more structured and institutionalised approach in the daily plan–do–review routines. The strong Vygotskian influence is demonstrated in the structured dialogue led by the teachers/educators.

The *Te Whāriki* model suggests that an appropriate curriculum and pedagogy for young children will be one determined with the needs of individual and specific groups of children, adults and communities in mind. Social constructivism suggests that children learn best when they are being supported by adults or their peers in actively developing their individual and group capability.

In the Quality and Diversity model much of the specific pedagogic guidance is embedded, and little explicit reference is made to the quality of adult–child interactions. Some of the observations do, however, provide hints regarding the specific adult roles that are favoured. At times it seems to be emphasising a 'low profile' and at others a high degree of direction.

Learning theory

One criticism of DAP has been associated with its allegedly uncritical application of 'developmental stage theory' in determining the early years curriculum and the suggestion that any particular set of classroom or nursery practices could be defined as objectively appropriate for all children at a certain stage of their development (New, 1994; Spodek and Saracho, 1991). A second line of criticism concerns the idea of 'developmental appropriateness' itself, which some see as premised on the idea of an essential child, of a child objectively knowable irrespective of time or place, context or perspective, moving along a biologically determined and common sequence of developmental stages.

The more extreme 'child-centred' or 'care' approaches to early childhood provision have been referred to. These approaches have often been defended in the past by reference to an especially crude application of constructivist learning theory where the idea that the child actively constructs his or her world through the natural processes of play and discovery learning are taken to the lengths of evoking the notion of the child as a 'lone scientist'. The approach has also been (quite mistakenly) attributed to Piaget (see Bennett et al., 1997: 2–4).

Piaget's theory on the role of social factors in early childhood development has been largely neglected (DeVries, 1997). Piaget argued that adult–child and peer relations influence every aspect of development and that affective and personality development are intimately related to intellectual and moral development. Perhaps most importantly, Piaget argued that reciprocity in peer relations provides the foundations for perspective-taking and for decentring. This suggests that collaborative play is exceptionally important for children. According to DeVries, Piaget proposed ways in which cooperative social interactions between children and between children and adults function to promote cognitive, affective and moral development, and as she says:

> If Piaget was correct, then we need to reconsider the structure and methods of education from the point of view of long-term effects on children's socio-moral, affective and intellectual development. (1997: 16)

Given the failure of many educationalists to recognise the full extent of Piaget's contribution, it is to Vygotsky that we are largely indebted for the foundations of a theory of teaching 'as assisted performance' (Tharp and Gallimore, 1991). As discussed by Jordan in Chapter 3, Vygotsky defined what he referred to as the 'zone of proximal development', that is the distance between the actual developmental level as determined by individual problem-solving and the level of potential development as determined through problem-solving under adult guidance or in collaboration with more capable peers (Vygotsky, 1978: 86). The notion has now been popularly extended beyond problem-solving to encompass performance in other areas of competence. The aims of teaching, from this perspective, are to assist children within this zone, and to provide the support and encouragement they require to perform successfully in areas that would otherwise be beyond them. The key challenge for educators becomes one of defining the limits of the zone, matching or 'tuning' the support, or of 'scaffolding' the learning (Wood, 1986) to a point just beyond each child's current independent capabilities. According to this account, any assistance provided that lies within the children's existing capability is wasted, while assistance beyond the limitations of the zone will be meaningless and potentially damaging to the child's self-confidence.

The academic understanding of learning that underpins current trends in early childhood education (Siraj-Blatchford, 1998; Siraj-Blatchford, 2007) are most significantly based upon principles of social constructivism that are drawn from both Vygotsky and Piaget.

If we consider learning to be the result of a process of cognitive construction that is achieved only when the child is interested and/or involved, it is entirely consistent to treat the part played by the effective educator in precisely the same way. The cognitive construction in this case is mutual, where each party engages with the understanding of the other and learning is achieved through a process of reflexive 'co-construction' involving 'sustained shared thinking'. A necessary condition will be that both parties are involved and, for the resultant learning to be worthwhile, that the content of their engagement should be in some way instructive.

Vygotsky (1978) argued that learning has a cultural and social dimension and that human consciousness is achieved through the internalisation of shared social behaviour. The work done by Vygotsky and other theorists interested in learning as situated social practice highlights the interactive aspects of learning and the importance of teaching in the process of learning. Stremmel (1993) has stressed the intersubjectivity of responsive teaching which concerns the sharing of purpose between child and teacher that is affirmed in the 'interactive patterns' (p. 2) established between the teacher and the child within a joint activity. In this process, the teacher must understand the cognitive, cultural and social perspective of the learner so that the child can be enabled to 'build bridges' (p. 3) between what he or she knows and what he or she is capable of knowing. 'Responsive teaching' seems to be very close to the patterns of exchange promoted in the exemplary models referred to above.

Social justice

In Siraj-Blatchford and Clarke (2000), I cite Article 2(1) of the United Nations Convention on the Rights of the Child (1989) in arguing that adults might be considered to have a responsibility as citizens for teaching young children in societies that are characterised by social injustice and inequality. I argue the case for a curriculum for early childhood that recognises their vulnerability, and that recognises the power that every adult has to affect (for good or bad) the self-identity, behaviour, actions, intentions, understandings and beliefs of the children they interact with. This does not mean that children are entirely powerless – far from it – but they are vulnerable around adults.

We need to consider how it is that young children who are in our care learn about and experience class bias, sexism and racism. We know that all children pick up stereotypical knowledge and understanding from their environment and try to make their own meanings from this experience. Outside experiences can come from parental views, media images and the child's own observations of how other individuals from their social class, gender, ethnic or language group are seen and treated. In the absence of strong and positive role models children are often left with negative perceptions. This bias can start from birth.

Research evidence produced by David Milner (1983) has shown that children have learned positive and negative feelings about racial groups from an early age. Milner suggests that children as young as 3 years demonstrate an awareness of a racial hierarchy 'in line with current adult prejudices' (1983: 122). A number of researchers (Lawrence, 1997; Siraj-Blatchford, 1994) have shown that positive self-esteem depends upon whether children feel that others accept them and see them as competent and worthwhile. Researchers have also shown the connection between academic achievement and self-esteem (Bernstein, 1992; Gilborn, 1990; Lloyd, 1987).

Cultural identity should therefore be seen as a significant area of concern within definitions of quality in early childhood education and for curriculum development (Siraj-Blatchford, 1996). All children and adults identify with classed, gendered and racialised groups (as well as other groups) but what is especially significant is that some cultural identities are seen as less academic (or intelligent) than others (often by the staff and children). Early years educators often display a profound sense of inadequacy when faced with sexism and racism from children (Walkerdine, 1987; Davies, 1989). Yet it is entirely natural for children to repeat the behaviours that they have been exposed to by parents and other significant adults. The early years curriculum must therefore provide children with experiences that counter these negative views.

We know that children can hold views about their 'masterful' or 'helpless' attributes as learners (Dweck and Leggett, 1988). Dweck and Leggett (1988) therefore emphasise the importance of developing 'mastery' learning dispositions in children. There is evidence that children who experience education through taking some responsibility for their actions and learning become more effective learners. They are learning not only the content of the curriculum but the processes by which learning takes place (Siraj-Blatchford, 1998, 2007).

Children need help from the adults around them in learning how to care for each other and to share things. In her research on the relationship between mothers and their babies and relationships between very young siblings, Judy Dunn (1988) suggests that mothers who talk to their children about 'feeling states' have children who themselves 'become particularly articulate about and interested in feeling states' (1987: 38). Consideration for others has to be learnt.

Children whose competence in English is still developing also find it difficult to take part in socio-dramatic play with English-speaking children without the support of staff (Clarke, 1996; Fraser and Wakefield, 1986). However, children also need the opportunity to use their first language in free play. Research (Clarke, 1996) shows that when bilingual children use their home-language in socio-dramatic play, the language used in these play situations is much more complex than the situations in which the children use English, even when the teacher tries to scaffold the play. This implies that cognitive development and stimulation is greater in the children when they use their 'more developed' language. This has interesting implications for the rest of the curriculum when bilingual children may be engaged in art, science or construction activities. Staff have to plan carefully for supporting children's learning in a range of groupings and with a range of support in both the home language and English.

What research tells us about effective teaching

In the preceding pages I have argued that teaching should be considered a legitimate aspect of early childhood professional practice on the grounds of learning theory, exemplary practice and social justice. In this concluding section a review of the research evidence regarding effective teaching in early childhood will be provided.

Longitudinal studies from the United States have provided powerful arguments and evidence for preschool education. The High/Scope Perry Preschool evaluation (Schweinhart et al., 1993) showed the substantial benefits to be gained through preschooling for children brought up in poverty and at high risk of school failure. Research findings from the longitudinal study in New Zealand, 'Competent Children' (Wylie, 1998), also suggest that by 6 years of age children gained higher or lower educational outcomes depending on factors including the age at which children started ECE (before age 3 had a better impact), the quality of staff interactions with children and the extent to which children were allowed to complete activities.

Some longitudinal studies have shown us that children provided with direct or 'programmed' instruction sometimes do better than those provided with other forms of pedagogy in the short term (e.g. Karnes, 1983). But the studies also suggest that when apparent, these gains are short-lived, with all the significant differences having 'washed out' within a year of the provision ending. Direct instruction has also been found to result in children showing significantly increased stress/anxiety behaviours (Burts et al., 1990). A more recent and rigorous longitudinal study conducted by Schweinhart and Weikart (1997) showed little difference in the academic performance of children provided with direct instruction but significantly more emotional impairment and disturbance leading to special educational provision. More importantly, the Schweinhart and Weikart study showed that the direct instruction group experienced more suspensions from work and more than double the rate of arrests than either of the other two groups.

Other studies have also shown that over-'formal' approaches to teaching young children are counterproductive (Nabuco and Sylva, 1996) and can hinder young children's learning, generating higher anxiety levels and lower self-esteem.

The Effective Provision of PreSchool Education (EPPE) study in the UK has recently reported significant effects on children's progress during the preschool years which can be attributed to attendance at early years settings (Sammons et al., 2002a, 2002b, 2003; Siraj-Blatchford, Sylva, Muttock et al., 2002). This, combined with the findings of the Researching Effective Pedagogy in the Early Years (REPEY) study (Siraj-Blatchford, Sylva, Muttock et al., 2002)[2] provides evidence of a wide range of pedagogical practices that affect child outcomes.

The evidential base of the EPPE study is particularly strong. The study involved 141 preschool centres randomly selected within six local education authorities in England. A 'home' sample of 300 children who had no significant group, preschool experience contributed to the total sample of more than 3000 children. The EPPE investigation identified effective settings by measuring child development (cognitive and social development) from age 3 to 7 and by controlling for child and family variables such as socioeconomic class. Systematic evaluations of the preschool settings was also carried out using Early Childhood Environment Rating Scales (ECERS)[3] and a number of 'quality characteristics' was identified that correlated strongly with highly effective settings. These characteristics were then investigated further in 14 in-depth, qualitative case studies of good to excellent settings in the REPEY project. The aim was to see how the quality characteristics worked in practice. In addition to the documentary analysis, 204 naturalistic observations of 28 staff were conducted and transcribed (a total of 400-plus hours); 42 staff and managers were interviewed, and 107 parents. The REPEY analysis was conducted using QSR NVivo software and the dataset included a total of 381 files (over one million words dataset). The REPEY findings were generally supportive of the three-part model of effective pedagogy, including adult and child *involvement*, *cognitive* (co-constructive) *engagement* and the use of *instruction* techniques such as modelling and demonstration, explanation and questioning.

The other major findings of the REPEY study were as follows:

- Effective pedagogues assess children's performance to ensure the provision of challenging yet achievable experiences.
- Effective pedagogues provide formative feedback during activities and differentiate their planning and teaching.
- Effective pedagogues model appropriate language, values and practices, encourage socio-dramatic play, praise, encourage, ask questions and, interact verbally with children.
- Effective pedagogy is both 'teaching' and the provision of instructive learning and play environments and routines.
- The most effective settings provide both teacher-initiated group work and freely chosen yet potentially instructive play activities.
- Excellent settings tend to achieve an equal balance between adult-led and child-initiated interactions, play and activities.
- Effective pedagogues have good curriculum knowledge and child development knowledge.
- The most highly qualified staff provide the most direct teaching but also the kind of interactions that guide but do not dominate children's thinking.
- Less qualified staff are better pedagogues when supervised and supported by qualified teachers.
- The most effective settings employ behaviour policies in which staff support children in rationalising and talking through their conflicts.
- Effective settings view cognitive and social development as complementary.
- The most effective settings have shared educational aims with parents supported by regular communication.

Adults and children in the excellent settings were more likely to engage at times in 'sustained shared thinking': episodes in which two or more individuals 'worked together' in an intellectual way to solve a problem, clarify a concept, evaluate activities or extend narratives etc. During periods of sustained shared thinking both parties contributed to the thinking and developed and extended the discourse.

When taken together, the research reported in this chapter points clearly to the importance of the role of the pedagogue or teacher in early childhood education. Not only do we need to foreground the role of the teacher, but we need to value and reposition teaching as central to quality early childhood education. In terms of the model provided in Figure 11.2, we should be moving away from the current polarities of approach towards the acceptance of a balanced curriculum and pedagogic framework that includes aspects of each of the open framework, child-centred and programmed approaches. Such a balance is already being realised in a minority of high-quality settings such as some of the Early Excellence Centres and Nursery Schools in the UK. The challenge for policy-makers is to provide more highly trained and professional teachers/educators to achieve this balance in all settings.

Notes

1. For further information about EPPE visit the EPPE website at: www.ioe.ac.uk/cdl/eppe/index.htm.
2. For further information about REPEY: www.dfes.gov.uk/research/data/uploadfiles/RR356.pdf.
3. For ECERS contact b.taggart@ioe.ac.uk or www.trentham-books.co.uk.

CHAPTER 12

QUESTIONING EVALUATION QUALITY IN EARLY CHILDHOOD

Valerie N. Podmore

Introduction

This chapter outlines and discusses issues of quality and evaluation in New Zealand, with reference to recent research-based developments. The first section provides an overview of New Zealand literature on aspects of quality in early childhood contexts. An emerging theme concerns the role of reflective early childhood practitioners who are attuned to children's perspectives (Podmore and Meade, with Kerslake Hendricks, 2000). The second section examines research-based initiatives, connected to *Te Whāriki*, the New Zealand early childhood curriculum, that focus on self-evaluation of quality provision.

Particular reference is made to projects that culminated in approaches known as *The Child's Questions* and *The Quality Journey*. *The Child's Questions* reflects socio-cultural perspectives, and the considerable research literature on young children's learning, together with observations of *Te Whāriki* in action (May and Podmore, 2000; Podmore et al., 2001). *The Quality Journey* is the Ministry of Education's (1999a, 2000b) resource for early childhood centre managers and practitioners, and home-based care providers, intended to establish 'quality improvement systems'. Connections between these documents and theory, research and practice are illustrated and appraised. Reference is also made to several developments and resources for early years teachers that draw on the framework of *The Child's Questions*.

Aspects of quality in early childhood education

It is evident from a range of international research studies that high-quality early childhood education has long-term benefits for children (Podmore and Meade, with

Kerslake Hendricks, 2000). New Zealand research supports the findings of both the concurrent and the long-term benefits for children. *Education to Be More*, the report of an early childhood working group formed by the government in the late 1980s, states that quality early childhood education is beneficial for children, for parents/*whanau* and for society (Department of Education, 1988).

Findings of the New Zealand Council for Educational Research's longitudinal '*Competent Children*' study, from a sample of children drawn from the predominantly urban/suburban/small-town region surrounding the capital city of Wellington, high-light the influence, up to the age of 14 years, of exposure to quality early childhood education (Hodgen, 2007; Wylie et al., 1996, 2001). Results pertaining to early child-hood education influences have been generally well supported,[1] and in turn have influenced aspects of early childhood policy development in New Zealand (Early Childhood Strategic Plan Working Group, 2001). A comprehensive, analytical litera-ture review prepared for the Ministry of Education provides further evidence, within and across international studies, of the long-term benefits of quality early childhood education (Smith et al., 2000).

There is a continuing need for more in-depth investigation of the specific compo-nents of, and processes within, local quality early childhood programmes. This inter-pretation of the findings outlined to date is congruent with Marilyn Fleer's proposition, in her overview of the longitudinal research, that 'more needs to be understood about the programmes offered in the early childhood centres' (Fleer, 2002b: 4).

At a New Zealand conference on quality in childcare centres, Smith (1996b) drew on research findings to list these nine criteria for quality in early childhood services: sensitive and responsive interactions between adults and children; adult–child ratios; staff training and education; staff stability; curriculum and programme focus; peer group harmony; communication with parents; favourable staff wages and working conditions; and safe and healthy physical environments. In addition, a review of inter-national research includes these further dimensions of quality: '... democratic parental participation, and language maintenance and cultural revival' (Podmore, 1993: 28).

In some recent New Zealand research, there is increased recognition of the com-plexities of concepts of quality, together with considerable emphasis on cultural con-texts. There is some evidence of questioning and repositioning of notions of quality, particularly with regard to cultural diversity. The approaches of a number of writers and researchers are somewhat consistent with an international trend towards viewing quality as a construct that 'needs to be contextualized, spatially and temporally, and to recognize cultural and other significant forms of diversity' (Dahlberg et al., 1999: 6). For example, the literature review prepared by Anne Smith et al. (2000) includes details of the components of high quality programmes that are linked to positive learning outcomes for children, and specifically mentions *Te Whāriki*, the New Zealand early childhood curriculum (Ministry of Education, 1996b). As concluded in Smith et al.'s review, there is clearly a need for the research on quality 'to be expanded ... to take a broader perspective on quality taking much more account of the impor-tance of sociocultural context ...' (Smith et al., 2000: 122).

A new policy initiative in New Zealand is providing funding over three-year periods for selected early childhood Centres of Innovation (COIs). The COIs are expected to be implementing high quality programmes that are specifically innovative (by including learning and teaching initiatives that are different from other centres), and to carry out research projects that incorporate practitioner–researcher collaboration. The COIs' research processes demonstrate effective collaboration and children's learning in action (Meade, 2006). Findings to date have relevance to learning and teaching in *Aotearoa*/New Zealand, for example to language development in Maori immersion programmes and quality transition practices in a Samoan-language immersion programme (Meade, 2007).

Concurrently, aspects of the structural components of quality remain a focus of recent policy initiatives, tempered by an accent on local context. Structural components set a framework for the quality learning processes that take place in early childhood settings. Structural dimensions under scrutiny include components of the traditional 'iron triangle' of quality: teacher education/training and qualifications, adult–child ratios and group size (Phillipsen et al., 1997). Government requirements for quality of early childhood services are currently the minimum standards specified in the Education (Early Childhood Centres) Regulations 1998 and the Education (Home Based Care) Order 1992,[2] together with the Revised Statement of Desirable Practices (DOPs) (Ministry of Education, 1996a). The DOPs incorporate two guiding principles, requiring services to work in partnership with parents/*whanau* to promote and extend learning and development of each child; and to develop and implement a curriculum that assists all children to become competent and confident learners. The DOPs include short excerpts from *Te Whāriki*, the New Zealand early childhood curriculum framework. The cultural relevance of some points about quality, as stated in the DOPs, is clearly evident. One example is: educators support and use children's home language and communication styles.

Teacher qualifications and continuing professional development have been appraised as important dimensions of quality provision in New Zealand, and have been found in turn to influence children's learning and development (Podmore and Meade, with Kerslake Hendricks, 2000). An emerging theme in local research and reviews concerns the role of reflective early childhood practitioners who are attuned to children's perspectives. This is evident in the Learning and Teaching Stories approach to assessment and to self-evaluation (Carr et al., 2000). A somewhat parallel trend is found in international work reappraising views of quality. A comparable notion about quality provision in early childhood centres can be seen, for example, in Dahlberg's comments about the importance of a 'pedagogy of listening' (Dahlberg, 2000; Dahlberg et al., 1999).

Self-evaluation of quality provision starting from the *Child's Questions* context of evaluation in New Zealand

Prior to the introduction of formal requirements for early childhood self-evaluation in New Zealand, there was wide consultation with the early childhood community and the development of a national curriculum (Carr et al., 2000). *Te Whāriki*, the New Zealand early childhood curriculum (Ministry of Education, 1996b), is a bicultural and socioculturally oriented curriculum (see Chapter 1 for details). *Te Whāriki,* which means 'woven mat', is a bicultural framework, with the document partly written in Maori, outlining the learning outcomes for children as working theories about the people, places and things in learners' lives, and as learning dispositions (Ministry of Education, 1996b: 44) (see also Cowie and Carr in Chapter 8). *Te Whāriki* invites practitioners to 'weave' their own curriculum, drawing on the framework of Principles, Strands and Goals as appropriate to the needs and interests of their own children and communities. This is consistent with the principle of empowerment, and *Te Whāriki* certainly challenges practitioners to make informed, reflective professional judgements.[3]

A subsequent literature review on quality evaluation found that it is important for practitioners to be involved in evaluating their own programmes. The review warns against inappropriate evaluation methods being imposed externally (Cubey and Dalli, 1996).

Evaluation and assessment projects: *Learning and Teaching Stories*

Follow-on research projects on assessment and on evaluation, funded by the Ministry of Education, formulated the frameworks of *Learning and Teaching Stories*. First, this research first developed approaches to holistic assessment, using *learning stories* that empower learners and communicate with families (Carr, 1998a, 1998b, 2001a, and Cowie and Carr in Chapter 8). Second, it developed holistic approaches to evaluation using *teaching stories* that create responsive, reciprocal and respectful relationships with people, places and things (May and Podmore, 2000; Podmore and May, with Mara, 1998). A further phase trialled the *Learning and Teaching Stories* approach to evaluation, using an action research design. The next section of this chapter includes a discussion of aspects of these approaches to evaluation, with reference to sociocultural theory.

The *Child's Questions*

This approach focuses on children's perspectives to define and evaluate quality practices in early childhood centres. Several writers, including Lilian Katz, have discussed how to evaluate early childhood programmes from multiple perspectives. Katz (1994) proposes that when developing indicators of quality a 'bottom-up' perspective should be included to reflect the subjective experiences of children. Katz suggests that there are possible questions children might ask, if they were able to; for example, 'Do I usually feel that I belong to the group and am not just part of the crowd?', 'Do I find most of my experiences satisfying rather than frustrating or confusing?' (Katz, 1994: 201).

The *Child's Questions*, developed contemporaneously in our evaluation research, reflect the considerable research literature on young children's learning, together with observations of *Te Whāriki* in action (May and Podmore, 2000; Podmore et al.,

Belonging	Do you appreciate and understand my interests and abilities and those of my family?	Do you know me?
Well-being	Do you meet my daily needs with care and sensitive consideration?	Can I trust you?
Exploration	Do you engage my mind, offer challenges and extend my world?	Do you let me fly?
Communication	Do you invite me to communicate and respond to my own particular efforts?	Do you hear me?
Contribution	Do you encourage and facilitate my endeavours to be part of the wider group?	Is this place fair for us?

Figure 12.1   The *Child's Questions* approach (Carr et al., 2002: 119)

2001). The 'child's voice' questions were developed initially from ethnographic studies of seven early childhood centres (Podmore and May, with Mara, 1998).

Sociocultural perspectives are relevant to the principles and strands of *Te Whāriki*. These perspectives also underpin the 'child's questions', which are linked to the five strands of *Te Whāriki*. The full and simplified forms of the 'Child's Questions' are shown in Figure 12.1.

In the action research trials of the *Learning and Teaching Stories* approach to evaluation, these 'child's voice' questions provided the initial questions that centres asked of themselves as they began their journey of evaluation. Practitioners participating in our research found the 'child's questions' a catalyst towards reflection on the role of the adult in early childhood centres (Carr et al., 2002; Podmore et al., 2001).

Practitioners worked alongside a research co-ordinator who was experienced at working with early childhood teachers in a professional development capacity. They selected a 'child's question', then trialled a self-evaluation tool for collecting data. The intention was to empower people in early childhood centres to assess and self-evaluate reflectively, using the 'child's questions'. The project developed and extended the idea that evaluation of an early childhood programme can be underpinned by a child's perspective of quality. Participants from the six centres engaged in the action research trials tended to find that the child's questions led to critical reflection and a clearer focus on children:

> If I am involved with a group of children, those questions flash through my mind. You know – 'Do you let me fly?' – am I doing that? (Staff member working with children aged under 2 years)

Action research process, *The Child's Questions* and self-evaluation

Case studies of the six early childhood centres participating in the action research described a shift in focus towards the child's perspective. There were shifts in practitioners' interests, from activities to the 'child's questions'. Centre participants who previously saw planning as being about deciding what activities to provide began to plan starting from the children's perspective; for example, by asking from the child's perspective, 'Is this place fair for us?'

There was also a shift from a concern about external accountability to placing priority on pedagogy.

> [Many centre participants in the evaluation project] became interested in criteria for responsive and reciprocal relationships between learners and people, places, and things (a pedagogical principle of *Te Whāriki*) by investigating and evaluating their own conversational styles and interactions, and episodes of peer inclusion and exclusion. (Carr et al., 2000: 59)

Co-construction and the *Child's Questions*

As part of the original evaluation project, the researchers outlined the theoretical underpinnings of the child's questions (May and Podmore, 2000; Podmore and May, 2003; Podmore and May, with Mara, 1998). This section extends the discussion of links between the child's questions and aspects of sociocultural theory, with reference to Barbara Rogoff's work on co-construction of knowledge in the context of communities of learners. (See also Jordan, in Chapter 1).

Belonging: Do you know me?

'Do you appreciate and understand my interests and abilities and those of my family?'

This question connects to ecological approaches to development, with an emphasis on responsive learning contexts (Bronfenbrenner, 1979), and a socialisation model which focuses on children's learning within family and cultural contexts (McNaughton, 1995, 2002). It is also linked to work on children's dispositions for learning (Carr, 1997; Katz, 1993).

This question appears pertinent to the concept of shared understanding, and the view that learning and development are inseparable from the concerns of families and interpersonal and community processes (Rogoff et al., 1995).

Well-being: Can I trust you?

'Do you meet my daily needs with care and sensitive consideration?'

This question emphasises the significance of respectful relationships with adults to the well-being of infants in early childhood centres (Gerber, 1984; May, 1991), and of the relationship between adults' reciprocal, sensitive interactions and infants' development (Howes et al., 1992; Smith, 1996b).

Exploration: Do you let me fly?

'Do you engage my mind, offer challenges and extend my world?'

This question includes concepts of guided participation and scaffolding, and is linked to Rogoff's (1990), Bruner's (1986) and Vygotsky's (1987) perspectives. It is consistent with the Pascal–Bertram framework for developing effectiveness in early learning settings, where the processes of adult engagement and child involvement are key components (Laevers, 1999; Laevers et al., n.d; Pascal, 1996, 1999). Clearly, this question is closely connected to the concepts of guided participation and co-construction (Rogoff, 1990; Rogoff et al., 1993).

Communication: Do you hear me?

'Do you invite me to communicate and respond to my own particular efforts?'

This question is linked to theoretical concepts of joint attention (Rogoff, 1990; Smith, 1996c), responsive communication (Howes, 1983, 1986; Howes et al., 1992), and inter-subjectivity (Bruner, 1995; Rogoff, 1990; Rogoff et al., 1993). It highlights the importance of reciprocal communication and shared understanding between adults and young children. These are among the key elements of communication that characterise high-quality interactive processes in early childhood centre settings.

Here, the emphasis on the child's voice potentially moves teachers beyond notions of scaffolding in which the child can sometimes be seen as passive. Sociocultural theorists Van der Veer and Valsiner (1994) have reappraised the metaphor of the scaffold, and see the structure of the scaffold as somewhat mechanical. According to Rogoff (1998), children's active participation is an essential component of co-construction.

Contribution: Is this place fair for us?

'Do you encourage and facilitate my endeavours to be part of the wider group?'

Affirmation of infants and young children through their interactions with adults and encouragement to learn alongside others are supported theoretically by work on joint attention (Rogoff, 1990), joint problem-solving and equal power (Smith, 1996c; see also Vygotsky, 1987).

This question, with its focus on the group, is potentially inclusive of the institutional and cultural context. As Rogoff writes:

> From a sociocultural perspective, developmental processes are not just within individuals but also within group and community processes. Hence individual children are not regarded as developing with everything else static. (1997: 269)

This question may also encompass Rogoff's view of development as 'a process of transformation of participation where individuals participate and contribute to ongoing activity' (1998: 695), and the concept of learning through shared endeavours.

Co-construction, individuals and groups: an appraisal

In an article appraising sociocultural assessment in early years education, Fleer notes that the 'learning stories' vignettes in Carr's early reports to the Ministry of Education were 'situated within an individualistic perspective' (2000: 111). One possible limitation of the 'child's questions' approach, too, is its apparently individualistic approach to evaluating teaching. This potential concern was raised initially when Pacific early childhood teachers participated in focus group interviews about self-evaluation research related to *Te Whāriki* (Mara, 1999). Their critique supports the need for further teaching and learning research that enhances understanding of mediation processes within groups in early childhood settings. As evident during our action research study, teachers' experiences and reflections do tend to include a group perspective when they focus on the *Te Whāriki* strand of 'Contribution' and the child's question 'Is this place fair *for us?*' The example below illustrates this point:

> At one early childhood centre participating in the action research trials, teachers collected observational records of play situations where one child was excluded by others. By focusing on the 'child's question' 'Is this place fair for us?' and on the group processes within the centre, they learned about when and where exclusion was happening. The teachers then planned and evaluated how, in specific situations, to work alongside children to develop shared understanding of concepts of fairness. (Adapted from Carr et al., 2000: 42)

This suggests there is scope to evaluate group processes among children and teachers, starting from *The Child's Questions*.

The Quality Journey

Policy initiatives are in place to encourage improved outcomes for children through teachers' self-evaluation. One resource developed in New Zealand, *The Quality Journey/He Haerenga Whai Hua*, is intended for practitioners in early childhood centres and in home-based services (Ministry of Education, 1999a, 2000a). Anne Meade and Anne Kerslake Hendricks, in consultation with the early childhood sector, developed the resource to guide services that are developing improvement systems, undertaking reviews and using quality indicators. The Ministry of Education's stated intention is that this resource should be used as a tool to improve quality through giving information and promoting reflection.

The Quality Journey/He Haerenga Whai Hua builds upon concepts and ideas in the revised statement of Desirable Objectives and Practices (the DOPs), *Quality in Action* and *Te Whāriki* (Podmore and Meade, with Kerslake Hendricks, 2000: 54). It defines a quality improvement system and specifies steps towards developing a review process.

Three core components for review are set out:

- teaching, learning and development;
- adult communication and collaboration;
- organisational management (Ministry of Education, 1999a: 10).

The examples of quality reviews and case studies provided in the resource are inclusive of cultural considerations and sensitive to aspects of the diversity of early childhood services in New Zealand. The fictitious story of a first quality review at a community-based city childcare centre 'Ngahuru' illustrates this point. The story portrays the process of implementing cycles of 'plan, do, study, act' to enhance quality at a centre. As part of the 'journey' tools such as a rating scale are developed and used to reflect on quality issues like the 'communication between educators and parents/*whanau*'. This process leads to revision of policies at the centre to extend communication with South-East Asian families, and to reflect the Treaty of Waitangi's principle of partnership between Maori and non-Maori (Ministry of Education, 2002: 60–8).

In this way, the resource uses case studies of reviews as concrete but fictitious examples of centres' journeys towards improving quality. A glossary and useful recommendations for further reading are also included. Uptake of *The Quality Journey/He Haerenga Whai Hua* is voluntary (Ministry of Education, 1999b).

Comparative synopsis

The two complementary approaches, evaluation starting from *The Child's Questions* using *Learning and Teaching Stories*, and *The Quality Journey*, are both connected to the strands of *Te Whāriki* through the DOPs (Ministry of Education, 1996b, 1998). These connections have been developed and presented in diagrammatic form (Carr et al., 2000: 75; Podmore and Meade, with Kerslake Hendricks, 2000: 55).

In *The Quality Journey/He Haerenga Whai Hua* there is a section on looking at practice 'through a child's eyes'. It is recommended there that, in order to see practice from a child's perspective when using the Teaching, Learning and Development indicators set out, 'it may be useful to keep in mind the five child's questions that link into the strands of *Te Whāriki*' (Ministry of Education, 2000b: 4). Clearly then, there are some directly acknowledged links between *The Child's Questions* using *Learning and Teaching Stories* and *The Quality Journey*. However, the *Learning and Teaching Stories* research appears to state more explicitly the relevance of the concept of co-construction.

Further developments

Sociocultural observations and teachers' self-evaluation, using the framework of *The Child's Questions*, continue to be incorporated into recent resources; for example, in a self-evaluation publication prepared for early childhood services and early years teachers (Ministry of Education, 2006); and a textbook on observation written primarily for early childhood practitioners and teacher researchers (Podmore, 2006). *The Child's Questions* has also influenced the naming and tone of an intervention programme resource developed for schools and special education services, '*Do you know me? E mohio ana koe ki ahau?*' (Gilmore et al., 2007).

A key resource, the Ministry of Education's (2006) *Ngā Arohaehae Whai Hua/Self-review Guidelines for Early Childhood Education*, was designed for internal reviews, that is, for teachers or services to evaluate their own practice. It includes references to both *The Quality Journey* and *The Child's Questions*. In the resource, *The Quality Journey* is cited to define 'self-review'; it is mentioned as one of several publications that assist early childhood services to evaluate their own practice; and it is included in a list of documents available for guiding reviews, with particular reference to its teaching and learning indicators. The Ministry of Education's (2006) resource specifies further that *The Child's Questions* is a conceptual framework, informed by *Te Whāriki*, that services can use to link their observations to theoretical ideas. It includes as an example a self-review carried out by a home-based service that used the framework of *The Child's Questions* to analyse their Learning Stories. The appendices in the resource include different forms designed for analysis of teachers' and services' reviews – their observations and Learning Stories. One form is developed from Rogoff's (2003) planes of analysis; another from *The Child's Questions* (Carr et al., 2002). *The Child's Questions* form includes each of the five 'child's questions' in its full form (in the left-hand column), and in relation to each of the child's questions asks these three specific questions for reflection: 'What should we be doing as adults?', 'What does our information tell us about what we actually do?', 'What changes do we need to make to our practice as a result?' (Ministry of Education, 2006: 68). In this way, *The Child's Questions* currently informs self-evaluation in a more formalised way, and potentially connects self-reviews to the theoretical constructs underpinning *Te Whāriki* and the original *Child's Questions* research. One challenge will be to provide appropriate teacher education and professional development to support teachers' understanding of the theoretical and research basis of the original (child's) questions. This knowledge would appear to be a prerequisite to informed, in-depth reflection on practice.

Summary

This chapter has overviewed research on quality and self-evaluation within New Zealand. The chapter emphasises the importance to quality learning environments of having highly qualified practitioners, continuing professional development and self-evaluation processes. There are clearly some differences between postmodern positioning on the relativism of dimensions of quality (Dahlberg et al., 1999) and this chapter's affirmation of policy moves towards local 'standardisation' of early childhood teacher qualification requirements. However, some clear consistency is noted between New Zealand research on 'teaching stories' starting from the 'child's questions', and support for a 'pedagogy of listening' (Dahlberg, 2000). Self-evaluation starting from the 'child's questions' incorporates children's perspectives, connects to a socioculturally oriented curriculum and can lead early childhood teachers towards insightful reflection and improvement of provision.

Acknowledgements

I acknowledge warmly the contributions of colleagues and participants to our research projects outlined in this chapter, with special thanks to Helen May and Margaret Carr for their collaborative research involvement. Pam Cubey, Ann Hatherly and Bernadette Macartney contributed as research facilitators to the action research project referred to in this chapter. The 'Learning and Teaching Stories' research projects were funded on contract to the Ministry of Education. This chapter also draws on a collaborative literature review concerned with aspects of quality in early childhood education, and I acknowledge Anne Meade's and Anne Kerslake Hendricks's work on jointly preparing that review.

A draft of this chapter was prepared while I was on research and study leave from Victoria University of Wellington, and based at the Children's Research Centre, Trinity College, Dublin. I am grateful to Professor Robbie Gilligan and colleagues for sharing their congenial and scholarly writing environment.

Notes

1. Although a critique of the 'Competent Children' study's quantitative analyses by Nash (2001) questioned whether alternative analysis designs (using more rigorous multivariate analysis methods) might be desirable to check the robustness of connections between some other specific variables.
2. There was an amendment to this Order in 1998.
3. A thoughtful critique by Joy Cullen (1996) cautioned that implementation of Te Whāriki might become superficial – suggesting the need for in-depth, reflective coverage of Te Whāriki in teacher education and professional development programmes.

CHAPTER 13

MULTIPLE PATHWAYS BETWEEN HOME AND SCHOOL LITERACIES

Susan Hill and Susan Nichols

We will be chatting and he will say 'What's that word mean? What's the one we were doing the other day in the car?' 'Contamination – I was talking about some contaminated soil, remember', and Tolly asked me what that meant and how does that happen, and I was saying about poisons and chemicals and then, what were chemicals? (Jess)

'Cat' was Christianne's first word. I said 'Well what happens if we change that first letter?' So we learned the 'at' words. Then I'd say 'What's going to happen if we change that letter?' And then I tried 'mat' and 'rat', working on that word family. She got the hint of that and then she changed the 'a' for the 'o' and she goes 'Cot'. I said 'Yeah, so what's that?' And we figured out that that was 'cot' and then when we tried to change that middle letter. (Robyn)

In this chapter about literacy and quality links between home and school we draw on recent sociocultural work by Rogoff (2003) and Larson and Marsh (2005), who view literacy learning occurring through participation in social, cultural and historical contexts that are mediated by interaction. To begin we define what we mean by the term 'literacy'. There are two over-arching theoretical constructs that recur in literacy theory and research which are important in understanding links between home and school. These constructs are 'representation' and 'practice'.

Next we use case studies of three children at home and then at school to raise questions about multiple pathways between home and school. These questions invite the reader to consider the children's meaning-making resources and use of literacy as a social practice.

Literacy as representation

Representation is the process of meaning-making using available resources (Hall, 1997). Traditional definitions of literacy have focused on the production and comprehension of print-based resources (writing and reading). Literacy is currently being redefined in order to encompass the kinds of representational resources that are increasingly supplementing or replacing traditional modes (Cope and Kalantzis, 2000: 229). This new approach is also termed the 'semiotic' orientation and can be summed up by the statement 'text is more than language' (Kress, 1999: 468). In the same way that we can ask how individuals and groups use print to make meanings, we can ask how meanings are made and goals accomplished using other 'semiotic resources' such as oral language, visual imagery, numerical symbols and music (Lemke, 1990: 226).

Early childhood research has made many important contributions to our understanding of how children make meaning using non-print resources such as drawing and speech. However, these have not generally been considered as part of literacy, at least as it is practised by expert users. Rather, these non-print representational practices have generally been understood as a necessary precursor to the acquisition of full literacy. While early picture books do require visual decoding skills as well as print literacy competence, children have traditionally been expected to move from these to print only texts. This is beginning to change as developments in information and communications technology require competence in a range of representational resources. Particularly with the advent of multimedia communication, the ability to use a range of representational resources and to understand the relationship between them is becoming crucial (Hill, 2007; Lankshear and Knoebel, 1997; Marsh, 2003; Mavers, 2007). For literacy educators this means that it is important to understand how children make meanings using a range of modalities, not just in the 'pre-literate' years but all through their learning. Indeed, a long tradition of ethnographic studies of practices around literacy has shown that, in both community and classroom settings, the use of print is accompanied with talk, gesture and action (Dyson, 1993; Heath, 1983; Ormerod and Ivanic, 2000). A semiotic definition of literacy enables us to think about how all these representational resources are employed, even when the focus remains primarily on the production of a print text.

The semiotic model does not replace older definitions of literacy. Rather, it is inclusive of, and adds to, both the traditional print-oriented and the more recent language-oriented communications model. Figure 13.1 illustrates this.

The inner circle represents the traditional print-oriented definition of literacy. Here there is an emphasis on encoding and decoding print. The middle circle represents a language-oriented definition of literacy, which includes print but extends the range of representational resources to include oral language. In the outer circle literacy encompasses print and language plus a broader range of representational resources or modalities. For example, in multimedia, print is combined with sound, movement and visual imagery to create complex texts that require the 'reader' to process in multiple modes simultaneously.

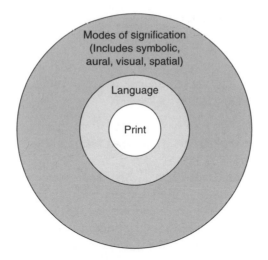

Figure 13.1   A semiotic model of literacy (Nichols, 2000)

Literacy as social practice

Understanding literacy as practice is important for understanding home and school links as this means attending to the circumstances where representations are produced. These circumstances may include the local and broader social contexts, the participants and their relations to each other, the purpose of the activity, the way it unfolds over time, and the physical characteristics of the setting.

Literacy ethnographers such as Heath (1983) and Tyler (1993) led the shift to practice-oriented approaches to literacy through their observational studies of literacy practices in diverse community settings. McNaughton (1995: 20) focused his investigation of family literacy on practices understood as 'systems of activity'. Activities, he points out, are always purposeful and identifying their purposes provides insights into the social and cultural values of families and communities. Writing about caregivers' decisions about literacy activities with their children, McNaughton observes 'Particularly in multilingual, multicultural, industrialised countries … multiple cultural meanings and messages exist in the socialisation process. … [Caregivers] select from and adapt to these multiple heterogenous "voices" which are available to them.' So in speaking of literacy as practice, it is more accurate to speak of multiple literacies in multiple social and cultural contexts interacting in complex ways.

Recent studies of literacy as social practice suggest that children's meaning-making is a complex activity shaped by the particular family structure and family narratives (Marsh, 2003; Pahl, 2002). In an ethnographic study of three diverse families Pahl (2002) writes that the concept of home pedagogy is not static but a vital and profound process made up of family narratives, the games children play, drawings and artefacts created, combined together with the 'idea of home' the adults construct. Nichols's (2002) study of parents reading to children demonstrates that home is a place of work and of domestic relationships within which literacy activities such as the bed-time story may be simultaneously pedagogic, instrumental and affective.

The notion of 'schooled' pedagogies, which have traditionally been clearly observable, has often been placed in opposition to 'home' pedagogies, which are less visible. Further research into the construction of meaning in homes will expand understanding of less visible home pedagogies.

Literacy as representation and practice

Complex studies of literacy, particularly those that are longitudinal and/or conducted in community as well as in school settings, tend to include both representation and practice in their definitions of literacy. Snow et al. (1991), for instance, define literacy as 'complex relationships among reading, writing, ways of talking, ways of learning, and ways of knowing'. Some studies focus primarily on the use of print within a social practice perspective. Purcell-Gates (1995) defines literacy in terms of being 'lettered' and thus is able to describe a household as 'non-literate' because its residents do not use print as a representational resource. However, she also understands literacy as a set of social practices around the use of print. Labbo (1996) takes a semiotic approach to investigating children's computer literacy. She points out that a semiotic approach inherently involves both representation and practice dimensions: 'Semiotic analysis gives equal credit to the cognitive contribution of the individual child's investigation of symbol usage as well as to the social contribution of the interactions that flow around and through those investigations' (Labbo, 1996: 359).

Literacy at home in the early years

Defining literacy as both representation and social practice is changing how we understand the connection between homes and schools, as the two main sites where young children's literate competence is acquired. In this chapter we will introduce you to three young children, as they move from their homes into school for the first time; discuss some of the theory and research that assists us to understand the complex connections between these sites; and consider how educators can best capitalise on, and extend, the forms of literate competence that children bring from their homes and communities.

Reading the cases

As you read the cases that follow, consider each child's home experiences in terms of the definition of literacy as representation and social practice.

- What meaning-making resources does each child have access to?
- What kinds of social goals are achieved using these resources?
- In what social practices does the child participate?
- What are his/her forms of literate competence, in terms of our definition?

Tolly at home

Tolly's early years were spent at home with his parents, Julie and Jess, and his part-time nanny. Tolly's language and communication skills developed in an environment of adults talking with him and about him. From an early age his parents included him in conversations, regardless of topic, and responded promptly to his requests for explanations. They involved him in decision-making as much as possible.

> We will be chatting and he will say 'What's that word mean? What's the one we were doing the other day in the car?' "Contamination" – I was talking about some contaminated soil, remember', and Tolly asked me what that meant and how does that happen, and I was saying about poisons and chemicals, and then, what were chemicals? (Jess)

When Tolly was quite young he was found to suffer from a chronic medical condition which necessitated regular hospital trips and affected his general energy levels. Because some of his treatment was distressing, Tolly developed the habit of using talk as a delaying tactic:

> We saw him try and talk some specialist out of doing a test on him and he was like talking very quickly, and he was projecting it in a very articulate fashion and was very reasonable. (Julie)

Tolly enjoyed imaginative play at home, creating scenarios and characters using toys, talking with 'pretend friends' and dressing up. He loved to imitate his parents, for instance talking on a toy phone in adult-like ways. He was also encouraged to join in with household activities such as cooking and sewing.

Christianne at home

We first met Christianne when she was 4 years old. Her preschool years were spent between her parents' house and her Grandmother Yaya's place, both of which she considered home. Her Grandmother Yaya, a Greek woman, read Greek storybooks to Christianne and translated English songs such as *Jingle Bells* into Greek so they could sing together. Yaya believed each child in her extended family was different and tried to provide them with activities they preferred. With Christianne it was 'books, books, books to read'.

At Yaya's house Christianne would sometimes spend time with her uncle, a boy 7 years her senior. Indeed, Yaya believed that Christianne was mature for her age

(Continued)

(Continued)

because she had spent so much time with the older child. Her uncle's old school books became props that Christianne would use to play school, acting teacher to her dolls.

Playing school was important for another reason. Christianne's mother, Robyn, was a primary school teacher. Even before she began school, Christianne was aware of the concept of 'homework' from watching Robyn, and would join in by doing her own 'homework' such as colouring in. Robyn consciously prepared Christianne for school by introducing literacy activities. Christianne was encouraged to learn her letters by looking at a pictorial alphabet board. Games such as 'I spy' were used to teach initial sounds. Her mother used a phonemic approach to teach word families.

> 'Cat' was her first word. I said 'Well what happens if we change that first letter?' So we learned the 'at' words. Then I'd say 'What's going to happen if we change that letter?' And then I tried 'mat' and 'rat', working on that word family.

Erin at home

Erin is the youngest of five children and, when we first met the family, both parents were unemployed. Erin's mother, Eva, suffered from clinical depression and Erin's father, Steve, decided to resign from his job to look after her. Both parents were regular visitors to the school attended by Erin's older siblings. Steve was Chair of the Wattles School Council. Erin always accompanied her parents in dropping off and picking up her siblings. Her mother said she was 'bored stupid' at home and wanted to go to school.

When she was old enough Erin joined her sisters at callisthenics three times a week. Callisthenics combines rhythmic gymnastics with dance and is highly competitive, with spectacularly costumed routines. Dressed for action, Erin looked fit and full of energy. Eva, a talented dressmaker, made all her daughter's callisthenics costumes.

In the girls' bedroom there are two bunks and three shelves of books. On these shelves are the children's collection of about 50 Golden Books and about 140 Lollipop Books. Eva bought the Lollipop Books, which cost about $2.00, each time she went to the supermarket and she also kept the girls' books neatly organised from easy texts to the more difficult Enid Blyton books. Eva said that Erin knew all the books off by heart. Erin learnt the books off by heart because the older children in the family had read them to her many times.

Research perspectives on the home–school link

We review here a number of key studies in the field of children's literacy to address questions about the relationship between literacy in home and school. It should be noted that 'home' is an umbrella term for a number of different sites. Researchers may focus on the household or look more broadly at communities or cultures, depending on their area of interest. Most 'school' studies focus on a particular kind of site within the school, the classroom. The relationship between these two domains is one of the key issues of educational, and more specifically of literacy, research and practice.

Home–school link: connecting systems

McNaughton (1995), following Bronfenbrenner (1979), takes a systems theory approach to the home–school relation, with a particular focus on emergent literacy. A system in this model has three characteristics: it 'is dynamic, it grows and adjusts to various forces, and is goal oriented' (McNaughton, 1995: 162). Systems operate on a number of levels: there are the immediate settings in which a person is situated, termed 'micro-systems', such as the family, the neighbourhood and the school; there are larger multi-site institutions such as the churches and corporations; and there are even broader and less tangible groupings of knowledge and practice such as cultures and ideologies. Sets of activities that take place within these settings can also be understood as forms of systems: reading and writing are two such activity systems.

According to this model, understanding a child's development involves considering, first, his or her participation in activities in different settings and, second, the relationships between these different forms of participation. Within the activity system of 'reading' for instance, one would need to understand how 'reading' is enacted in all the settings in which a child undertakes or observes 'reading' and how the child perceives reading across the various settings. This would further entail attending to the teaching/learning strategies and how novice–expert relationships are made available to the child within the activity systems in different settings. And it would involve understanding the practice and meaning of 'reading' at all system levels: the micro (home, classroom), the exo (institution, geographic area) and the macro (culture, ideology).

Close case studies of individual children show how they negotiate the different demands of participation in their micro-systems. In such studies we see how forms of knowledge and practice are relayed between sites and transformed in the process. Based on her close observations of young children in and out of their classrooms, Dyson (1993: 183) has generated the concepts of 'worlds' and 'borders' to describe the relationship between the domains children inhabit. She describes three worlds, each with its set of participant practices involving language and behaviour: the official school world, the peer world and the home world or 'sociocultural community'. Her detailed observations show that children are often trying to accomplish multiple social goals simultaneously. Representational practices are a tool in children's negotiations around social identities. For instance, chanting, drawing, writing and performing as characters in their stories provide children with ways of establishing themselves as socially, as well as academically, adept. They can be used to please or to challenge a teacher, to win friends or to get rid of an unwanted acquaintance.

Dyson's work challenges what she sees as 'the too-neat boundaries drawn between children, languages, and cultures' (1993: 183). She is referring here, not only to the boundaries between home and school, but between popular culture and school curriculum, between the mainstream and the alternative. Her argument is that children already do make connections between these worlds, bringing together languages, genres and domains of knowledge in creative and unpredictable ways.

Serpell (1997) writes that the relation between school and home can be a 'handover' or a 'bridge'. In the first, the two domains are seen as having different sets of responsibility in relation to the child. The parents 'hand over' the child to the school for an education while the school 'hands over' the child to the parent for socialisation and emotional care. In the second model, there is 'negotiation of a shared understanding of how the responsibilities of the two parties are conceptually related ..., and of how the child is expected to integrate the demands of these two worlds' (1997: 595). Where there are cultural differences, bridging the two domains is seen to require a form of 'bicultural mediation', which Serpell describes as a translation of concepts across meaning systems.

Interactions in homes and schools

One of the major similarities between homes and schools, from children's perspective, is that in both settings adults are ultimately in charge. However, the way in which adults and children interact may be very different, not only between homes and schools but between different kinds of families and even different classrooms. For the child, negotiating how to interact with adults in these diverse social settings is one of the key challenges of moving between micro-systems.

There is now a long tradition of research into adult–child interaction in homes and schools which can help us understand these challenges more fully (e.g. Freiburg and Freebody, 1995; Tizard and Hughes, 1984; Wells, 1986). A common finding is that adult–child interaction patterns in the home are significantly different from teacher–student interaction patterns in classrooms. In Freiberg and Freebody's (1995) analysis of adult–child interactions around learning, teachers were observed frequently to ask questions requiring children to possess general knowledge not directly related to the specific task at hand. Parents rarely did this; when assisting their children with homework their questions called on specific task-related knowledge. The 'pedagogic events' enacted at home and school were qualitatively different. Teachers responded positively or neutrally to all children's responses while parents gave evaluations, naming responses as 'right' or 'wrong' and supplying 'right' answers when the child was unable to. Despite their apparent acceptance of children's responses, teachers took the 'expert' position in that they framed the questions and shaped the discussion towards their intended outcomes. Parents shifted from 'expert' to 'non-expert' partner depending on their child's knowledge of the task.

Children of low socioeconomic backgrounds are often thought to suffer from deficiencies in oral language development which then negatively impact on their acquisition of school literacy. Bernstein's (1973) theory of class codes has had a strong influence on this view. He claimed children of low socioeconomic status (SES) are disadvantaged at school because their parents socialise them into a 'restricted' (context-specific) oral language code. That is, talk in these families is said to revolve around the here-and-now, not around ideas, events or objects outside the immediate context. Freiburg and Freebody's (1995) findings, which did not compare families by social class, suggest that this specificity may be more prevalent in homes in general than in classrooms. Thus they see the home–school difference as more salient than the social class difference.

Another challenge to Bernstein's theory was mounted by Wells (1986), who set out to investigate this claim in a landmark longitudinal study. This study found no differences in oral language competence between working-class and middle-class children from two and a half years until school entry. The association between low SES and the restricted code was disrupted by the finding that working-class parents were not less likely to extend on their children's utterances and to refer to ideas and information from outside the immediate context than middle-class parents. Indeed, Tizard found that adult–child interactions were more cognitively challenging in out-of-school settings (e.g. Tizard and Hughes, 1984). In classroom interactions with teachers, children are much less likely to initiate conversation topics and much more likely to be required to answer questions. They are also less likely to find that their contributions are taken up and extended by their adult speaking partner.

Participation practices in homes and schools

For children crossing constantly between different micro-systems, knowing how to participate effectively in each setting is crucially important. McNaughton (1995) argues that the closer the similarity between participation practices in different settings, the easier it is for children to move between them. Difference can also be seen as productive. Dyson (1993) draws attention to children's creativity in producing new meanings and forms of practice as a result of their participation in different worlds. Both would agree that transition for children does not cease at the end of the first school term, but is a continual process, which for some children is more complex than for others.

Ethnographic studies that cross home and school sites have helped us to understand the differences and similarities in participation practices, and the impact of these on children from diverse social and cultural communities. The groundbreaking study of Heath (1983), in three different communities, has been highly influential. Heath observed family and community literacy practices in an African-American working-class neighbourhood, in a white fundamentalist Christian working-class neighbourhood and in a white middle-class neighbourhood. She took a broad view of literacy, incorporating both print and oral language as representational resources, and a diverse range of practices of participation, including individual and group, formal and informal. She tracked focus children from their homes and communities into school and observed similarities and differences in the participation practices in these two sites.

Heath's broad conclusion is that middle-class homes and school classrooms share some important participation practices, or what she calls 'norms of conduct' (p. 236). These mainstream norms include: linearity as a means of organising space and time (e.g. the use of hour-by-hour schedules); the privileging of expert knowledge; the formalisation of rules for group activities; and voluntariness in social activities. The link between these broader norms and more specific literacy practices can be seen, for example, in the privileging of expert knowledge. Heath notes, in middle-class homes and in classrooms, secondary sources are valued over information gained through immediate social networks (unlike in the two working-class communities). These secondary sources often take the form of print texts so that it is these texts that are then understood as carrying authority. This association of print literacy products with valued knowledge is a key foundation of school approaches to learning, not just of literacy but of all subjects. Those who don't have these forms of competence are then considered in deficit terms.

It is important to be aware that Heath's work was undertaken in a setting where social divisions constituted communities as distinct, culturally and socio-economically. In different social circumstances, with more blending between social groups (for instance in circumstances of high immigration into established areas) these divisions may not be so distinct. Australian researchers Cairney and Ruge (1998) also found that children from families that constructed power relations and knowledge in similar ways to those operating in the classroom were advantaged at school. However, these differences did not fall out neatly along socioeconomic or cultural lines, as with Heath's study. There were examples of working-class families where parents employed school-like pedagogies in facilitating their children's learning and there were professional families in which parents allowed their children greater participation rights than they were granted in the classroom, which in some cases disadvantaged these children.

The foregoing discussion on domains of development reveals that children's lives are grounded in the environments they inhabit. These environments are important influences on development. When there are complementarities between them, children have the opportunity to develop and practise repertoires that link one environment to another and moving from one micro-system to another can be relatively unproblematic. When there are differences, however, children are involved in negotiating 'how to be' in the different micro-systems.

Moving from home to school

We now return to the three children introduced previously in this chapter, and watch them move first from home to a form of preschool, and then from preschool to the first year of formal schooling. While the preschool year is often overlooked in literacy research, it is important to consider children's experiences in this setting, in terms of their access to representational resources and social practices. Indeed, the practices of preschool settings are different from both homes and classrooms, giving children the considerable challenge of making two transitions in little more than two years.

Reading the cases

As you read these cases, consider the insights from theory and research which have been discussed previously in this chapter:

- What activity systems operate in each child's educational setting?
- How do the participation practices in homes, preschools and schools relate to each other?
- Are adult–child interactions across these settings similar or different?
- To what extent are the children able, at school, to capitalise on the forms of literate competence (representational resources and social practices) which they have learned at home?

Tolly at school

At 3-and-a-half Tolly began preschool at the Pemberton Early Learning Centre. This preschool is run on Reggio Emilia lines, employing a holistic, theme-oriented, child-centred pedagogy. Most of the children go on from here to Pemberton Grammar School, a private school with a particularly strong reputation in boys' literacy learning.

Tolly loved preschool. He interacted easily with adults and was confident enough to try out all the activities that were offered to him. He was able to continue familiar play practices such as story creation and role-play but now with the possibility of an expanded cast of characters. Recognising his imaginative strengths, staff encouraged Tolly to develop and extend his scenarios. His major challenge was in interacting with his child peers. Partly, this was about learning to share. Tolly was particularly keen to use certain resources (such as the computer), which were in high demand, and so his negotiation skills came to the fore.

As Tolly continued in the same school, his transition to Reception was eased somewhat. However, there were aspects that were very different. Literacy was a high priority and was taught through an intensive structured phonics programme. Along with his classmates, Tolly was introduced to worksheets and the expectation that tasks should be completed. There was time for free play, but this was greatly reduced compared with previously at the ELC.

(Continued)

(Continued)

Tolly's participation in classroom activities was highly visible owing to his advanced oral language. In class discussion times he always had a contribution to make and was skilled in holding the floor. When the task involved making something, Tolly would keep up a running commentary.

Tolly's reading developed according to expectations but his writing was slower to come on. He was often among the last to complete worksheets, after many gentle but firm reminders. When it was writing time, Tolly would often create a simultaneous alternative activity, entertaining himself and his table mates. For instance, pencils would be made to assume characters and act out scenes. While Tolly associated reading with stories, something he enjoyed, he associated writing with work, once remarking to the researcher that there was 'too much work and not enough play' at school.

Christianne at school

Christianne attended a child–parent centre attached to the primary school she would be later attending. The child–parent centre was set up every day with a range of activities for children to choose. For instance, there might be train track outside on the verandah, some gym equipment on the lawn and a making activity inside. There was abundant print displayed in the preschool. Children's names were everywhere, e.g. on a birthday chart, on their coat pegs.

Christianne's orientation to print was obvious in this environment. She could often be found in the book corner, 'reading' by retelling familiar stories. She also chose to copy writing from books.

Christianne found she was able to continue one of her favourite activities in this new environment – playing teacher, except here it was called 'helping'. For instance, she would jump at the opportunity to take on adult-like tasks such as calling out children's names or handing out resources. Her liking for responsibility and control was not always seen positively though, by either adults or her peers. She had one friend and when this child, Justine, was not present, she would play alone. A teacher commented that Christianne was 'strong willed'.

Christianne found the transition to the first year of school extremely easy. As her mother, Robyn, taught at the same school, they travelled to and from the school together and could talk about school issues both morning and afternoon. It was very easy for the teachers at the school to talk about Christianne's progress with her mother who sat with the other teachers in the staff room. At home, Christianne's mother continued to work in a teacherly way with her using homework sessions as opportunities to supplement her instruction. For instance, for one homework task Christianne captioned a picture with 'this mermaid is singing'. Robyn wrote the word 'mermaid' above Christianne's invented version and put 'ing' in a box for emphasis.

As well as regular school, each Saturday from 9.00 a.m. to 12.00 p.m. Christianne attended Greek school where she learned Modern Greek language, dancing and other aspects of culture. The instruction was adult-directed with an emphasis on memorisation and children were tested regularly. Christianne often wrote in her school journal what she had done at Greek school.

In Year 2, or the third year of school, Christianne moved to the grammar school, where her mother was both an 'old scholar' and a teacher, having moved there from the Wattles. At the Queens Baptist school there were weekly tests and Christianne liked to do these. She usually got 10/10 for spelling. When the class did writing, which was on most days, Christianne would write a page or more. At age 8 she was reading texts with a readability score of beyond Year 12 of high school.

Erin at school

Erin attended the same preschool as Christianne (see above). Erin was a lively participant and displayed an interest in a wide range of the activities offered, for example the sand pit, at the writing table and in the book corner, with others and alone. Apparently uninfluenced by gender stereotypes, Erin could often be found playing with cars and trucks, or swinging and climbing on the gym equipment. She related well to other children and would join in with collaborative story-building play, often using the trucks as characters.

Erin would often handle books but clearly understood 'real reading' as decoding print, a skill she had not yet learned, saying 'I don't know how to read.' She would compose and retell stories using a mixture of book-like and oral language. Erin's attention to the visual in texts was also obvious: for instance she was seen to comment on a mismatch between illustrations in one text.

The following year Erin began school. Her Reception class was taught by an experienced teacher with a strong belief in the value of an integrated curriculum and in the effectiveness of positive feedback. Opportunities to read and write were presented in many different ways and activities were changed regularly. Erin encountered school literacy through Big Books, word study, collaborative story-making, three-way partner reading and in diverse other ways. Children read to an adult not daily but about once every fortnight.

Erin was considered by her teacher to be well-organised and motivated. She worked quietly, whatever the task, and rarely asked for help. However, her

(Continued)

(Continued)

self-assessment was not so positive or, to look at it another way, was determinedly realistic. When asked about reading, she said she couldn't read very well. She would select books she could read confidently but, when offered, did not want to try higher levels.

Despite her own assessment, Erin made good progress in literacy in her Reception year. She progressed to writing sentences of several lines, correctly spaced. She performed well on a test of phonemic awareness, correctly identifying words by their initial sounds (onsets) and rhymes.

Each of our three focus children had personal circumstances that potentially placed them in risk categories for schooling and literacy. Tolly had a chronic illness, Christianne was partly raised by a non-English speaking relative and Erin's family experienced parental unemployment and depression. Yet before entering the school system, each child was versed in activity systems that offered opportunities to use language, process information and produce representations. Tolly's relationship with his parents and nanny was rich in talk and their willingness to engage in conversation with him built his skills in self-representation, information-seeking, story-telling and negotiation. Christianne encountered texts in both English and Greek and was introduced to the concept of translation, so beneficial to understanding language as a system; additionally she had access to school-like participation practices through her mother's profession and her uncle's old school books. Erin also similarly experienced peripheral participation in school through her older siblings and her father, counter to expectations of working-class men, was actively involved in school management. She saw books valued in the way they were budgeted for, treated as objects of care and used regularly.

Preschool, for each child, appeared to operate as a very open activity system owing to the degree of choice possible. It is interesting to see the participation practices these children brought into the preschool setting from home. Tolly was able to continue his conversational interactions with adults and to extend his imaginative play with new props and actors. Christianne was clearly eager for opportunities to show her knowledge of school routines and quickly stepped into the role of teacher's helper even though the preschool setting encouraged play more than formal learning. Erin found in the play equipment a way to enjoy gymnastic motion – though this was read as tomboy-like by observers unaware of her callisthenics training.

What was new for each child in preschool was their insertion into a much larger social grouping of peers than they had experienced previously. While play is often considered natural to children, we can see from these cases that interacting with peers makes social, and specifically linguistic, demands. Sharing was hard for Tolly, a single child, and Christianne found playing with other children much less predictable, and therefore harder to know how to succeed in, than the structured and scaffolded interactions she was used to in her family.

On the other hand, school tasks, which are often considered to represent the major challenge in transition, were not as problematic as might have been expected, particularly for the two girls. It is not surprising that Erin, whose mother arranged her books at home in order of difficulty, was judged 'well-organised' by her teacher or that a child used to tough competition in callisthenics would also appear 'motivated'. Tolly, in contrast, had not been trained into work practices and the fatigue caused by his illness, which his constant chatting often masked, made completing his worksheets a hard slog.

Conclusion

Teachers are increasingly working with students who are culturally and linguistically diverse, and these students have differing cultural capital that can be used as rich cultural resources for teaching (Dyson, 1999). The challenge for early childhood educators is:

> to see the task of making connections not as one of getting rid of the diversity that they encounter in the make up of their populations, nor of dealing with diversity as something that has to be coped with, but rather as one of incorporating diversity to the advantage of effective pedagogy. (McNaughton, 2002: 31)

To build quality connections between home and school demands that educators explore the worlds of children, their activities, practices and funds of knowledge. Literacy is not print alone nor language but the ways meaning is represented in signs, logos, music, animation and forms of multimedia. As teachers and children explore the great wealth of texts present in children's worlds, the notion that the rules for producing different kinds of texts, whether spoken, written or visual, are somehow natural, universal and accessible to all is not substantiated by the research into home and school continuities. Rather the arbitrary rules for reading and producing different genres are community-specific and situation-specific. Once this idea is taken on board by teachers then all kinds of language can be analysed and explored and language can be treated as an 'object of contemplation' not just a tool for communication (Hemphill and Snow, 1996: 198). The development of this awareness that language is an 'object of contemplation' has a further significance. It enables teachers and children to develop critical literacy with greater power to reflect on social inequalities. Some cultural groups' ways of speaking may not be viewed and treated as legitimate in the classroom, reflecting a minority status (McNaughton, 2002).

In Christianne's case increasing the quality of home–school links means increasing and ever-widening the range of texts she meets and building textual dexterity. Being successful with school literacies may not be enough to work with the range of changing texts that we will meet on the Internet and CD-ROM. In Tolly's case this may mean capitalising on his oral stories and techniques for negotiating and making links from the spoken to the written form. The narrow repetitive print-oriented curriculum is not taking him from where he is 'at'. For Erin, it may mean recognising the range of practical ways in which literacy is used at home (for instance in all the activities of designing and making a callisthenics costume) and encouraging Erin to see her competence as extending beyond the reading of a narrow range of beginner books.

In schools where there is considerable diversity in children's homes, communities and cultures, it is not possible for teachers to predict each child's unique forms of literate competence. Rather, teachers have to become enquirers into the literacies of their children's worlds. In turn, children need to be informants about their participation in social practices of literacy, and the representational resources that they are competent in using. Young children, as demonstrated in the case studies in this chapter, are problem-solvers and very flexible socio-linguists who are able to speak, read, write and view a range of written and spoken language genres at home and at school. Teachers also live in multiple worlds and have access to a range of literacies. By bringing their own lives into the classroom, they can show the way in crossing the boundaries that divide their classroom from other worlds. Finally, educational policy development that focuses on home and school pedagogies may be greatly informed by attending to the rich literacy practices and representational resources used by young children and their families.

PART 5

CONCLUSION

CHAPTER 14

A FRAMEWORK FOR CONCEPTUALISING EARLY CHILDHOOD EDUCATION

Marilyn Fleer, Angela Anning and Joy Cullen

Introduction

Vygotsky argued that children are cultural beings, living in particular communities at particular times and living and constructing a particular history. Research framed from a sociocultural-historical perspective is less about revealing 'the eternal child' and more about uncovering 'the historical child' (Vygotsky, 1987). Sociocultural-historical perspectives take into account the social, historical and cultural dimensions of everyday activities and seek to better understand children within this richly framed research context.

In this book the authors have taken a sociocultural-historical view of research and practice for framing their analysis of early childhood education in the United Kingdom, New Zealand and Australia. Many scholars have built on Vygotsky's original writing, with important strands in activity theory, social-constructivism and socio-historical research. The materials introduced in the chapters of this book have foregrounded existing taken-for-granted practices, illuminated historically located activities and problematised cultural practices. As such, the authors have located the historical and the contemporary side-by-side in order to envisage new directions for early childhood education.

This final chapter brings together the emerging themes and concepts presented in the preceding four parts of the book with a discussion of the theoretical underpinnings and their implications for early childhood pedagogy, knowledge, assessment and quality. Collectively, the material contained in this book gives a glimpse of the cultural baggage as well as the cultural capital that we have acquired. Through the rich material presented in each of the chapters, it is possible to see both the transformations of early childhood education in practice and the building of cultural capital for our profession. In bringing together respected scholars of sociocultural theory in early childhood education from three nations, we seek to build a new community of practice, with new conceptual tools for strengthening our understanding of and practice in early childhood education.

Outcomes of sociocultural-historical research in early years education

Importance of the role of the teacher

One of the significant features of the outcomes of cultural-historical research in the early years has been a growing awareness of the importance of the role of adults, particularly their knowledge base and their capacity for 'sustained shared thinking' (Siraj-Blatchford, this volume) with children. Wood (Chapter 2) argues that 'while there is substantial evidence on *learning* through play, there is relatively little evidence on *teaching* through play'. This observation can be applied to much of the research in early years education. Government funding has been directed towards determining what learning has resulted from early years education, with only more recent efforts directed towards differentiating between programme types, different pedagogical strategies and the diversity of professional knowledge underpinning the delivery of good quality education and care (Siraj-Blatchford, Chapter 11; Fleer, 2001). This also mirrors the traditional focus on the children and their interactions with the materials, as observed by the non-mediating and objective teacher.

In Chapter 2 Wood points directly to the high level of skills required of practitioners when considering play in relation to 'teaching'. Teachers must carefully balance the role of 'teacher directed' and 'child initiated' interactions in centres. This balance has also been shown by Jordan (Chapter 2) to be significant for optimising and generating authentic learning opportunities for children. Like Williams-Kennedy (Chapter 7), Siraj-Blatchford (Chapter 11) has shown that where programmes place all the responsibility for learning with children, through teachers positioning themselves as 'providing resource-rich environments', without planning for their role in mediating these resources, some children will be disadvantaged. She argues that the prevailing approach to early years education has always privileged children from middle-class homes who have the necessary cultural capital already to maximise the use of preschool experiences in ways that support Western linear developmental trajectories. Wood's research also centres on the role of the teacher, and provides rich evidence for the importance of the teacher critically reflecting and planning for his or her role in children's play.

Practitioners' concept development

Anning (Chapter 5) also generated a community of practice (Lave and Wenger, 1991) for building a curriculum with staff from a wide range of early childhood settings. Like Cullen (Chapter 6), Anning found significant tension to arise for staff because of a difference in expectations and theoretical perspectives for guiding what constituted quality practice. Anning found that the discourse and focus for childcare professionals sat uncomfortably with an emphasis on 'the mind' and they 'were intimidated by the prospect of working' with education authorities. Those perceiving themselves to be 'educators' were equally uncomfortable with the emphasis on 'the body' of those trained as carers and health workers. Through an action research project that drew upon the theoretical work of Lave and Wenger (1991), a community of practice was generated that allowed the group to move towards a sociocultural-historical approach for learning. Significantly, Anning noted that the practitioners found educational 'value in everyday' practice, and they were able to ascribe meaning 'to materials and activities in their everyday working lives'. They had to develop a language to share their reflections in spoken and written versions and sometimes to confront conflicts with other professionals in the project team and in the broader community. With the integration of childcare services with the Department of Education in both Australia and the UK, the outcomes of Anning's research are highly significant for the transitional work that will need to occur at all levels of practice, policy and research.

Theoretical tools

One area that does not appear to have been researched using a sociocultural-historical framework is work on the nature of gendered interactions or gendering. Whether this is problematic for researching from a sociocultural-historical perspective has not been determined. However, it is more likely that post-structuralist theorisation and development in research methodologies and methods have progressed more rapidly and provided a powerful approach for early childhood researchers to draw upon. MacNaughton (Chapter 4) draws upon this tradition, but with links to social constructivism, to investigate the relations between an artefact (perfume bottle) and a child (boy) in order to better understand gendering. Through this single case example, MacNaughton has 'documented preschool children's gendered play, talked with children about how they understood gender, and explored how gender equity is created in the classroom'. She specifically notes how this boy has understood that the perfume bottle is gender-laden, but has constructed a social and conceptual space in which he can play with this particular artefact within the context of an early childhood setting. The action research model that is used by MacNaughton for working with practitioners to explore gender has generated a community of learners who together were able to critique their own practices and come to new understandings about gendering.

Changing theoretical lenses

What is evident from the studies reported in this book that have used sociocultural-historical theory is that changing theoretical lenses is very difficult for practitioners. This work has also shown the complexity of adult–child interactions, and the necessity to foreground content knowledge, theorisation and new practices for working differently with children in early years settings. Importantly, teacher thinking about their practice also requires institutional change, as working in a sociocultural-historical way needs the sanctioning of authorities (such as through *Te Whariki*), active engagement (as with *Loving to Learn* action research by Anning), and critical analysis (as seen through Cullen's research with EI and practitioners in New Zealand). In the next section, the socio-political context is examined, as societal expectations shape what and how institutions operate and can change – to support or constrain changes in theoretical thinking.

The four themes: current research evidence and future directions

Part 1: Learning and pedagogy

A legacy of the developmental, play-based curriculum philosophy in early years settings is the pervasive view of the practitioner as manager of the learning environment and facilitator of children's development. As sociocultural-historical theories of learning have gained greater recognition, one of the biggest challenges for early childhood practitioners has been how to reconcile their understanding of their facilitation role with the more proactive pedagogical approach promoted by sociocultural-historical theorists. The sociocultural-historical approach adopted in this book foregrounds the learner in the contexts of learning–teaching relationships: peers learning together in play settings, adults and children learning together in instructional settings, and adults learning together as planners, teachers, assessors and evaluators of curricula for young children. In accordance with sociocultural-historical principles, adult and child learners are viewed as situated in particular institutional, social, cultural and historical contexts, reflected in the beliefs, artefacts and practices that constrain learning. Hence community and home-based funds of knowledge, and the values and expectations for learning that emanate from these contexts, contribute to learning in early childhood settings, either explicitly or implicitly. The extent to which early childhood practitioners explicitly understand the cultural beliefs and practices embedded in homes and communities, as well as their professional settings, is emerging as a key pedagogical issue in early years settings.

Collectively, the authors in Part 1 provide evidence from early childhood settings that argues for a strong focus on the pedagogical skills of teaching teams. The three chapters illustrate movement from teacher as facilitator to teacher as co-learner and co-player to teacher as challenger and informant to policies. Wood's call (Chapter 2) for a more secure pedagogy of play that includes greater emphasis on cultural repertoires could plausibly apply across the areas of assessment and evaluation, planning, teachers' professional development, community relations and advocacy. Jordan's study (Chapter 3) signals the importance of collaborative planning with parents if the intersubjectivity that allows for co-constructed learning between adults and learners is to occur. Intersubjectivity, in this sense, involves shared understandings of children's funds of knowledge and interests that may arise in home and community settings. MacNaughton's view (Chapter 4) that knowledge and learning is always social and therefore embodies ethics, values and politics signals a need for sensitive awareness of cultural and community contexts that extends beyond the identification of funds of knowledge or interests. Maintaining this degree of sensitivity is a challenge in contemporary multicultural societies. As the work of various authors in this book has shown, there may be mismatches in the meanings that activities portray to children on the basis of their home and community experiences and the institutional expectations embedded in the learning environment. Moreover, issues of power relationships and the conditions of power affecting learning, as debated by MacNaughton, are not easily recognised in a sector that has a long history of nurturing children's development.

Increasing teacher competence to work with community knowledge, beliefs and practices would not necessarily address the issue of how family funds of knowledge and capital interface with the disciplinary-based (or formal) knowledge through which children eventually become contributing members of society. As Hedegaard (2008) has debated, institutions may need to consider differing developmental trajectories for children whose learning has been embedded in cultural practices that differ from institutional norms. A sociocultural curriculum such as New Zealand's *Te Whariki* that builds on children's interests and cultural practices raises issues regarding the nature of outcomes for children (Cullen, 2003). In other words, without addressing the issues raised by Hedegaard, a sociocultural curriculum could beg the question of whether children will attain the skills and competencies required to function as members in contemporary societies.

The role of tools and artefacts in mediating learning takes particular significance when reconceptualising pedagogical implications of the historical dimensions of teachers' work. Multi-agency developments in early childhood highlight the impact of differing professional philosophies and practices on collaborative services and the challenges this can pose for establishing a shared community of practice. A community of practice approach to professional development is signalled by such pedagogical challenges. While the notion of reflective practice is well accepted in teacher education and professional development, examination of the role of significant beliefs and practices within professional communities has not been salient in this discourse. A cultural perspective on pedagogy suggests that the shared knowledge of communities of practice could be reified (Wenger, 1998) or stultified if a culture of enquiry is not sustained. Along these lines, future research would likely 'address the relative value of implicit versus academic theory and of research by teachers versus that done by academics' (Genishi et al., 2001: 1205). In Chapter 11, Siraj-Blatchford presents an argument for teachers as key to an effective pedagogy, based on REPEY evidence about quality early years programmes. A future direction that could build upon the solid base of the REPEY research would be to promote teacher research to develop a pedagogy of practice. In this regard the teacher-researchers in New Zealand's Centre of Innovation research projects are reporting findings that extend our understanding of sociocultural pedagogy in practice (Haworth et al., 2006; Meade, 2007).

Part 2: The nature of knowledge in early years settings

Debates about the nature of knowledge operate at the dual levels of *curriculum knowledge* appropriate for the education of young children and *professional knowledge* appropriate for practitioners responsible for promoting young children's learning.

At the level of *curriculum models*, Siraj-Blatchford in Chapter 11 argues that there is still confusion about the impact of attendance at types of settings as opposed to exposure to versions of knowledge (discussed by Anning in Chapter 5) on children's attainments. The truth is we have little empirical evidence about the effectiveness of different curriculum models. In all three countries, the debate about curriculum models polarises 'developmentally appropriate practice', with a strong emphasis on children's choice in determining what they want to learn and 'subject or project-based curricula' with an emphasis on adult-initiated decisions about what children need to learn. Decisions about versions of knowledge run parallel to decisions about appropriate pedagogy as discussed in the introduction to Part 1 of this book. A third debate is evidenced in the tension between a curriculum geared for where children are now (as in the culturally sensitive *Te Whāriki* approach in New Zealand), where they will be next (as preparation for schooling in the Foundation Stage in the UK) or where they will be in the future (as in the Innovation/Futures models in some Australian states).

It is clearly unethical to set up controlled, experimental studies designed to test the effectiveness of different curriculum models on young children's attainment. Children get only one chance at a good start to education. Moreover, in the messy, real world of curriculum delivery by different practitioners, to a variety of children, in diverse settings, research designed to measure impact is fraught with practical problems in controlling variables. A cogent example of this in the UK was the attempt to unravel variations in patterns of delivery of services and their impact/outcomes for children and parents in the National Evaluation of Sure Start (Anning et al., 2007). However, there may be opportunities, implicit in this book, for quasi-experimental studies of naturally occurring contrasts at cross-national levels. How interesting it would be, for example, to follow cohorts of matched samples (on the lines of the EPPE project – see Siraj-Blatchford in Chapter 11) of children progressing through early education based on *Te Whāriki*, the Foundation Stage Curriculum and a Futures Curriculum.

Debates about *professional knowledge* also tend to be strong on assertion but weak on evidence. By tradition, the preparation of practitioners to 'teach' young children has been driven by hierarchical/status divisions, with graduate teachers managing teams of poorly paid classroom assistants or nursery officers. It has also been dogged by political interference. The training of teachers has been caught up in a torrent of government initiatives in all three countries. Examples are raising standards in 'the basics' or 'subjects' (as Tymms and Merrell point out in Chapter 9), or social control in 'citizenship', or preparing a workforce in 'skills in ICT and related technology'. The training of nursery officers/childcare workers, traditionally strong on child development, has been influenced by the rapid expansion of childcare designed to release women as cheap, part-time labour. Combined systems offering education and care have been rebranded 'educare'; but as Anning argues in Chapter 5, the sharing and redistribution of professional knowledge in integrated services centres is a complex and time-consuming process.

In all three countries the imperative to deliver services to young children by multi-agency teams has compounded debates about professional knowledge. What are the core, generic knowledge domains and expertise/skills required of all team members delivering children's services (speech therapists, physiotherapists, psychologists, teachers, social workers, health workers, administrators)? Which are specific to a role or post within the team? How can knowledge be exchanged in the best interests of practitioners, children and their parents? (See Cullen in Chapter 6.) As argued in Chapter 5, activity theory provides a useful theoretical model on which to base research in this field.

Part 3: Assessment in early years settings

While sociocultural-historical theory in early years has progressed significantly, with many countries now reporting that they have evolved their teaching practices accordingly (Edwards, 2007), few have put the same amount of effort into reshaping or retheorising their assessment practices (Carr, 2001a; Fleer, 2006; Hatherly and Richardson, 2007). It is now evident that there is a general lag between early childhood teaching practice and early childhood assessment practices (Fleer and Richardson, 2004). For instance, although we know a great deal more about how to make judgements about children's learning gained through dynamic and dialectical means, Australia still predominantly uses individualistically framed tools in preschools, and is about to embark upon the national assessment of all children entering school using an instrument that has been designed in Canada and tweaked for Australian contexts (Australian Early Development Index). Meanwhile in England practitioners are required to complete a lengthy and detailed profile for every child, based on a statutory curriculum for all children from birth to 5 years old, and to return the scores to both local and national authorities (see Chapter 1 for details).

When a sociocultural-historical perspective is taken, it is evident that richer and more immediately useful data on children's learning is gained. Sociocultural-historical theory has helped build communities of practice that are both unique and dynamic – for example, as teachers map, record and analyse evidence of the transformation of participation rather than some end point (Carr, 2001a). However, the complexities of this type of assessment practice have two major shortcomings.

First, Tymms and Merrell in Chapter 9 argue that governments, as in England, will put pressure on practitioners to use assessment instruments that will enable them to compare the effectiveness of different kinds of provision across centres, local authorities/states and even countries. Learning stories, discussed by Cowie and Carr in Chapter 8, are not appropriate for quick and easy comparative purposes. There is clearly a need for further research in this area. What kinds of assessment tools are needed for government's macro policy imperatives? Further research is needed if countries are to avoid importing tools from other cultural contexts, and using these with only minor changes.

Secondly, Fleer and Richardson in Chapter 10 demonstrate that teachers who have spent their whole professional careers using individualistic lenses to observe children, who have been benchmarking their assessment of children based on particular developmental stages, and who have reduced their observations to domains, have found it very difficult to use sociocultural-historical theory for documenting children's learning. It has already been noted that introducing curricula (such as *Te Whāriki*, as discussed by Cullen in Chapter 6), and culturally framed pedagogy (as discussed by Williams-Kennedy in Chapter 7, and Hill and Nichols in Chapter 13) which are informed by sociocultural-historical theory is problematic for teachers. With an ageing population, and a correspondingly ageing teaching force, more thought and resourcing needs to be put into supporting practitioners with making the transition from a constructivist developmental perspective to a sociocultural-historical perspective. It is through this major paradigm shift, that teachers, for example, can begin to think and assess differently in their centres, and begin to see more clearly the significance of the cultural contexts in which diverse learners grow.

In working towards the future, early childhood teachers need two types of conceptual tool. The first tool is built upon sociocultural-historical theory, where documentation of learning moves beyond an individualistic orientation and acknowledges that learning is owned by a community of learners. In building learning stories and in mapping the transformation of understanding greater insights can be gained about children's learning and teachers' teaching. Secondly, the profession needs instruments that can extract from this rich web of assessment activity discrete measures of understanding as matched to government priorities. In all three countries current government priorities are numeracy and literacy.

When governments wish to use these instruments for accountability purposes, then we should look toward approaches to assessment exemplified in, for example, PIPs (Performance Indicators in Primary Schools), as discussed by Tymms and Merrell in Chapter 9, where teachers can expertly document entry and exit points. As discussed by Cowie and Carr (Chapter 8), New Zealand is currently examining the ways in which government can gain information about the nature and quality of learning in early childhood education. Australia has developed a sociocultural-historical assessment tool for reporting to government, but only for centres that have Indigenous students. The social, cultural and political context of each country determines to what extent the early childhood profession needs and receives resources to support assessment practices.

Part 4: Evaluation and quality in early years settings

Quality in early childhood settings is a much contested phenomenon in the UK (Dahlberg et al., 1999), in Australia (Fleer and Kennedy, 2000; Raban et al., 2007), in New Zealand (Duncan, 1997; Farquhar, 1999a, 1999b; Smith, 1997, 1999; Smith and Barraclough, 1997), and in the United States (National Research Council, 2000, 2001; Scarr et al., 1994). The concept of quality has been debated in many forums (Colbung et al., 2007; Fleer et al., 2006; Smith and Taylor, 1996), has been the focus of research reports for parents and government departments (Wylie, 1996, 1999), and has been the subject of consultation with communities (e.g. Australian Commonwealth Child Care Advisory Council, 2000).

> [quality] now plays a dominant role in our thinking, our language and practices. The 'age of quality' is now well and truly upon us, and not just in relation to early childhood institutions, but every conceivable type of product and services. (Dahlberg et al., 1999: 4)

Farquhar (1999a: 7) has commented on this trend, and warns against a 'one-word-fits-all' construct or a universal perspective. Her thoughtful critique of the research literature and her analysis of quality-related documentation in New Zealand suggest the need to introduce 'more precise terminology focused on what we actually mean and are interested in' when we discuss quality. Better conceptual tools are needed if the level of debate is to progress beyond a universal perspective and, as implied by Tymms and Merrell in Chapter 9, to be used for more than an accountability instrument by the government for measuring the success of the profession.

Podmore points out in Chapter 12 that easily measurable indicators of quality have been noted in the research literature, including: structural (e.g. staff–child ratios, group size, staff training, education and experience, staff wages and working conditions, and staff stability) and procedural (e.g. staff qualifications) indicators. Ratios have been reported as making a significant contribution to outcomes for children in some countries (McGurk et al., 1995; Scarr et al., 1994), including Australia (MacNaughton, 2000b; Russell, 1985) and New Zealand (Smith et al., 1989), but with Wylie (1989) cautioning that there is no guaranteed formula for determining quality provision in the early years.

The OECD report *Starting Strong II* (2006) and the influential EPPE project in the UK (Sylva et al., 2003) present strong evidence of a causal relationship between the level of teacher education and professional qualifications and the quality of the programme provided to young children (Cassidy et al., 1995). Other studies have also pointed indirectly to staff qualifications as quality measures. For example, Scarr et al. (1994: 131) have found that 'Regulatable measures did not prove to be acceptable measures of quality care, except for teachers' wage (which is linked to qualifications and experience), which were highly correlated with process measures of quality'. They argued that teacher salary was a useful indicator of centre quality, stating that 'other well-known measures, such as ratios of caregivers to children, group sizes, and staff turnover were less well correlated' (1994: 148).

Process quality indicators are much more difficult to isolate and measure, and as a result research efforts in this area have been limited. Process quality indicators are measures of actual programme experiences by children, such as the social relationships and the interactions between staff and children. Although it is widely acknowledged that process quality indicators are the most important element for measuring quality, very few studies have been directed towards examining the link between process indicators of quality and long-term cognitive outcomes for children. Siraj-Blatchford's work, reported in Chapter 11, is an exception.

Smith et al. (2000: 49) have reported that 'It is difficult to isolate the effect of a single quality indicator because good things go together – especially ratios, group size and caregiver training'. Rogoff (1998) has argued that research that reduces complex processes to isolated variables (as has been the tradition in branches of psychology) no longer captures the dynamic and interrelated nature of complex concepts such as quality. A sociocultural-historical perspective on quality would build rather than reduce all the contributing variables. A problem with such research is that it is expensive to fund on the kind of large-scale basis of the EPPE funded project and the National Evaluation of Sure Start in the UK (www.ness.bbk.ac.uk and www.surestart.gov.uk). A second problem is that making generalisations from less expensive, small-scale studies is inappropriate. However, methodologies have been developed for the meta analyses of many small-scale studies to generate common findings, as has been done in examining evaluations of intervention programmes such as Head Start in the United States. This may prove a useful way forward.

While research literature provides some evidence of ways of measuring quality, caution needs to be exercised in accepting only structural and procedural elements in investigations of quality provision and links to subsequent achievement. Farquhar (1999a: 4) states:

> The focus has been on physical capital (e.g. number of staff) rather than on human capital (e.g. staff motivation). Today quality and money are commonly considered to go hand in hand, that is, inputs cost money and therefore the maintenance of positive structural conditions [is] related to the programme's financial status and funding. Yet we know from the literature outside of early childhood education that quality cannot be bought and that the view of quality as consisting merely of inputs is a very narrow one. (Farquhar, 1999a: 4)

Sociocultural theory has provided early childhood professionals and researchers with alternative lenses to examine issues of quality. In this book a diversity of perspectives on quality was offered. In using a sociocultural-historical approach, authors have framed their contributions in ways that illustrate more fully the complexities surrounding the concept of quality. For example, Podmore in Chapter 12 implicitly argued that 'quality' can be demonstrated when teachers move their programming framework from 'planning as being about deciding what activities to provide' to planning 'starting from the children's perspectives or questions'. She argued for the building of a community of learners where co-construction of knowledge takes place. Although the focus is on the individual learner, she foregrounds the role of the adult in this process. This approach to research is richer than simply measuring the variable 'teacher salary' or 'qualifications' in relation to student outcomes.

On the other hand Hill and Nichols, in Chapter 13, focus their lens on the cultural and social construction of literacy in the home and in the school, arguing that quality early childhood practice is evident when pedagogy is built upon an understanding of the multiple pathways between home and school literacy. However, as Jordan argues in Chapter 3, these connections can be built only when the interactional patterns and perspectives of the teacher are examined in relation to children's home interactional patterns and worldviews. Siraj-Blatchford also foregrounds the role of the teacher in quality provision. She argues that teachers have a responsibility to teach. This is counter-intuitive to how teachers have been positioned in early childhood education, where traditionally their role has been perceived as enablers rather than teachers. Clearly, quality cannot be considered without repositioning the role of the adult back into teaching–learning dynamics. Podmore also found when she questioned quality that participants in her study shifted from a concern about external accountability to placing priority on pedagogy, highlighting the importance of factoring the teaching process within a quality framework for research.

As we have argued throughout this text, a result of the (mis)interpretations of Piaget's research and theory by early childhood educators is that the role of the teacher has been de-emphasised. In this volume, it is evident that issues of quality and evaluation can be framed only when the teacher is placed back into the teaching and learning context. This of course is consistent with sociocultural-historical theory, where the role of the teacher is important for building a community of learners (Wenger, 1998), for guided participation (Lave and Wenger, 1991), for everyday cognition (Rogoff, 1998, 2003), for moving from an inter-psychological level of functioning to an intra-psychological level (Vygotsky, 1978) and for supporting scaffolded learning (Bruner, 1996). Perspectives on quality, research into measures of quality and discussions around evaluation processes are better understood when the role of the teacher is embedded in the research process. Examining these sociocultural interactional sequences as embedded within a complex cultural and social milieu challenges the rather primitive understandings that we have about quality. Clearly, further research is urgently needed if we are to appreciate fully the complexities and diversity of quality that are enacted in our early childhood settings. A sociocultural-historical perspective has much to offer us for framing our research and in building new theoretical models to examine and explain quality in early childhood education. Resources that draw upon these theoretical models have slowly developed over time and provide support for professionals in the field (e.g. Fleer and Raban, 2007; Ministry of Education, 1996b).

Future directions across nations

In the following country sections, policy initiatives and associated dilemmas and challenges for practitioners are debated.

United Kingdom

In the last decade in the UK the Labour government has focused unprecedented attention and public spending on early childhood services. For example, between 1990 and 2000 daycare provision quadrupled (www.daycaretrust.org.uk); by 2006 expenditure on the early intervention programme, Sure Start, launched in 1998, reached £1.5 billion (www.ness.bbk.ac.uk); and all 3- and 4-year-olds are guaranteed two and a half (soon to be three) hours of free preschool education a day for 38 weeks of the year. The Blair years were characterised by an almost obsessive imperative to reform public services. The mantra of 'joined up thinking' impacted on all those responsible for delivering children's services in the UK, compelling single agencies to work together in multi-agency teams for the benefit of families.

But government policy initiatives, welcome in their overall vision of improving the life chances of young children and their families in the name of social justice, brought dilemmas for those charged with making reforms work on the ground. First, as childcare and preschool education expanded rapidly, it was difficult to maintain high-quality provision. The growth in the sector was further complicated by the government imperative to work in 'the third way', that is by commissioning more and more services out to the private and voluntary sector. There have been tensions in reconciling the needs of the private sector (now responsible for 80% of daycare in the UK and increasingly operated by global brand market leaders) to make profits with their accountability to provide high-quality services, monitored by rigorous inspections from Ofsted. Ofsted is a self-standing inspection system, but closely linked with the government agenda for standards in early education and childcare. Futhermore, the voluntary sector (in particular providers of traditional preschool playgroups and charitable family support services) have felt undervalued and marginalised as services have been reshaped.

Many voluntary sector services have a very local history and flavour, and this brings us to a second set of dilemmas. The rhetoric of reforming public services at a national level has been underpinned by strategies to involve local communities in decisions about the kind of services they want and need. Services are to be seen as a shared enterprise between a range of stakeholders – parents, practitioners, children and their communities and local businesses. Sure Start was an exemplification of this model. Yet the reality is that social engineering at a national level sits uneasily with empowering communities at a local level. Sure Start local programmes were constantly being charged with achieving national targets; for example, the expansion of childcare, which conflicted with the demands of their local communities, who favoured not returning to work until their children reached school age and using informal childcare networks. The commitment was to sustain the Sure Start intervention for ten years (from 1998 to 2008); but at the first sign of slow impact, in 2004 the government rebranded and reshaped Sure Start local programmes into Children's Centres. Local authorities were pulled back in to administer and control decision-making about service planning and delivery from local Children's Centres. Communities (often those whose voices were rarely heard) who had felt committed to and excited by the Sure Start initiative felt let down yet again.

A third set of dilemmas relate to the practicalities of implementing the ambitious agenda embodied in *Every Child Matters*. The vision requires all those delivering children's services to work together for the benefit of the whole child, nested within their family and community. Within single agency services, there are well documented problems with the status, pay and working conditions of the (predominantly feminised) workforce. These problems are compounded by the assumptions that professionals will work harmoniously in multi-agency teams, sharing spaces, documentation and professional knowledge. Teachers of young children, for example, will be expected to liaise closely with those delivering play, recreation, health, family support and parenting programmes either from Children's Centres (many of which for pragmatic and cost reasons are being built alongside primary schools) or under the Extended Schools initiative (see Chapter 1). At the same time, England has for the first time a statutory curriculum (The Foundation Stage) for birth to 5-year-olds, which practitioners in a wide range of settings (daycare, childminding, preschool playgroups, nursery and reception classes) are charged with delivering. Though the Foundation Stage curriculum has been carefully designed to offer a balanced approach to educating 'the whole child' it still places an emphasis on subject knowledge. Many practitioners see themselves as trained to 'care' and 'play with' young children, rather than to educate them, and feel alienated from the imperative to prepare very young children for school. And health, family support, teachers and social workers feel anxious about how their specialist roles, status, knowledge and skills will be protected in the imperative to work in multi-agency teams.

Yet we still have a weak evidence base of what works best for children and their families in terms, for example, of curriculum for children and the content of parenting programmes for adults. We have little hard evidence of the cost benefits of different ways of delivering services; for example, in single- or multi-agency teams. Devolution of power since 1999 to Scotland, Wales and Northern Ireland has freed up these nations to operate differently in aspects of delivering children's services. In other respects they are still bound into UK policy by complex layers of legislations. For example, in Scotland education, health and care policies are devolved, while employment remains the remit of the UK government. Childcare tax credits, designed to promote a consumer demand-led approach to buying daycare, are UK-wide. This diversity has enabled Wales to develop a distinct, more play-based, curriculum for children up to the age of 7. Scotland is exploring the policy of school starting age being 6, rather than 5, bringing them into line with other European countries with whom they feel more affinity than perhaps with England. Ironically, devolution with the potential for divisiveness between the four nations offers a window of opportunity to set up comparative research to explore evidence of the effectiveness and impact of different models.

Aotearoa-New Zealand

It is timely to adopt a sociocultural-historical framework to consider a vision for early childhood education in New Zealand, five years into the ten-year Strategic Plan for

Early Childhood, *Pathways to the Future: Nga Huarahi Aratiki* (Ministry of Education, 2002), which establishes core goals and strategies for the sector. The three core goals of the plan form a structure for this analysis.

Increasing participation in quality ECE services

Structural provisions such as equity funding and 20 free hours of ECE indicate the government's commitment to this goal. From a sociocultural-historical perspective structural provisions need to be viewed against a cultural backdrop that emphasises cultural meanings and goals for young children. Government support for language immersion programmes for indigenous Maori and Pacific Island groups is consistent with the focus on increasing participation; an ongoing challenge is for teachers in mainstream centres to provide learning environments that can produce the authentic links with diverse ethnic communities that would promote wider participation. Ironically, the drive to improve teacher qualifications has worked against parent-led services, as some playcentres and *Kohanga Reo* have struggled to meet licensing requirements. Clearly there is an ongoing need to consider the contribution of parent-led services alongside the increasing professionalism of the early childhood sector.

Improving quality of ECE services

Two recent government-funded initiatives support the implementation of a sociocultural curriculum: nationwide professional development to support the release of early childhood assessment exemplars, and the Centre of Innovation programme. Teachers have embraced the concept of sociocultural assessment developed by Carr and colleagues in their narrative assessment (learning story) approach. This credit view of the child as learner incorporates cultural and community meanings through its stress on multiple perspectives, although an inherent tension between individual and socially mediated assessment remains in that the narrative typically starts with the individual child. As the Centre of Innovation publications are beginning to attest, experienced teachers who are supported to analyse their practice can negotiate this tension (Meade, 2007); others more immersed in a developmental tradition may be less likely to explore sociocultural nuances of assessment. The Centre of Innovation teacher research is indicating that collaborative research on a community of learners model can have positive outcomes for children, centres and communities, in a sociocultural-historical sense. The challenge now is to explore means of extending teacher-research as a form of professional development to a wider range of centres.

Promoting collaborative relationships

The third goal, with its focus on relationships, encapsulates the core of a sociocultural-historical pedagogy. New Zealand's inclusive early intervention policy, the move to multi-agency work across education and health sectors, and the pedagogy of relationships inherent in the Maori child-rearing and educational perspectives have meant that early childhood teachers have strong pressures to develop collaborative educational approaches. As the revised New Zealand Curriculum (Ministry of Education 2007) aligns goals for primary education more clearly with the early childhood curriculum, the separateness of the two sectors may lessen as early childhood and primary teachers explore common approaches to areas such as assessment and literacy. Such developments will require increasing willingness to explore the funds of knowledge and practices of communities, agencies and education sectors. They will also necessitate an educated and confident early childhood teaching sector, conversant with both disciplinary knowledge *and* the sociocultural-historical pedagogy that supports appropriate ways of working with young children of all cultures.

Australia

Australia has seen the election of a new government, with an agenda that seeks to generate an education revolution. The Labor Government has appointed a Parliamentary Secretary for Early Childhood Education and Development, who works directly to the Prime Minister. Early childhood has been named as an important area for government activity and policy development. New directions for early childhood education have already been enacted at the federal level through the bringing together of the administrative centres for childcare provision and education under the Group called Early Childhood Education and Care. These federal administrative changes provide a useful backdrop for ensuring that innovation and change can occur more swiftly as the federal department liaises with the states and territories. Key directions for the future include:

- new funded places in universities to increase the number of early childhood teacher graduates;
- 50% reduction in university fees for those graduates who teach in the country for a period of five years;
- the development of a national curriculum framework;
- national assessment of all children entering school;
- qualified teachers to be appointed to centres (preschools and childcare centres) that run a preschool programme for 4-year-old children;
- universally available preschool for all 4-year-old children.

Workforce issues have taken centre stage in Australia, alongside curriculum development, and concerns for quality provision. The structural changes at the federal level, and the forthcoming innovations, will see Australia with a very new system for early years education. These important developments should be matched with strong research for implementation and for evaluation. This agenda is yet to be articulated and realised. However, the former changes are welcomed by Australian researchers and practitioners and their announcement has been long overdue. As always, these impending changes are fraught with difficulties and challenges. Three main issues must be observed closely as the new policies are rolled out in Australia. First, the national assessment of children will use an instrument that was originally developed in Canada and which seeks to map deficiencies across the system. This deficit, rather than credit, model of assessment is cause for concern within communities who have already felt the effects of disadvantage. Second, the development of a national curriculum will require a system-wide effort in collaboration, something the sector has not had a long history of achieving. Finally, the expansion of the early childhood sector will cause resourcing problems for the rural and remote communities. Without careful strategic planning of how early years practitioners can be supported in their upgrading of qualifications, the new policies will simply remain a 'wish' rather than an 'outcome'. These initiatives come at a time when the workforce is likely to see massive retirements, and a national downturn in interest in enrolling in education awards in universities.

A vision for the future

This book has aimed to conceptualise early childhood education through a sociocultural-historical lens on the basis of cross-national research. This organisational and analytic device has yielded a body of debate that itself reflects key dimensions of a sociocultural-historical perspective – in particular, a dynamic and evolving professional context. Further, the cross-national perspective has elicited dilemmas and challenges that face early years professionals in the three countries.

Governments in the UK, Australia and New Zealand are taking increasing interest in the sector, fiscally and in terms of services and curricula for young children. While this may be welcome news for the sector, it also poses philosophical and practical dilemmas for early years professionals. The flipside of increased funding is that governments view early childhood as the first step towards developing a successful workforce and socially inclusive society. This is an instrumental view of early childhood education and care, however worthy the intended outcomes. Certainly, these goals are part of our agenda but there is also a long-established tradition that we should provide programmes to enrich the lives of young children and their families. A developmental philosophy has often been invoked to support this traditional agenda. If governments perceive lack of support from the field for their policies, in defensive reactions by practitioners to their long-term goals (for example, raising standards in literacy and numeracy), the early years 'voice' may be marginalised.

As practitioners strive to minimise the effects of prescribed curricula, a focus on holistic development and children's interests, associated with a traditional developmentally oriented approach, could be perceived as promoting an uncritical continuation of 'play-based/child-centred' programmes. This book argues instead for a critical pedagogy of play. Sociocultural-historical pedagogical principles, sensitive to cultural contexts and implemented by proactive adults, provide a way forward. A challenge will be to ensure that professionals working in multi-agency teams to deliver children's services will be prepared in their training to understand these principles.

The important role of teachers has been emphasised throughout this book. This has been supported in the three countries, at government level, through goals for upgrading the qualifications of the early childhood sector. This agenda too has inherent dilemmas. For example, the ultimate goal of a fully qualified (i.e. three-year training) workforce in New Zealand has resulted in the transfer of newly qualified teachers to managerial positions in some childcare centres to meet the transitional training requirement for a 'person-responsible' in a centre. In the UK, requirements for a new graduate qualification for the responsible person, an Early Years Professional, will not necessarily be as trained teachers. Such pragmatic responses could interfere with the objectives of government policy of universal entitlement to high-quality early years education and care. In Australia the promise of more resourcing for the early childhood sector will in principle ensure that there are enough qualified teachers for all the newly funded preschool programmes that can now be delivered by a qualified early childhood teacher regardless of the context (e.g. preschool centre or childcare centre). However, the increases in university places for the education of these qualified teachers will put strain upon the university sector. Will there be enough qualified academics to educate the 1200 new preschool teachers? Similarly, the lower salaries of early childhood teachers when compared with primary teachers in many of the states and territories of Australia means that graduates of these programmes may well not go into preschools or childcare centres, but rather into the school sector. On a more positive note, the additional tertiary places give more opportunity for upgrading two-year qualified staff to four-year degree status, especially for rural communities and for staff whose second or third language may be English. Having linguistically diverse early childhood practitioners and more appropriately qualified teachers in the rural communities is important and urgently needed.

From a sociocultural-historical perspective we should also accept that researchers have a responsibility to provide a critical perspective on policy and to advocate for a reflexive relationship between policy, research and practice. This could mean willingness to work constructively with government agendas, in preference to conducting theoretically-driven research in isolation from social and political contexts. Yet researchers must retain their academic integrity. In a sector that is subject to political influence it is imperative that researchers contribute an analytic and evidence-informed perspective on policy.

In 2004 we proposed an agenda for research that would illuminate practice and inform policy in early years education. In 2008 we state more firmly that the following propositions regarding quality early years education and care, which are justified, either logically and/or empirically, by the research evidence debated by contributing authors, should inform policy and research *and* guide practice. The challenge for international early childhood researchers and practitioners from a sociocultural-historical perspective is to establish and maintain a dialectical relationship in which researchers, practitioners and policy-makers increase their dialogue and co-construct common educational goals for a society's youngest members.

Propositions for quality early years education

* Effective practice reflects a culture of enquiry that involves a research-based discourse.
* Teaching and learning are central to quality early childhood services.

- Pedagogical leadership is integral to achieving quality early childhood education.
- Professional development is conceptualised as the co-construction of a community of practice and learners – including parents, children and professionals.
- An appropriate curriculum is co-constructed between children and significant others (peers and adults) and is underpinned by close home and centre partnerships that build on cultural and community practices and meanings.
- Children's perspectives, interests and knowledge are respected as the core of an early childhood curriculum.
- Children's learning and development is conceptualised holistically as the dialectical relations between emotional, social, cognitive, physical, spiritual and cultural dimensions.
- Socioculturally/historically framed assessment practices view knowledge as owned by a community of learners, rather than residing in individuals.
- Assessment is about recording how participants move through understanding rather than simply mapping the end product or outcome.
- Enacting sociocultural-historical theory into practice requires active reconceptualisation of the teaching–learning process.

As argued by Nuttall and Edwards (2007: 21):

The curriculum that any given community develops for its children is inevitably influenced by contemporary social concerns, its dominant beliefs and collective knowledge, and, perhaps most importantly, the hopes it holds for its children's future. This complexity means that examination of curriculum construction at any level of education requires consideration of the knowledge, beliefs and practices that inform participation within a community, as well as the nature of the knowledge about learning and development held by that community at that time. It is for this reason that curriculum frameworks are not just theoretical and pedagogical texts, but political texts, both in the bureaucratic sense and in the generic sense of dominant beliefs and practices.

GLOSSARY

AECA. The Australian Early Childhood Association (now named Early Childhood Australia) is a peak national non-government organisation acting in the interests of young children from birth to age 8. It actively promotes the provision of high-quality services for all young children and their families.

Aotearoa. Maori name for New Zealand.

Assessable moment. An opportunity in which a teacher can make a more authentic assessment of a group of children or a child since they are engaged in a particular learning task and appear to be working at their optimal level.

Babies into Books. In the UK there is a number of schemes operating which involve introducing the parents of babies to the idea that books can be enjoyed by parents and their babies almost from birth.

Centre. In New Zealand, a chartered early childhood setting licensed to provide for children up to the age of 5 years, at which age children generally start formal schooling.

Child's Questions, The. An approach to practitioners' evaluation of their early childhood education programmes. Each of five questions connects to a specific strand of *Te Whāriki*.

Community childcare centre. In Australia, a non-profit early childhood centre that has full-time or sessional provision. Such centres are usually organised by a city council and administered by a management committee or trust.

Department for Children Schools and Families (DCSF). Since mid-2007, the UK national department for the delivery of educational services. Its name has frequently changed in line with ideologies and structural changes. See DfEE; DfES.

Department for Education and Employment (DfEE). Former name for the UK national department for the delivery of educational services. Superseded by the Department for Education and Skills.

Department for Education and Skills (DfES). Former name for the UK national department for the delivery of educational services. Previously the Department for Education and Employment (DfEE). In mid-2007 became the Department for Children, Schools and Families (DCSF).

Department of Education, Science and Training (DEST). In Australia, the Commonwealth department with responsibility for educational services. Formerly the Department of Education, Training and Youth Affairs (DETYA).

Department of Education, Training and Youth Affairs (DETYA). Former name for the Commonwealth department with responsibility for educational services in Australia. Formerly the Department of Employment, Education, Training and Youth Affairs (DEETYA); superseded by the Department of Education, Science and Training (DEST).

DEST. See Department of Education, Science and Training.

DfEE. See Department for Education and Employment.

DfES. See Department for Education and Skills.

Early childhood services – New Zealand. Includes chartered and licensed centre-based and home-based services catering for children in the years prior to school entry, usually at 5 years. Includes sessional kindergartens, childcare centres, play centres (parent co-operatives), *Kohanga reo* (Maori immersion), Pacific centres and programmes with specific philosophies such as Rudolph Steiner, Montessori.

Foundation Stage Curriculum. In response to mounting anxiety about the 'too formal too soon' nature of education being offered to 4-year-olds in Reception classes in primary schools in the UK, a Foundation Stage Curriculum was introduced for the education of 3- to 5-year-olds in all early years settings, including primary schools. In September 2008 the Foundation Stage was extended to from birth to 5.

Indigenous. In Australia, refers to Aboriginal Australian population and culture.

Intersubjectivity. A term introduced by Newson and Newson (1975), in Berk and Winsler (1995: 27), which 'refers to the process whereby two participants who begin a task with a different understanding arrive at a shared understanding'.

Learning and teaching stories. Holistic approaches to assessment and evaluation, using *learning stories* that empower learners and communicate with families, and *teaching stories* that create responsive, reciprocal and respectful relationships with people, places and things.

Local authority. The UK regional structures for the planning, financing and delivery of services. The authority consists of elected members who oversee structural systems operated by permanent employees. Money to pay for the services is partly raised through local rates. Under New Labour, local authorities whose services are deemed to have 'failed' inspections have been privatised.

Maori. The indigenous people of New Zealand.

Ofsted. The Office for Standards in Education is an independent agency contracted by the English government to inspect all local authorities, schools and (since 2002) providers of preschool services. Though independent, their agenda is strongly influenced by government policy; for example, the imperative to drive up standards in literacy and numeracy in England.

Pacific Nations people. Immigrants to New Zealand from Pacific Islands and New Zealanders of Pacific heritage; also known as Pasifika.

Quality Journey, The. A resource developed for practitioners in early childhood centres and in home-based services in New Zealand, intended as a tool to improve quality through information and reflection.

Reception class. In the UK, the first year of schooling. Children normally attend Reception classes from the ages of 4 to 5. They then transfer to Year 1 and begin the National Curriculum for Key Stage 1 (for 5- to 7-year-olds). Increasingly Early Years Units in primary schools cater for 3-to 5-year olds.

SAE. Standard Australian English, the dominant language spoken in Australia. It is also the primary language of instruction used by teachers in most of government schools.

Te Whāriki. The early childhood curriculum in New Zealand. A bicultural curriculum, it is designed for diverse early childhood services, including Maori and Pasifika immersion programmes. *Te Whāriki* means 'a mat' that weaves together the principles, strands and goals of the curriculum, and acknowledges the diverse philosophies, structures and environments of services.

Whanau. Maori word for 'family' (inclusive of extended family); members of an extended family and its support network who form a context for the care and guidance of a child.

BIBLIOGRAPHY

Alexander, R. (2007) *Interim Report of the Condition and Future of Primary Education in England: The Primary Review*. Based at the University of Cambridge and funded by the Esmee Fairbairn Foundation. Final Report due 2008.

Ames, C. (1992) 'Classrooms: goals, structures and student motivation', *Journal of Educational Psychology*, 84: 261–71.

Anning, A. (2007) 'Play and the legislated curriculum. Back to basics: an alternative view', in J. Moyles (ed.), *The Excellence of Play, 2nd edition*. Maidenhead: Open University Press. pp. 15–26.

Anning, A. and Ball, M. (2008) *Improving Children's Services: From Sure Start to Children's Centres*. London: Sage Publications.

Anning, A. and Calder, P. (2008) 'Early childhood education care and professional profiles in the United Kingdom: Multi-agency teamwork and transdisciplinary challenges', in E. Baker, B. McGaw and P. Peterson (eds), *International Encyclopaedia of Education*, 3rd edition. Oxford: Elsevier.

Anning, A. and Edwards, A. (2006) *Promoting Children's Learning from Birth to Five*, 2nd edition. Buckingham: Open University Press.

Anning, A., Cottrell, D., Frost, N., Green, J. and Robinson, M. (2006) *Developing Multi-professional Teamwork for Integrated Children's Services*. Maidenhead: Open University Press.

Anning, A., Stuart, J., Nicholls, M., Goldthorpe, J. and Morley, A. and the NESS team (2007) *Understanding Variations in Effectiveness amongst SureStart Local Programmes*. Report 024. Nottingham: DfES Publications.

Athey, C. (1990) *Extending Thought in Young Children: A Parent Teacher Partnership*. London: Paul Chapman.

Australian Commonwealth Child Care Advisory Council (2000) 'Review of the Quality Improvement and Accreditation System – Information Sessions on Latest Proposals'. Letter and paper sent to all Long Day Care Centre Providers and Commonwealth Childcare Programmes, 1 February.

Awdurdod Cymwysterau Cwricwlwm Ac Asesu Cymru (ACCAC)/Qualifications and Curriculum Authority for Wales (2004) *The Foundation Phase in Wales*. Cardiff: Welsh Assembly Government.

Bailey, D.B., McWilliam, R.A., Buysse, V. and Wesley, P.W. (1998) 'Inclusion in the context of competing values in early childhood education', *Early Childhood Research Quarterly*, 13 (1): 27–47.

Baumrind, D. (1971) 'Current patterns of parental authority', *Developmental Psychology Monographs*, 4: 1–113.

Beatty, B. (1995) *Pre-school Education in America: The Culture of Young Children from the Colonial Era to the Present*. New Haven, CT, and London: Yale University Press.

Bellamy, C. (2001) *The State of the World's Children 2001*. New York: United Nations Children's Fund.

Belsky, J., Barnes, J. and Melhuish, E. (eds) (2007) *The National Evaluation of Sure Start: Does Area-based Early Intervention Work?* Bristol: The Policy Press.

Bennett, N., Wood, E. and Rogers, S. (1997) *Teaching Through Play: Reception Teachers' Theories and Practice*. Buckingham: Open University Press.

Berk, L. and Winsler, A. (1995) *Scaffolding Children's Learning: Vygotsky and Early Childhood Education*. Washington, DC: National Association for the Education of Young Children.

Bernstein, B. (1973) *Class, Codes and Control*. London: Routledge & Kegan Paul.

Bernstein, B. (1981) 'Codes, modalities and the process of cultural reproduction: a model', *Language and Society*, 10: 327–63.

Bernstein, B. (1992) *The Structuring of Pedagogic Discourse. Volume IV: Class, Codes and Control*. London: Routledge.

Bishop, A., Swain, J. and Bines, H. (1999) 'Seizing the moment: reflections on play opportunities for disabled children in the early years', *British Journal of Educational Studies*, 47 (2): 170–83.

Bishop, R. and Glynn, T. (1999) *Culture Counts: Changing Power Relations in Education*. Palmerston North, NZ: Dunmore Press.

Black, P. and Wiliam, D. (1998) 'Assessment and classroom learning', *Assessment in Education*, 5 (1): 7–74.

Blaise, M. (2005) *Playing It Straight – Uncovering Gender Discourses in the Early Childhood Classroom*. London: Routledge.

Blenkin, G. and Kelly, A.V. (eds) (1994) *The National Curriculum and Early Learning: An Evaluation*. London: Paul Chapman.

Blenkin, G. and Kelly, A.V. (eds) (1997) *Principles into Practice in Early Childhood Education*. London: Paul Chapman.

Bond, T.G. and Fox, C.M. (2001) *Applying the Rasch Model: Fundamental Measurement in the Human Sciences*. Mahwah, NJ: Lawrence Erlbaum Associates.

Bourke, R., Bevan-Brown, J., Carroll-Lind, J., Cullen, J., Kearney, A., Mentis, M., Poskitt, J., Prochnow, J., Ward, A., O'Neill, J., McAlpine, D., Bevan-Brown, W., Grant, S. and Morton, M. (2002) *Special Education 2000: Policy Monitoring and Evaluation Project*. Final report to Ministry of Education, IPDER, Massey University, New Zealand. Retrieved 4 March 2008 from http://specialeducation-research.massey.ac.nz/

Bowman, B., Donovan, S. and Burns, M. (eds) (2001) *Eager to Learn: Educating Our Pre-schoolers*. Washington, DC: National Academy Press.

Bredekamp, S. and Copple, S. (eds) (1997) *Developmentally Appropriate Practice in Early Childhood Programs Serving Children from Birth Through 8*, revised edition. Washington, DC: National Association for the Education of Young Children.

Bredekamp, S. and Rosegrant, T. (1992) 'Reaching potentials: introduction', in S. Bredekamp and T. Rosegrant (eds), *Reaching Potentials: Appropriate Curriculum and Assessment for Young Children, Volume 1*. Washington, DC: National Association for the Education of Young Children. pp. 2–8.

Bredekamp, S. and Rosegrant, T. (eds) (1995) *Reaching Potentials: Transforming Early Childhood Curriculum and Assessment, Volume 2*. Washington, DC: National Association for the Education of Young Children.

Broadhead, P. (2004) *Early Years Play and Learning: Developing Social Skills and Co-operation*. London: Routledge Falmer.

Bronfenbrenner, U. (1979) *The Ecology of Human Development*. Cambridge, MA: Harvard University Press.

Brown, A.L., Ash, D., Rutherford, M., Nakagawa, K., Gordon, A. and Campione, J.C. (1993) 'Distributed expertise in the classroom', in G. Salomon (ed.), *Distributed Cognitions: Psychological and Educational Considerations*. Cambridge: Cambridge University Press. pp. 188–228.

Bruner, J. (1986) *Actual Minds, Possible Worlds*. Cambridge, MA: Harvard University Press.

Bruner, J. (1995) 'From joint attention to meeting of minds: an introduction', Foreword in C. Moore and P.J. Dunham (eds), *Joint Attention: Its Origins and Role in Development*. Hillsdale, NJ: Lawrence Erlbaum Associates. pp. 1–14.

Bruner, J. (1996) *The Culture of Education*. Cambridge, MA: Harvard University Press.

Burman, E. (2008) *Deconstructing Developmental Psychology*, 2nd edition. London: Routledge.

Burts, D., Hart, C., Charlesworth, R. and Kirk, L. (1990) 'A comparison of frequency of stress behaviours observed in kindergarten children in classrooms with developmentally appropriate versus developmentally inappropriate instructional practices', *Early Childhood Research Quarterly*, 5: 407–23.

Bussye, V., Wesley, P.W. and Able-Boone, H. (2001) 'Innovations in professional practice: creating communities of practice to support inclusion', in M.J. Guralnick (ed.), *Early Childhood Inclusion: Focus on Change*. Baltimore, MD: Paul H. Brookes. pp. 179–200.

Butterworth, B. (1999) *The Mathematical Brain*. London: Macmillan.

Cairney, T.H. and Ruge, J. (1998) *Community Literacy Practices and Schooling: Towards Effective Support for Students*. Executive Summary. Canberra, ACT: Department of Employment, Education, Training and Youth Affairs.

Cannella, G. (2001) 'Natural born curriculum: popular culture and the representation of childhood', in J.A. Jipson and R.T. Johnson (eds), *Resistance and Representation: Rethinking Childhood Education*. New York: Peter Lang. pp. 15–22.

Cannella, G.S and Viruru, R. (2004) *Childhood and Postcolonization: Power, Education, and Contemporary Practice*. London: Routledge.

Carr, M. (1997) 'Persistence when it's difficult: a disposition to learn in early childhood', in *Early Childhood Folio*, 3: 9–12. Wellington: New Zealand Council for Educational Research.

Carr, M. (1998a) *Assessing Children's Experiences in Early Childhood: Final Report to the Ministry of Education. Part One*. Wellington: Research Division, Ministry of Education.

Carr, M. (1998b) *Project for Assessing Children's Experiences: Final Report to the Ministry of Education. Part Two: Five Case Studies*. Hamilton: University of Waikato.

Carr, M. (1999) *A BWECCIAN Approach to Assessment in Early Childhood: Learning Stories*. Keynote address presented at New Zealand Early Intervention Association Conference, Nelson.

Carr, M. (2000a) 'Technological affordance, social practice and learning narratives in an early childhood setting', *International Journal of Technology and Design Education*, 10: 61–79.

Carr, M. (2000b) 'Seeking children's perspectives about their learning', in A. Smith, N. Taylor and M. Gollop (eds), *Children's Voices: Research, Policy and Practice*. Auckland: Pearson Education. pp. 37–55.

Carr, M. (2001a) *Assessment in Early Childhood Settings: Learning Stories*. London: Paul Chapman.

Carr, M. (2001b) 'Let me count the ways. Analysing the relationship between the learner and everyday technology in early childhood', *Research in Science Education*, 31: 29–47.

Carr, M. and Claxton, G. (2002) 'Tracking the development of learning dispositions', *Assessment in Education*, 9 (1): 9–38.

Carr, M. and May, H. (1994) 'Weaving patterns: developing national Early Childhood Curriculum guidelines in Aotearoa–New Zealand', *Australian Journal of Early Childhood*, 19 (1): 25–33.

Carr, M., Lee, W. and Jones, C. (2004) *Kei Tua o Te Pae. Assessment for Learning: Early Childhood Exemplars. Books 1–9.* Wellington: Learning Media.

Carr, M., May, H. and Podmore, V.N. (2002) 'Learning and teaching stories: action research on evaluation in early childhood in Aotearoa–New Zealand', *European Early Childhood Education Research Journal*, 10 (2): 115–26.

Carr, M., May, H. and Podmore, V.N., with Cubey, P., Hatherly, A. and Macartney, B. (2000) *Learning and Teaching Stories: Action Research on Evaluation in Early Childhood.* Wellington: New Zealand Council for Educational Research.

Cassidy, D.J., Buell, M.J., Pugh-Hoese, S. and Russell, S. (1995) 'The effect of education on child care teachers' beliefs and classroom quality: Year One evaluation of the TEACH Early Childhood Associate Degree Scholarship program', *Early Childhood Research Quarterly*, 10: 171–83.

Curriculum, Evaluation and Management (CEM) Centre (2007) Retrieved 1 October 2007 from www.cem.dur.ac.uk

Chaiklin, S. (2001) (ed.) *The Theory and Practice of Cultural-historical Psychology.* Aarhus, Denmark: Aarhus University Press.

Chaiklin, S. (2003) 'Vygotsky's doctrine of scientific concepts: its role for contemporary education', in Alex Kozulin, Boris Gindis, Vladimir S. Ageyev, Suzanne M. Miller (eds) *Vygotsky's Educational Theory in Cultural Context.* Cambrige: Cambridge University Press. pp. 65–82.

Chak, A. (2007) 'Teachers' and parents' conceptions of children's curiosity and exploration', *International Journal of Early Years Education,* 15 (2): 141–59.

Chambers, I. and Curti, L. (1996) *The Post-Colonial Question: Common Skies, Divided Horizons.* London: Routledge.

Clarke, P. (1996) 'Investigating second language acquisition in preschools: a longitudinal study of four Vietnamese-speaking four-year-olds' acquisition of English'. Unpublished PhD thesis. LaTrobe University, Melbourne, Australia.

Claxton, G.L. (1995) 'What kind of learning does self-assessment drive? Developing a "nose" for quality: comments on Klenowski', *Assessment in Education*, 2 (3): 339–43.

Colbung, M., Glover, A., Rau, C. and Ritchie, J. (2007) 'Indigenous peoples and perspectives: early childhood education', in L. Keesing-Styles and H. Hedges (eds), *Theorising Early Childhood Practice. Emerging Dialogues.* Castle Hill, NSW: Pademelon Press. pp. 137–61.

Cole, M. and Wertsch, J. (1996) 'Beyond the individual–social antinomy in discussions of Piaget and Vygotsky', *Human Development*, 39 (5): 250–56.

Comber, B. (2000) 'What really counts in early literacy lessons', *Language Arts*, 78 (1): 39–49.

Cope, B. and Kalantzis, M. (eds) (2000) *Multiliteracies: Literacy Learning and the Design of Social Futures.* Melbourne: Macmillan.

Cowie, B.M. (2000) 'Formative assessment in science classrooms'. PhD thesis. University of Waikato, New Zealand.

Cowie, M. (2002) 'The introduction of baseline assessment in Aberdeen: the proof of the pudding is in the eating'. Paper presented at the European Conference on Educational Research, Lisbon.

Crain, W. (2005) *Theories of Development: Concepts and Applications*, 5th edition. Upper Saddle River, NJ: Pearson/Prentice Hall.

Crooks, T. (1993) 'Principles to guide assessment practice'. Paper presented at the Assessment and Learning in New Zealand – Challenges and Choices Conference, Palmerston North.

Crozier, G. and Davies, J. (2007) 'Hard to reach parents or hard to reach schools? A discussion of home–school relations, with particular reference to Bangladeshi and Pakistani parents', *British Educational Research Journal*, 33 (3): 295–313.

Cubey, P. and Dalli, C. (1996) *Quality Evaluation of Early Childhood Programmes: A Literature Review*. Wellington: Institute for Early Childhood Studies, Victoria University of Wellington.

Cullen, J. (1994) 'Why retain a development focus in early education?', in E. Mellor and K. Coombe (eds), *Issues in Early Childhood Services: Australian Perspectives*. Dubuque, IA: Wm C. Brown. pp. 53–64.

Cullen, J. (1996) 'The challenge of *Te Whāriki* for future development in early childhood education', *Delta*, 48 (1): 113–25.

Cullen, J. (1999) 'Learning opportunities for young children with special needs', *Early Education*, 21 (Spring/Summer): 5–10.

Cullen, J. (2001) 'Ethics and assessment in early childhood programmes', *Early Education*, 27 (Spring/Summer): 5–11.

Cullen, J. (2002) 'Discourse, policy and practice: an inclusive approach to early intervention', *Delta: Policy and Practice in Education*, 54 (1/2): 133–48.

Cullen, J. (2003) 'The challenge of *Te Whāriki*: catalyst for change', in J. Nuttall (ed.), *Weaving Te Whāriki: New Zealand's Early Childhood Curriculum Document in Theory and Practice*. Wellington: New Zealand Council for Educational Research. pp. 269–96.

Cullen, J. and Bevan-Brown, J. (1999) *Resourcing Special Education in Early Childhood: Database and Best Practice Validation*. Final report to Ministry of Education, IPDER, Massey University, New Zealand.

Cullen, J. and Carroll-Lind, J. (2005) 'An inclusive approach to early intervention', in D. Fraser, R. Moltzen and K. Ryba (eds), *Learners with Special Needs in Aotearoa New Zealand,* 3rd edition. Southbank, Victoria: Thomson Dunmore Press. pp. 220–43.

Dahlberg, G. (2000) Keynote address at the NZEI Te Riu Roa Early Childhood Millennium Conference, Victoria University of Wellington, 11 July.

Dahlberg, G. and Moss, P. (2005) *Ethics and Politics in Early Childhood Education*. London: Routledge Falmer.

Dahlberg, G., Moss, P. and Pence, A. (1999) *Beyond Quality in Early Childhood Education and Care: Postmodern Perspectives*. London: Falmer Press.

Daniels, H. (2001) *Vygotsky and Pedagogy*. London: Routledge.

Darder, A. (ed.) (2002) *Reinventing Paulo Friere: A Pedagogy of Love*. Boulder, CO: Westview Press.

Davies, B. (1989) *Frogs and Snails and Feminist Tales.* St Leonard's, NSW: Allen & Unwin.

Davies, B. (1990) 'Agency as a form of discursive practice. A classroom scene observed', *British Journal of Sociology in Education*, 11 (3): 341–61.

Davydov, V.V. and Zinchenko, V.P. (1993) in H. Daniels (ed.), *Charting the Agenda. Educational Activity after Vygotsky*. London: Routledge.

Department for Children, Schools and Families (DCSF) (2007) *The Children's Plan*. London: DCSF.

Department for Education and Employment (DfEE) (1997) *Excellence in Schools*. London: HMSO.

Department for Education and Employment (DfEE) (1999) *Early Years Development Partnerships and Plans*. Guidance 1998–99. London: DfEE.

Department for Education and Employment/Qualifications and Curriculum Authority (DfEE/QCA) (2000) *Curriculum Guidance for the Foundation Stage*. London: QCA.

Department for Education and Skills (DfES) (2002) *Birth to Three Matters: A Framework for Supporting Children in Their Earliest Years*. London: DfES.

Department for Education and Skills (DfES) (2004a) *Every Child Matters: Change for Children*. London: The Stationery Office.

Department for Education and Skills (DfES) (2004b) *Every Child Matters: The Next Steps*. London: The Stationery Office.

Department for Education and Skills (DfES) (2005) *Ten Year Strategy for Childcare*. London: The Stationery Office.

Department for Education and Skills (DfES) (2007a) *The Early Years Foundation Stage: Setting the Standards for Learning, Development and Care for Children from Birth to Five*. Nottingham: DfES Publications.

Department for Education and Skills (DfES) (2007b) *Letters and Sounds: Principles and Practice of High Quality Phonics Six-Phase Teaching Programme*. Nottingham: DfES Publications.

Department of Education (1988) *Education to Be More: Report of the Early Childhood Care and Education Working Group* (Meade Report). Wellington: Department of Education.

Department of Education, Science and Training (DEST) (2006) *National Report to Parliament on Indigenous Education and Training*, 2004. Retrieved 31 October 2007, from www.dest.gov.au/sectors/indigenous_education/publications_resources/profiles/

Department of Education, Training and Youth Affairs (DETYA) (2000) *The National Literacy Plan*. Canberra, ACT: DETY Affairs.

Department of Education, Training and Youth Affairs (DETYA) (2001) *Preschool Profile. Notes for Early Childhood Educators to assist in monitoring and reporting on the literacy and numeracy skills of children in the preschool/kindergarten/childcare centre years*. Retrieved 30 November 2007 from www.dest.gov.au/sectors/indigenous_education/publications_resources/profiles/

DeVries, R. (1997) 'Piaget's social theory', *Educational Researcher*, 26 (2).

Dewey, J. (1933) *Experience and Education*. New York: Macmillan.

Dockett, S. and Fleer, M. (1999) *Play and Pedagogy in Early Childhood: Bending the Rules*. Marrickville, NSW: Harcourt Brace.

Donaldson, M. (1992) *Human Minds*. London: Penguin.

Drummond, M.J. (2000) 'Starting with children – towards an early years curriculum', in C. Clouder, S. Jenkinson and M. Large (eds), *The Future of Childhood*. Stroud, UK: Hawthorn Press. pp. 27–36.

Duncan, J. (1997) 'Implications of quality research for practice.' Paper presented at a seminar entitled 'Quality Contexts for Children's Development', Invercargill, 12 March.

Dunn, J. (1988) *The Beginnings of Social Understanding*. Oxford: Blackwell.

Dunn, L. (2002) 'Children with special rights', *Early Education*, 30 (Spring/ Summer): 17–22.

Dunn, L. (2006) 'A community of practice for early childhood special education.' Paper presented at 10th Early Childhood Conference and Symposium, Porirua, NZ, December.

Dweck, C.S. and Leggett, E.L. (1988) 'A social-cognitive approach to motivation and personality', *Psychological Review*, 95 (2): 256–73.

Dyson, A.H. (1993) *Social Worlds of Children Learning to Write in an Urban Primary School*. New York: Teachers' College Press.

Dyson, A.H. (1999) 'Writing (Dallas) Cowboys: a dialogic perspective on the "What did I write?" question', in J.S. Gaffney and B.J. Askew (eds), *Stirring the Waters: The Influence of Mary Clay*. Portsmouth: NH: Heinemann. pp. 127–47.

Eades, D. (1993) *Aboriginal English*. Marrickville, NSW: Primary English Teaching Association.

Early Childhood Education Forum (1998) *Quality in Diversity in Early Learning: A Framework for Early Childhood Practitioners*. London: National Children's Bureau.

Early Childhood Strategic Plan Working Group (2001) *Final Report of the Strategic Plan Group to the Minister of Education*. Wellington: Early Childhood Strategic Plan Working Group.

Eckersley, R. (2004) *The Green State: Rethinking Democracy and Sovereignty*. Cambridge, MA: MIT Press.

Education Department of Western Australia (1994) *First Steps Developmental Continua/First Steps Resource Books*. Melbourne: Longman Australia.

Edwards, S. (2007) 'From developmental-constructivism to sociocultural theory and practice. An expansive analysis of teachers' professional learning in early childhood education', *Journal of Early Childhood Research*, 5 (1): 83–106.

Engestrom, Y., Meittenen, R. and Punamaki, R.L. (eds) (1999) *Perspectives on Activity Theory*. Cambridge: Cambridge University Press.

Eraut, M. (1999) 'Nonformal knowledge in the workplace – the hidden dimension of life-long Learning: A framework for analysis and the problems it poses for the researcher'. Paper presented at the First International Conference on Researching Work and Learning, Institute for Life-Long Learning, University of Leeds, UK.

Farquhar, S. (1999a) 'Research and the production of "worthwhile" knowledge about quality in early years education'. Paper presented at AARE–NZARE conference, Melbourne, Australia, December.

Farquhar, S. (1999b) 'The trouble with "quality"', *The First Years: New Zealand Journal of Infant and Toddler Education*, 1 (1): 10–14.

Fitz-Gibbon, C.T. (1996) *Monitoring Education: Indicators, Quality and Effectiveness*. London: Cassell.

Fitz-Gibbon, C.T. and Tymms, P.B. (2002) 'Technical and ethical issues in indicator systems: doing things right and doing wrong things', *Education Policy Analysis Archives*, 10 (6). Retrieved 29 February 2008 from http://epaa.asu.edu/epaa/v10n6/

Fleer, M. (1992) 'From Piaget to Yygotsky: moving into a new era of early childhood education', in B. Lambert (ed.), *The Changing Face of Early Childhood*. Canberra, ACT: Australian Early Childhood Association. pp. 134–49.

Fleer, M. (ed.) (1995) *DAP Centricism: Challenging Developmentally Appropriate Practice*. Watson, ACT: Australian Early Childhood Association.

Fleer, M. (2000) *An Early Childhood Research Agenda: Voices from the Field*. Canberra: Department of Education, Training and Youth Affairs.

Fleer, M. (2001) 'Literacy learning across cultures', in E. Elliot (ed.), *Every Child*. Canberra, ACT: Australian Early Childhood Association.

Fleer, M. (2002a) 'Sociocultural assessment in early years education – myth or reality?', *International Journal of Early Years Education*, 10 (2): 105–20.

Fleer, M. (2002b) 'Early childhood education: a public right and not a privilege', *Australian Journal of Early Childhood*, 27 (2): 1–12.

Fleer, M. (2006) 'Potentive assessment in early childhood education', in M. Fleer, S. Edwards, M. Hammer, A. Kennedy, A. Ridgway, J. Robbins and L. Surman (eds), *Early Childhood Learning Communities. Sociocultural Research in Practice*. Frenchs Forest, NSW: Pearson Education. pp. 161–74.

Fleer, M. and Kennedy, A. (2000) 'Quality assurance: whose quality and whose assurance?', *New Zealand Research in Early Childhood Education*, 3: 12–20.

Fleer, M. and Raban, B. (2007) *Early Childhood Literacy and Numeracy: Building Good Practice*. Canberra, ACT: Department of Education, Science and Training,

Fleer, M. and Richardson, C. (2003) 'Collective mediated assessment: moving towards a sociocultural approach to assessing children's learning', *Journal of Australian Research in Early Childhood Education*, 10 (1): 41–55.

Fleer, M. and Richardson, C. (2004) *Observing and Planning in Early Childhood Settings: Using a Sociocultural Approach*. Canberra, ACT: Early Childhood Australia.

Fleer, M. and Robbins, J. (2004a) 'Beyond ticking the boxes: From individual developmental domains to a sociocultural framework for observing young children', *New Zealand Research in Early Childhood Education*, 7: 23–39.

Fleer, M. and Robbins, J. (2004b) 'Moving from a constructivist-developmental framework for planning to a sociocultural approach: foregrounding the tension between individual and community', *Journal of Australian Research in Early Childhood Education*, 10 (2): 47–62.

Fleer, M. and Udy, G. (2002) 'Early years education in Australia', in *2002 Year Book Australia*. Canberra, ACT: Australian Burean of Statistics. pp. 287–92.

Fleer, M. and Williams-Kennedy, D. (2001) *Building Bridges: Literacy Development in Young Indigenous Children*. Canberra, ACT: Department of Education, Science and Training.

Fleet, A., Patterson, C. and Robertson, J. (eds) (2006) *Insights: Behind Early Childhood Pedagogical Documentation*. Castle Hill, NSW: Pademelon Press.

Forman, G. (1996) 'The project approach in Reggio Emilia', in C.T. Fosnot (ed.), *Constructivism: Theories, Perspectives, and Practices*. New York: Teachers' College Press. pp. 172–81.

Foucault, M. (1982) 'The subject and power', in H. Dreyfus and P. Rabinow (eds), *Michel Foucault: Beyond Structuralism and Hermeneutics*. Chicago: University of Chicago Press. pp. 208–26.

Fraser, S. and Wakefield, P. (1986) 'Fostering second language development through play in a multilingual classroom', *TESL Canada Journal/Revue TESL du Canada*, Special Issue, (1): 19–27.

Freiberg, J. and Freebody, P. (1995) 'Analysing literacy events in classrooms and homes: conversation-analytic approaches', in *Everyday Literacy Practices In and Out of Schools in Low Socio-Economic Urban Communities, Volume 1*. Nathan, Qld: Griffith University.

Freire, P. (1995) *Letters to Christina: Reflections on My Life and Work* (trans. Donaldo Macedo). New York: Routledge.

Frome, P. and Eccles, J. (1998) 'Parents' influence on children's achievement-related perceptions', *Journal of Personality and Social Psychology*, 74: 435–52.

Genishi, C., Ryan, S., Oschner, M. and Yarnall, M.M. (2001) 'Teaching in early childhood education: understanding practices through research and theory', in V. Richardson (ed.), *Handbook of Research on Teaching*, 4th edition. Washington, DC: American Educational Research Association. pp. 1175–210.

Gephart, R. (1999) 'Paradigms and research methods', *Research Methods Forum*, 4 (Summer). Retrieved 29 February 2008 from http://division.aomonline.org/rm/1999_RMD_Forum_Paradigm_Research_Methods.htm

Gerber, M. (1984) 'Caring for infants with respect', *Zero to Three*, 4 (3).

Ghandi, L. (1998) *Postcolonial Theory: A Critical Introduction*. Sydney: Allen & Unwin.

Giddens, A. (1989) *Sociology*. Cambridge: Polity Press.

Gilborn, D. (1990) *Race, Ethnicity and Education*. London: Allen & Hyman.

Gilmore, B., Haslam, R., Hitaua, R., Kent, B., Tavui, E., Tu'ionetoa, A. and Crosswell, M. (2007) 'Do you know me? E mohio ana koe ki ahau?', *Kairaranga: Weaving Educational Threads, Weaving Educational Practice*, 8 (2): 32–7.

Gipps, C. (2002) 'Sociocultural perspectives on assessment', in G. Wells and G. Claxton (eds), *Learning for Life in the 21st Century*. Oxford: Blackwell. pp. 73–83.

Gonzalez, N., Moll, L.C. and Amanti, C. (eds) (2005) *Funds of Knowledge: Theorizing Practices in Households, Communities and Classrooms*. Mahwah, NJ: Lawrence Erlbaum Associates.

Greenfield, P.M. (1984) 'A theory of the teacher in the learning activities of everyday life', in B. Rogoff and J. Lave (eds), *Everyday Cognition: Its Development in Social Context*. Cambridge, MA: Harvard University Press. pp. 117–38.

Greeno, J.G. (1997) 'On claims that answer the wrong questions', *Educational Researcher*, 26 (1): 5–17.

Grenfell, M. and James, D. with Hodkinson, P., Reay, D. and Robbins, D. (1998) *Bourdieu and Education: Acts of Practical Theory*. London: Falmer Press.

Gutierrez, K. and Rogoff, B. (2003) 'Cultural ways of learning: Individual traits or repertoires of practice', *Educational Researcher*, 32: 19–25.

Hall, S. (1997) 'Introduction', in S. Hall (ed.), *Representation: Cultural Representations and Signifying Practices*. London: Sage.

Harms, T., Clifford, R. and Cryer, D. (1998) *Early Childhood Rating Scale*, revised edition. New York: Teachers' College Press.

Harries, A.V. (2002) 'Baseline in Lesotho: some preliminary observations'. Paper presented at the European Conference on Educational Research, Lisbon.

Hatherly, A. and Richardson, C. (2007) 'Building connections: assessment and evaluation revisited', in L. Keesing-Styles and H. Hedges (eds), *Theorising Early Childhood Practice. Emerging Dialogues*. Castle Hill, NSW: Pademelon Press. pp. 51–70.

Haworth, P., Cullen, J., Simmons, H., Schimanski, L., McGarva, P. and Woodhead, E. (2006) *The Flight of Our Kite: The Wycliffe Nga Tamariki Kindergarten Story. Centre of Innovation*. Final Research Report to Ministry of Education. Napier, NZ: Napier Kindergarten Association.

Heath, S.B. (1983) *Ways With Words*. Cambridge, MA: Cambridge University Press.

Hedegaard, M. (2008) 'Child development from a cultural-historical approach: children's activity in everyday local settings as foundation for their development'. *Mind Culture and Activity* (in press). (Paper presented at the triennial conference of the International Society for Culture and Activity Research, Sevilla, Spain.)

Hedges, H.D. (2002) 'Subject content knowledge in early childhood curriculum and pedagogy'. Unpublished MEd thesis, Massey University, New Zealand.

Hedges, H. and Nuttall, J. (2008) 'Macropolitical forces and micropolitical realities: implementing *Te Whāriki*', in V.M. Carpenter, J. Jesson, P. Roberts and M. Stephenson (eds), *Nga Kaupapa Here: Connections and Contradictions in Education*. Melbourne: Cengage Publishing. pp. 77–87.

Hemphill, L. and Snow, C. (1996) 'Language and literacy development: discontinuities and differences', in D.R. Olson and N. Torrance (eds), *The Handbook of Education and Human Development*. Oxford: Blackwell. pp. 173–201.

Hill, S. (2007) 'Multiliteracies: towards the future', in L. Makin, C. Diaz & C. McLachlan (eds), *Literacies in Childhood: Changing Views, Challenging Practice*, 2nd edition. Sydney: Elsevier. pp. 56–70.

Hill, S., Comber, B., Louden, W., Rivalland, J. and Reid, J. (1998) *100 Children Go to School: Connections and Disconnections in Literacy Development in the Year Prior to School and the First Year of School, 3 Volumes*. Canberra, ACT: Department of Education, Training and Youth Affairs.

Hodgen, E. (2007) *Early Childhood Education and Young Adult Competencies at Age 16: Technical Report 2 from the Age-16 Phase of the Longitudinal Competent Children, Competent Learners Study*. Wellington: Ministry of Education. Retrieved 7 March 2008 from http://action.web.ca/home/crru/rsrcs_crru_full.shtml?x=107705

Horner, R. and Topfer, C. (2003) 'Assessing emerging literacy. Action Research Project 2002.' Unpublished manuscript, Department of Education, Hobart, Tasmania.

Howes, C. (1983) 'Caregiver behaviour in centre and family day care', *Journal of Applied Developmental Psychology*, 4: 99–107.

Howes, C. (1986) 'Quality indicators for infant–toddler childcare'. Paper presented at the annual meeting of the American Educational Research Association. San Francisco, CA: ED 273385.

Howes, C., Phillips, D. and Whitebrook, M. (1992) 'Thresholds of quality: implications for the social development of children in center-based childcare', *Child Development*, 63: 449–60.

Howie, S. (2002) *English Language Proficiency and Contextual Factors Influencing Mathematics: Achievement of Secondary School Pupils in South Africa*. Enschede, Netherlands: University of Twente Press.

Hughes, P. (2005) 'Baby, it's you: international capital discovers the under threes', *Contemporary Issues in Early Childhood*, 6 (1): 30–40.

Indigenous Higher Education Advisory Council (2006) *Improving Indigenous Outcomes and Enhancing Indigenous Culture and Knowledge in Australian Higher Education*. Report to the Minister for Education, Science and Training, Australian Government, Canberra, ACT.

James, A. and Prout, A. (1997) *Constructing and Reconstructing Childhood: Contemporary Issues in Sociological Study of Childhood*. London: Falmer Press.

Johnson, J.E., Christie, J.F. & Wardle, F. (2005) *Play, Development and Early Education*. Boston, MA: Pearson Education.

Jordan, B. (1999) 'Planning for Children's Thinking in Early Childhood'. Paper presented at the 11th Australasian Human Development Association Conference, Sydney.

Jordan, B. (2003) 'Professional development making a difference for children: Co-constructing understandings in early childhood centres'. Unpublished PhD thesis, Massey University, New Zealand.

Joseph Rowntree Foundation (2007) *Experiences of Poverty and Educational Disadvantage*. York: Joseph Rowntree Foundation.

Kalliala, M. (2006) *Play Culture in a Changing World*. Maidenhead: Open University Press.

Karnes, M.B. (ed.) (1983) *The Underserved: Our Young Gifted Children*. Reston, Virginia: The Council for Exceptional Children.

Katz, L. (1993) *Dispositions: Definitions and Implications for Early Childhood Practices*, Perspectives from ERIC/EECE: A Monograph Series. Urbana, Il: ERIC Clearinghouse on Elementary and Early Childhood Education.

Katz, L. (1994) 'Perspectives on the quality of early childhood programmes', *Phi Delta Kappan*, 75 (Nov.): 200–5.

Kemp, D. (2000) *National Indigenous English Literacy and Numeracy Strategy, 2000–2004*. Canberra, ACT: Department of Education, Training and Youth Affairs.

Kincheloe, J. (2005) *Critical Constructivism Primer*. New York: Peter Lang.

Kohlberg, L. and Mayer, R. (1972) 'Development is the aim of education', *Harvard Education Review*, 42 (4): 449–96.

Konzal, J.L. (2001) 'Collaborative inquiry: a means of creating a learning community', *Early Childhood Research Quarterly*, 16: 95–115.

Kozulin, A. (1998) *Psychological Tools: A Sociological Approach to Education*. Cambridge, MA: Harvard University Press.

Kress, G. (1999) 'Genre and the changing contexts for English Language Arts', *Language Arts*, 76 (6): 461–9.

Krogh, S. and Slentz, K. (2001) *The Early Childhood Curriculum*. New York: Lawrence Erlbaum Associates.

Kuschner, D. (2007) 'Children's play in the journal, *Young Children*: an analysis of how it is portrayed and why it is valued', in D. Justus Sluss & O.S. Jarrett (eds), *Investigating Play in the 21st Century. Play and Culture Studies, Volume 7*. Lanham, MD: University Press of America. pp. 55–69.

Labbo, L.D. (1996) 'A semiotic analysis of young children's symbol making in a classroom computer center', *Reading Research Quarterly*, 31 (4): 356–85.

Laevers, F. (1999) 'The project "Experiential Education": concepts and experiences at the level of context, process and outcome', in *Keynote Papers, Proceedings of the Seventh Early Childhood Convention, Volume 1*. Nelson: Whakatu. pp. 17–26.

Laevers, F., Vandenbussche, E., Kog, M. and Depondt, L. (n.d.) *A Process-Oriented Child Monitoring System for Young Children*. Experiential Education Series, No. 2. Leuven, Belgium: Centre for Experiential Education.

Lankshear, C. and Knoebel, M. (1997) 'Literacies, texts and difference in the electronic age', in C. Lankshear (ed.), *Changing Literacies*. Buckingham: Open University Press.

Larson, J. and Marsh, J. (2005) *Making literacy real: theories and practices for learning and teaching*. London: Sage.

Lave, J. and Wenger, E. (1991) *Situated Learning: Legitimate Peripheral Participation*. Cambridge: Cambridge University Press.

Lawrence, D. (1997) *Enhancing Self-Esteem in the Classroom*. London: Paul Chapman.

Leach, J. and Moon, B. (1999) *Learners and Pedagogy*. London: Paul Chapman/Open University Press.

Leau, H.R., Flamig, K., Frankenstein, Y., Koch, S., Schneider, K. and Schweiger (2007) *Bildungs – und Lergeschichten*. Berlin: Verlag das netz Weimar.

Lemke, J. (1990) *Talking Science: Language, Learning and Values*. Norwood, NJ: Ablex.

Lindfors, J.W. (1999) *Children's Inquiry: Using Language to Make Sense of the World*. New York: Teachers' College Press.

Livingstone, D. (2003) 'Reclaiming early childhood teacher education: A critical constructivist approach'. Paper presented at the 50th Annual Meeting of the Southeastern Regional Association of Teacher Educators, Savannah, GA, 19–22 November, ED481713.

Lloyd, B. (1987) 'Social representations of gender', in J. Bruner and H. Haste (eds), *Making Sense: The Child's Construction of the World*. London: Routledge. pp. 147–62.

Losardo, A. and Notari-Syverson, A. (2001) *Alternative Approaches to Assessing Young Children*. Baltimore, MD: Paul H. Brookes.

Luke, C. (2000) 'What next? Toddler Netizens, Playstation thumb, techno-literacies', *Contemporary Issues in Early Childhood*, 1 (1): 94–9.

Lunt, I. (1993) 'The practice of assessment', in H. Daniels (ed.), *Charting the Agenda. Educational Activity After Vygotsky*. London: Routledge.

McGurk, H., Mooney, A., Moss, P. and Poland, G. (1995) *Staff–Child Ratios in Care and Education Services for Young Children*. London: HMSO.

Macmillan, A. (2006) 'Call to scrap set age for school entry', *Scotland on Sunday*.

MacNaughton, G. (1995) 'A post-structuralist analysis of learning in early childhood settings' in M. Fleer (ed.), *DAPcentrism: Challenging Developmentally Appropriate Practice*. Canberra, ACT: Australian Early Childhood Association. pp. 35–54.

MacNaughton, G. (2000a) *Rethinking Gender in Early Childhood Education*. Sydney: Allen & Unwin; London: Paul Chapman.

MacNaughton, G. (2000b) *The Tasmanian Early Childhood Review: Towards a Future Vision*. Final report prepared for the Department of Education, Hebart, Tasmania.

MacNaughton, G. (2001) 'Silences and subtexts of immigrant and non-immigrant children', *Childhood Education*, 78 (1): 30–6.

MacNaughton, G. (2005) *Doing Foucault in Early Childhood Studies*. London: Routledge Falmer.

MacNaughton, G. (2008) 'Constructing gender in early years education', in C. Skelton, B. Francis and L. Smulyan (eds), *The Sage Handbook of Gender and Education*. London: Sage. pp. 127–38.

MacNaughton, G. and Williams, G. (1998) *Techniques for Teaching Young Children: Choices in Theory and Practice*. Frenchs Forest, NSW: Longman.

McNaughton, S. (1995) *Patterns of Emergent Literacy: Processes of Development and Transition*. Auckland: Oxford University Press.

McNaughton, S. (2002) *Meeting of Minds*. Wellington: Learning Media.

McWilliam, R.A., Wolery, M. and Odom, S.L. (2001) 'Instructional perspectives in inclusive preschool classrooms', in M.J. Guralnick (ed.), *Early Childhood Inclusion: Focus on Change*. Baltimore, MD: Paul H. Brookes. pp. 503–27.

Malaguzzi, L. (1993) 'For an education based on relationships', *Young Children*, 49 (1): 9–13.

Mallory, B.L. (1998) 'Educating young children with developmental differences: principles of inclusive practice', in C. Seefeldt and A. Galper (eds), *Continuing Issues in Early Childhood Education*, 2nd edition. Columbus, OH: Merrill. pp. 213–37.

Mallory, B.L. and New, R.S. (1994) 'Social constructivist theory and principles of inclusion: chal-lenges for early childhood special education', *Journal of Special Education*, 28 (3): 322–37.

Mara, D. (1999) *Implementation of Te Whāriki in Pacific Islands Early Childhood Centres.* Wellington: New Zealand Council for Educational Research.

Marsh, J. (2003) 'One-way traffic? Connections between literacy practices at home and in the nursery', *British Educational Research Journal*, 29 (3): 369–82.

Marsh, J. (ed.) (2005) *Popular Culture, New Media and Digital Literacy in Early Childhood.* London: Routledge Falmer.

Mavers, D. (2007) 'Semiotic resourcefulness: A young child's email exchange as design', *Journal of Early Childhood Literacy*, 7 (2): 155–76.

May, H. (1991) 'A philosophy of practice in infant–toddler care: a case study of Magda and RIE (Resources for Infant Educators)', in M. Gold, L. Foote and A. Smith (eds), *Proceedings of Fifth Early Childhood Convention, Dunedin, New Zealand.* Dunedin. pp. 284–94.

May, H. (1999) 'The price of partnership: the Before Five decade', *New Zealand Journal of Educational Studies*, 43 (1): 18–27.

May, H. and Podmore, V.N. (2000) '"Teaching Stories": an approach to self-evaluation of early childhood programmes', *European Early Childhood Education Research Journal*, 8: 61–74.

Meade, A. (1995) 'Good practice to best practice in early childhood education: Extending poli-cies and children's minds.' Paper presented to the Start Right Conference, London, 20–22 September.

Meade, A. (2000) 'If you say it three times, is it true? Critical use of research in early childhood education', *International Journal of Early Years Education*, 8 (1): 15–26.

Meade, A. (ed.) (2006) *Riding the Waves: Innovation in Early Childhood Education.* Wellington: New Zealand Council for Educational Research.

Meade, A. (ed.) (2007) *Cresting the Waves: Innovation in Early Childhood Education.* Wellington: New Zealand Council for Educational Research.

Mellor, D. and Epstein, D. (2007) 'Appropriate behaviour? Sexualities, schooling and heter-gender', in C. Skelton, B. Francis and L. Smulyan (eds), *The Sage Handbook of Gender and Education.* London: Sage. pp. 378–91.

Merrell, C. and Tymms, P. (2007) 'What children know and can do when they start school and how this varies between countries', *Journal of Early Childhood Research*, 5 (2): 115–34.

Milner, D. (1983) *Children and Race: Ten Years On.* London: Ward Lock Educational.

Ministry of Education (1996a) *Te Whāriki He Whāriki Matauranga: Early Childhood Curriculum.* Wellington: Learning Media.

Ministry of Education (1996b) 'Revised statement of desirable objectives and practices (DOPs) for chartered early childhood services in New Zealand', *New Zealand Gazette*, 3 October.

Ministry of Education (1997) *The Quality Journey.* Wellington: Learning Media.

Ministry of Education (1998) *Quality in Action: Te Mahi Whai Hua. Implementing the Revised Statement of Desirable Objectives and Practices in New Zealand Early Childhood Services.* Wellington: Learning Media.

Ministry of Education (1999a) *The Quality Journey: He Haerenga Whai Hua. Improving Quality in Early Childhood Services.* Wellington: Learning Media.

Ministry of Education (1999b) *Pitopito Korero*, No. 21. Wellington: Ministry of Education.

Ministry of Education (2000a) *Including Everyone: Te Reo Tataki.* Wellington: Learning Media.

Ministry of Education (2000b) *The Quality Journey: He Haerenga Whai Hua*, 2nd edition. Wellington: Learning Media.

Ministry of Education (2002) *Pathways to the Future: Nga Huarahi Aratiki. A 10-year Strategic Plan for Early Childhood Education.* Wellington: Learning Media.

Ministry of Education (2005) *Kei Tua o Te Pae: Assessment for Learning. Early Childhood Exemplars.* Wellington: Learning Media.

Ministry of Education (2006) *Nga Arohaehae Whai Hua: Self-review Guidelines for Early Childhood Education*. Wellington: Learning Media.

Ministry of Education (2007) *The New Zealand Curriculum*. Wellington: Learning Media. Available at http://nzcurriculum.tki.org.nz

Mortimore, P. (ed.) (1999) *Understanding Pedagogy and Its Impact on Learning*. London: Paul Chapman.

Mosier, C. and Rogoff, B. (2000) *Privileged Treatment of Toddlers: Cultural Aspects of Autonomy and Responsibility*. Santa Cruz, CA: University of California Press.

Moss, P. and Pence, A. (1994) *Valuing Quality in Early Childhood Services*. London: Paul Chapman.

Moss, P. and Penn, H. (1996) *Transforming Nursery Education*. London: Paul Chapman.

Moyles, J., Adams, S. and Musgrove, A. (2002) *Study of Pedagogical Effectiveness in Early Learning*. Research Report No. 363. London: Department for Education and Skills.

Munn, P. (1994) 'Perceptions of teaching and learning in pre-school centres', in M. Hughes (ed.), *Perceptions of Teaching and Learning*. Clevedon: Multi-Lingual Matters.

Nabuco, E. and Sylva, K. (1996) 'The effects of three early childhood curricula on children's progress at primary school in Portugal.' Paper presented at the ISSBD Conference in Quebec, Canada.

Nash, R. (2001) 'Competent children: a critical appreciation', *New Zealand Journal of Educational Studies*, 36 (1): 115–20.

National Research Council, Youth and Families Board on Children, and Committee on Integrating the Science of Early Childhood Development (2000) *From Neurons to Neighborhoods: The Science of Early Childhood Development* Jack P. Shonkoff and Deborah A. Phillips (eds). Washington, DC: National Academy Press.

National Research Council, Committee on Early Childhood Pedagogy (2001) *Eager to Learn: Educating Our Preschoolers*. Committee on Early Childhood Pedagogy, Commission on Behavioral and Social Sciences and Education, National Research Council. Barbara T. Bowman, M. Suzanne Donovan, and M. Susan Burns (eds). Washington, DC: National Academy Press.

New, R. (1994) 'Culture, child development and developmentally appropriate practices: teachers as collaborative researchers', in B. Mallory and R. New (eds), *Diversity and Developmentally Appropriate Practices*. New York: Teachers' College Press.

Nichols, S. (2000) 'Unsettling the bedtime story: Parents' reports of home literacy practices', *Contemporary Issues in Early Childhood*, 1 (3): 315–28.

Nichols, S. (2002). 'Parents' construction of their children as gendered literate subjects: a critical discourse analysis', *Journal of Early Childhood Literacy*, 2 (2): 123–44.

Nutbrown, C. (1994) *Threads of Thinking*. London: Paul Chapman.

Nuttall, J. and Edwards, S. (2007) 'Theory, policy, and practice: three contexts for the development of Australasia's early childhood curriculum documents', in L. Keesing-Styles and H. Hedges (eds), *Theorising Early Childhood Practice: Emerging Dialogues*. Castle Hill, NSW: Pademelon Press.

OECD (2001) *Starting Strong: Early Childhood Education and Care*. Paris: Organisation for Economic Co-operation and Development.

OECD (2004) *Starting Strong: Curricula and Pedagogies in Early Childhood Education and Care: Five Curriculum Outlines*. Directorate for Education, Organisation for Economic Co-operation and Development. Retrieved 4 March 2008 from www.oecd.org/dataoecd/23/36/31672150.pdf

OECD (2006) *Starting Strong II: Early Childhood Education and Care*. Paris: Organisation for Economic Co-operation and Development.

Olson, D.R. and Bruner, J.S. (1996) 'Folk psychology and folk pedagogy', in D.R. Olson and N. Torrance (eds), *The Handbook of Education and Human Development: New Models of Learning, Teaching and Schooling*. Oxford: Blackwell.

Ormerod, F. and Ivanic, R. (2000) 'Texts in practice: interpreting the physical characteristics of children's project work', in D. Barton, M. Hamilton and R. Ivanic (eds), *Situated Literacies: Reading and Writing in Context*. London: Routledge.

Pahl, K. (2002) 'Ephemera, mess and miscellaneous piles: text and practices in families', *Journal of Early Childhood Literacy*, 2 (2): 145–66.

Palinscar, A.S., Brown, A.L. and Campione, J.C. (1993) 'First-grade dialogues for knowledge acquisition and use', in E.A. Forman, N. Minick and C.A. Stone (eds), *Contexts for Learning*. New York: Oxford University Press. pp. 43–57.

Pascal, C. (1996) *Evaluating and Developing Quality in Early Childhood Settings: A Professional Development Programme*. Worcester, UK: Centre for Early Childhood Research, Worcester College of Higher Education.

Pascal, C. (1999) 'The effective early learning project: achievements and reflection', in *Keynote Papers, Proceedings of the Seventh Early Childhood Convention, Volume 1*. Nelson: Whakatu. pp. 43–52.

Penn, H. (2007) 'Childcare market management: How the United Kingdom government has reshaped its role in developing early childhood education and care', *Contemporary Issues in Early Childhood*, 8 (3): 192–207.

Perkins, D.N. (1993) 'Person-plus: a distributed view of thinking and learning', in G. Salomon (ed.), *Distributed Cognitions: Psychological and Educational Considerations*. Cambridge: Cambridge University Press.

Phillips, G., McNaughton, S. and MacDonald, S. (2001) *Picking Up the Pace: Effective Literacy Interventions for Accelerated Progress over the Transition into Decile 1 Schools*. Auckland: Child Literacy Foundation and Woolf Fisher Research Centre.

Phillipsen, L.C., Burchinal, M., Howes, C. and Cryer, D. (1997) 'The prediction of process quality from structural features of child care', *Early Childhood Research Quarterly*, 12: 281–303.

Piaget, J. and Inhelder, B. (1969) *The Psychology of the Child*. New York: Basic Books.

Podmore, V.N. (1993) *Education and Care: A Review of International Studies of the Outcomes of Early Childhood Experiences*. Wellington: New Zealand Council for Educational Research/Ministry of Women's Affairs.

Podmore, V.N. (2006) *Observation: Origins and Approaches to Early Childhood Research and Practice*. Wellington: New Zealand Council for Educational Research.

Podmore, V.N. and May, H. (2003) '"The child's questions": narrative explorations of infants' experiences of *Te Whāriki*', *Australian Research in Early Childhood Education*, 10 (1): 69–80.

Podmore, V.N., May, H. and Carr, M. with Cubey, P., Hatherly, A. and Macartney, B. (2001) *The Child's Questions: Programme Evaluation Using 'Teaching Stories'*. Wellington: Institute for Early Childhood Studies, Victoria University of Wellington.

Podmore, V.N. and May, H. with Mara, D. (1998) *Evaluating Early Childhood Programmes Using the Strands and Goals of Te Whāriki, the National Early Childhood Curriculum*. Final Report on Phases One and Two to the Ministry of Education. Wellington: New Zealand Council for Educational Research and Ministry of Education.

Podmore, V.N. and Meade, A., with Kerslake Hendricks, A. (2000) *Aspects of Quality in Early Childhood Education*. Wellington: New Zealand Council for Educational Research.

Pollard, A., Broadfoot, P., Croll, P., Osborn, M. and Abbott, D. (1994) *Changing English Primary Schools: The Impact of the Education Act at Key Stage One*. London: Cassell.

Press, F. and Hayes, A. (2000) *OECD Thematic Review of Early Childhood Education and Care Policy: Australian Background Report*. Canberra, ACT: Department of Education, Training and Youth Affairs.

Primary National Strategy (2007) *Letters and Sounds: Principles and Practice of High Quality Phonics*. London: The Stationery Office.

Prince, C. (2007) 'A knowledge creation approach to environmental education in early child-hood: Creating a community of learners'. Unpublished EdD thesis, Massey University, New Zealand.

Prout, A. and James, A. (1997) 'A new paradigm for the sociology of childhood? Provenance, promise and problems', in A. James and A. Prout (eds), *Constructing and Reconstructing Childhood*, 2nd edition. London: Falmer Press. pp. 1–7.

Pugh, G. (ed.) (2001) *Contemporary Issues in the Early Years: Working Collaboratively for Children*, 2nd edition. London: Paul Chapman.

Purcell-Gates, V. (1995) *Other People's Words: The Cycle of Low Literacy*. Cambridge, MA: Harvard University Press.

Purdie, N. and Hattie, J. (1996) 'Cultural differences in the use of strategies for self-regulated learning', *American Educational Research Journal*, 33 (4): 845–71.

Purdue, K., Ballard, K. and MacArthur, J. (2001) 'Exclusion and inclusion in New Zealand early childhood education: disability, discourses and contexts', *International Journal of Early Years Education*, 9 (1): 37–49.

Raban, B. (2000) *Just the Beginning* ... Canberra, ACT: Commonwealth Department of Education, Training and Youth Affairs.

Raban, B., Nolan, A., Waniganayake, M., Ure, C., Brown, R. and Deans, J. (2007) *Building Capacity. Strategic Professional Development for Early Childhood Practitioners*. South Melbourne: Thomson Social Science Press.

Radford, G. (2001) 'Can "Learning Stories" increase opportunities for closer relationships and partnerships between families and kindergartens?' Unpublished research paper, University of Waikato, New Zealand.

Reay, D. (2007) 'Compounding inequalities: gender and class in education', in C. Skelton, B. Francis and L. Smulyan (eds), *The Sage Handbook of Gender and Education*. London: Sage. pp. 339–49.

Resnick, L., Levine, J. and Teasley, S. (eds) (1991) *Perspectives on Socially Shared Cognition*. Washington, DC: American Psychiatric Association.

Rinaldi, C. (2006) *In Dialogue With Reggio Emilia – Listening, Researching and Learning*. London: Routledge.

Rogoff, B. (1990) *Apprenticeship in Thinking: Cognitive Development in Social Context*. Oxford: Oxford University Press.

Rogoff, B. (1994) 'Developing understandings of the idea of communities of learners', *Mind, Culture, and Activity*, 1 (4): 209–29.

Rogoff, B. (1997) 'Evaluating development in the process of participation: theory, methods and practice building on each other', in E. Amsel and K.A. Renninger (eds), *Change and Development: Issues of Theory, Method and Application*. Mahwah, NJ: Lawrence Erlbaum Associates. pp. 265–85.

Rogoff, B. (1998) 'Cognition as a collaborative process', in D. Kuhn and R.S. Siegler (eds), *Handbook of Child Psychology, Volume 2*, 5th edition. New York: John Wiley. pp. 679–744.

Rogoff, B. (2003) *The Cultural Nature of Human Development*. New York: Oxford University Press.

Rogoff, B., Baker-Sennett, J., Lacasa, P. and Goldsmith, D. (1995) 'Development through participation in sociocultural activity', in J. Goodnow, P. Miller and F. Kessel (eds), *Cultural Practices as Contexts for Development: New Directions for Child Development*. San Francisco: Jossey–Bass. pp. 45–65.

Rogoff, B., Mistry, J.J., Goncu, A. and Moser, C. (1993) 'Guided participation in cultural activity by toddlers and caregivers', *Monographs of the Society for Research in Child Development*, 58 (8): 1–179.

Rogoff, B., Turkanis, C.G. and Bartlett, L. (2001) *Learning Together: Children and Adults in a School Community*. New York: Oxford University Press.

Roskos, K.A. and Christie, J.F. (eds) (2000) *Play and Literacy in Early Childhood: Research from Multiple Perspectives*. Mahwah, NJ: Lawrence Erlbaum Associates.

Roth, W.M. and Roychoudhury, A. (1994) 'Science discourse through collaborative concept mapping: new perspectives for the teacher', *International Journal of Science Education*, 16 (4): 437–55.

Rouse, D. (1990) 'The first three years of life: children trusting, communicating and learning', in D. Rouse (ed.), *Babies and Toddlers: Carers and Educators – Quality for Under Threes*. London: National Children's Bureau.

Russell, A. (1985) *An Observational Study of the Effect of Staff–Child Ratios on Staff and Child Behaviour in South Australian Kindergartens*. Adelaide: Flinders University.

Sadler, D.R. (1989) 'Formative assessment and the design of instructional systems', *Instructional Science*, 18: 119–44.

Sakharov, L.S. (1930) 'On the method of investigating concepts', *Psikhologija*, 3: 3–32 (translated by Michel Vale and published in *Soviet Psychology*, 1990, 23, 35–66) in Rene van der Veer and Jaan Valsiner (eds) (1998) *The Vygotsky Reader*. Cambridge, MA: Blackwell. pp. 73–98.

Salomon, G. (ed.) (1993) *Distributed Cognitions: Psychological and Educational Considerations*. Cambridge: Cambridge University Press.

Sammons, P., Sylva, K., Melhuish, E., Siraj-Blatchford, I., Taggart, B. and Elliot, K. (2002a) *Technical Paper 8a – Measuring the Impact of Pre-School on Children's Cognitive Progress over the Pre-School Period*. London: Institute of Education.

Sammons, P., Sylva, K., Melhuish, E., Siraj-Blatchford, I., Taggart, B. and Elliot, K. (2002b) *Technical Paper 8b – Measuring the Impact of Pre-School on Children's Social/Behavioural Development over the Pre-School Period*. London: Institute of Education.

Sanders, W.L. and Horn, S. (1995) *An Overview of the Tennessee Value-Added Assessment System (TVAAS) – Answers to Frequently Asked Questions*. Knoxville, TN: University of Tennessee.

Saracho, O. and Spodek, B. (2002) *Contemporary Perspectives on Early Childhood Curriculum*. Greenwich, CT: Information Age Publishing.

Scarr, S., Eisenberg, M. and Deater-Deckard, K. (1994) 'Measurement of quality in child care centres', *Early Childhood Research Quarterly*, 9: 131–51.

Schaffer, H.R. (1992) 'Joint involvement episodes as contexts for cognitive development', in H. McCurk (ed.), *Childhood and Social Development: Contemporary Perspectives*. Hove: Lawrence Erlbaum Associates.

Schoenfeld, A.H. (1999) 'Looking toward the 21st century: challenges of educational theory and practice', *Educational Researcher*, 28 (7): 4–14.

School Curriculum and Assessment Authority (SCAA) (1996) *Nursery Education: Desirable Outcomes for Children's Learning on Entering Compulsory Education*. London: DfEE/SCAA.

Schweinhart, L.J. and Weikart, D.P. (1997) 'The High/Scope Preschool Curriculum Comparison through age 23', *Early Childhood Research Quarterly*, 12: 117–43.

Schweinhart, L.J. and Weikart, D.P. (1999) 'The advantages of High/Scope: helping children lead successful lives', *Educational Leadership*, 57 (1): 76–8.

Schweinhart, L.J., Barnes, H.V. and Weikart, D.P. (1993) *Significant Benefits: The High/Scope Perry Preschool Study through Age 27*. Ypsilanti, MI: High/Scope Educational Research Foundation.

Scrivens, C. (2002) 'Early childhood education in New Zealand: the interface between professionalism and the New Right', in L.K.S. Chan and E.J. Mellor (eds), *International Developments in Early Childhood Services*. New York: Peter Lang. pp. 153–70.

Selleck, D. (2007) 'Early Years provision in Wales', *Nursery World*, July, p. 5.

Serpell, R. (1997) 'Literacy connections between school and home: how should we evaluate them?', *Journal of Literacy Research*, 29 (4): 587–616.

Shorrocks-Taylor, D. (1999) *National Testing Past, Present and Future*. Leicester: BPS Books.

Simmons, H., Schimanski, L., McGarva, P., Woodhead, E., Cullen, J. and Haworth, P. (2005) 'Teachers researching young children's working theories', *Early Childhood Folio*, 9: 18–22. Wellington: New Zealand Council for Educational Research.

Siraj-Blatchford, I. (1994) *The Early Years: Laying the Foundations of Racial Equality*. Stoke-on-Trent: Trentham Books.

Siraj-Blatchford, I. (1996) 'Why understanding cultural differences is not enough', in G. Pugh (ed.), *Contemporary Issues in the Early Years*. London: Paul Chapman.

Siraj-Blatchford, I. (ed.) (1998) *A Curriculum Development Handbook for Early Childhood Educators*. Stoke-on-Trent: Trentham Books.

Siraj-Blatchford, I. (1999) 'Early childhood pedagogy, practice, principles and research', in P. Mortimore (ed.), *Understanding Pedagogy and Its Impact on Learning*. London: Paul Chapman.

Siraj-Blatchford, I. (2007) 'Creativity, communication and collaboration: the identification of pedagogic progression in sustained shared thinking', *Asia–Pacific Journal of Research in Early Childhood Education,* 1 (2): 1–13.

Siraj-Blatchford, I. and Clarke, P. (2000) *Supporting Identity, Diversity and Language in the Early Years*. Buckingham: Open University Press.

Siraj-Blatchford, I. and Siraj-Blatchford, J. (2001) 'An ethnographic approach to researching young children's learning', in G. MacNaughton, S. Rolfe and Siraj-Blatchford, I. (eds), *Doing Early Childhood Research: International Perspectives on Theory and Practice*. Sydney: Allen & Unwin; Buckingham: Open University Press.

Siraj-Blatchford, I., Sylva, K., Muttock, S., Gilden, R. and Bell, D. (2002) *Researching Effective Pedagogy in the Early Years*. (Research Report No. 356 Department for Education and Skills). London: HMSO.

Siraj-Blatchford, I., Sylva, K., Taggart, B., Sammons, P. and Melhuish, E. (2002) *Technical Paper 10 – Intensive Study of Selected Centres*. London: London Institute of Education.

Smiley, P.A. and Dweck, C.S. (1994) 'Individual differences in achievement goals among young children', *Child Development*, 65: 1723–43.

Smith, A.B. (1993) 'Early childhood educare: seeking a theoretical framework in Vygotsky's work', *International Journal of Early Years Education*, 1 (1): 47–61.

Smith, A.B. (1996a) 'The early childhood curriculum from a sociocultural perspective', *Early Child Development and Care*, 115: 51–64.

Smith, A. (1996b) 'Is quality a subjective or objective matter?', in A. Smith & N. Taylor (eds), *Assessing and Improving Quality in Early Childhood Centres*. University of Otago, NZ: Children's Issues Centre. pp. 81–90.

Smith, A.B. (1996c) *'Quality childcare and joint attention'*. Paper presented at the Annual Conference of the New Zealand Association for Research in Education, Nelson Polytechnic, December.

Smith, A.B. (1997) 'Defining and choosing quality: messages from research'. Paper presented at a seminar entitled 'Quality Contexts for Children's Development', Invercargill, NZ, 12 March.

Smith, A.B. (1998) *Understanding Children's Development: A New Zealand Perspective*, 4th edition. Wellington: Bridget Williams Books.

Smith, A.B. (1999) 'Quality childcare and joint attention', *International Journal of Early Years Education*, 7 (1): 85–98.

Smith, A.B. and Barraclough, S.J. (1997) 'Quality childcare: do parents choose it?', *Early Childhood Folio*, 3: 19–22. Wellington: New Zealand Council for Educational Research.

Smith, A. and Taylor, N.J. (eds) (1996) 'Assessing and improving quality in early childhood centres', in *National Seminar Proceedings*. University of Otago, NZ: Children's Issues Centre, May.

Smith, A. and Taylor, N. (2000) 'The sociocultural context of childhood: Balancing dependency and agency', in A. Smith, N. Taylor and M. Gollop (eds), *Children's Voices: Research, Policy and Practice*. Auckland: Pearson Education. pp. 1–17.

Smith, A.B., McMillan, B.W., Kennedy, S. and Ratcliff, B. (1989) 'The effect of improving preschool teacher/child ratios: an experiment in nature', *Early Child Development and Care*, 42: 123–38.

Smith, A.B., Grima, G., Gaffney, M., Powell, K., Masse, L. and Barnett, S. (2000) *Strategic Research Initiative Literature Review: Early Childhood Education*. Wellington: Research Division, Ministry of Education.

Snow, C.E., Barnes, W.S., Chandler, J., Goodman, I.F. and Hemphill, L. (1991) *Unfulfilled Expectations: Home and School Influences on Literacy*. Cambridge, MA: Harvard University Press.

Spodek, B. and Saracho, O. (eds) (1991) *Issues in Early Childhood Curriculum*. New York: Teachers' College Press.

Stephen, C. (2006) *Insight 28: Early Years Education: Perspectives from a Review of the International Literature*. Scottish Executive Education Department. Retrieved 7 March 2008, from www.york.ac.uk/res/e-society/projects/3/0021792.pdf

Stipek, D. and Byler, P. (1997) 'Early childhood education teachers: Do they practise what they preach?', *Early Childhood Research Quarterly*, 12: 305–25.

Stone, C.A. (1993) 'What is missing in the metaphor of scaffolding?', in E.A. Forman, N. Minick and C.A. Stone (eds), *Contexts for Learning*. New York: Oxford University Press. pp. 169–83.

Stremmel, A.J. (1993) 'Responsive teaching: a culturally appropriate approach', in V.R. Fu, A.J. Stremmel and C. Treppe (eds), *Papers from the European Forum for Child Welfare and NAEYC Conferences, Hamburg and Denver, 1991 and 1992*.

Sutton-Smith, B. (1997) *The Ambiguity of Play*. Cambridge, MA: Harvard University Press.

Sylva, K. (1994) 'School influences on children's development', *Journal of Child Psychology and Psychiatry*, 35 (1): 135–70.

Sylva, K. (1999) 'The role of research in explaining the past and shaping the future', in L. Abbott and H. Moylett (eds), *Children and the Millennium*. London: Falmer Press. pp. 165–78.

Sylva, K. (2001) *The Effective Provision of Pre-school Education (EPPE) Project. An Introduction to EPPE and Its Methodology*, The EPPE Symposium at the British Educational Research Association (BERA) Annual Conference, Cardiff, 13–15 September.

Sylva, K. and Sammons, P. (2000) *An Introduction to EPPE, The Effective Provision of Pre-school Education (EPPE) Project: A longitudinal study funded by the DfEE (1997–2003)*. The EPPE Symposium at the British Educational Research Association (BERA) Annual Conference, Cardiff University, 7–9 September.

Sylva, K., Sammons, P., Melhuish, E., Siraj-Blatchford, I. and Taggart, B. (1999) *Technical Paper 1: An Introduction to the EPPE Project*. London: London Institute of Education.

Sylva, K., Melhuish, E., Sammons, P., Siraj-Blatchford, I., Taggart, B. and Elliott, K. (2003) *The Effective Provision of Pre-School Education (EPPE) Project: Findings from the Pre-School Period. Research Brief No. RBX 15-03*. London: Department of Education and Skills.

Sylva, K., Taggart, B., Siraj-Blatchford, I., Totsika, V., Ereky-Stevens, K., Gilden, R. and Bell, D. (2007) 'Curricular quality and day-to-day learning activities in preschool', *International Journal of Early Years Education*, 1 (1): 49–65.

Taylor Nelson Sobres with Aubrey, C. (2002) *The Implementation of the Foundation Stage in Reception Classes*. Confidential Report to the DfES. Richmond, UK: Taylor Nelson Sofres.

Tharp, R. and Gallimore, R. (1991) 'A theory of teaching as assisted performance', in P. Light, S. Sheldon and M. Woodhead (eds), *Learning to Think*. London: Routledge.

Timperley, H.S. and Robinson, V.M.J. (2001) 'Achieving school improvement through challenging and changing teachers' schema', *Journal of Educational Exchange*, 2: 281–300.

Tizard, B. and Hughes, M. (1984) *Young Children Learning: Talking and Thinking at Home and at School*. London: Fontana.

Twiss, D., Stewart, B. and Corby, M. (1997) 'Early intervention services in Aotearoa/New Zealand: inclusion of infants and young children in regular early childhood settings – current provisions, issues and challenges', in B. Carpenter (ed.), *Families in Context: Emerging Trends in Family Support and Early Intervention*. London: David Fulton. pp. 90–106.

Tyler, D. (1993) 'Making better children', in D. Meredyth and D. Tyler (eds), *Child and Citizen: Genealogies of Schooling and Subjectivity*. Nathan, Qld: Griffith University Press.

Tymms, P. (1999a) *Baseline Assessment and Monitoring in Primary Schools: Achievements, Attitudes and Value-added Indicators*. London: David Fulton.

Tymms, P. (1999b) 'Baseline assessment, value added and the prediction of reading', *Journal of Research in Reading*, 22 (1): 27–36.

Tymms, P. (2001) 'The development of a computer-adaptive assessment in the early years', *Educational and Child Psychology*, 18 (3): 20–30.

Tymms, P. and Albone, S. (2002) 'Performance indicators in primary schools', in A.J. Visscher and R. Coe (eds), *School Improvement Through Performance Feedback*. Lisse/Abingdon/Exton, PA/Tokyo: Swetz & Zeitlinger. pp. 191–218.

Tymms, P., Brien, D., Merrell, C., Collins, J. and Jones, P. (2003) 'Young deaf children and the prediction of reading and mathematics', *Journal of Early Childhood Research* 1 (2): 197–212.

Tymms, P., Merrell, C., Henderson, B., Albone, S. and Jones, P. (2007) 'Links between children's starting points and finishing points in primary school'. Paper presented at EARLI Conference, Budapest, August 2007.

United Nations (1989) *UN Convention on the Rights of the Child*. New York: United Nations.

Van der Hoeven-van Doornum, A. (2002) 'What baseline assessment is doing for children's progress and teachers' actions'. Paper presented at the European Conference on Educational Research, Lisbon.

Van der Veer, R. and Valsiner, J. (eds) (1994) *The Vygotsky Reader*. Oxford: Blackwell.

Vygotsky, L. (1926, trans. 1997) *Educational Psychology*. Boca Raton, FL: St Lucie Press.

Vgotsky, L.S. (1929a) 'The problem of the cultural development of the child: II', *Journal of Genetic Psychology*, 36: 415–32.

Vygotsky, L. (1929b) *Mind in Society*. Cambridge, MA: Harvard University Press.

Vygotsky, L. (1932) *Thought and Language*. Cambridge, MA: MIT Press.

Vygotsky, L. (1978) *Mind in Society: The Development of Higher Mental Processes* (trans. and ed. M. Cole, V. John-Steiner, S. Scribner and E. Souberman). Cambridge, MA: Harvard University Press.

Vygotsky, L.S. (1987) 'Thinking and speech', in *The Collected Works of L. S. Vygotsky, Volume 1* (trans. N. Minick, eds R. Reiber and A. Carton). New York: Plenum Press. pp. 39–285.

Vygotsky, L.S. (1997) *The Collected Works of L.S. Vygotsky, Volume 3. Problems of the Theory and History of Psychology* (trans. R. van der Veer; eds R.W. Rieber and J. Wollock). New York: Plenum Press.

Vygotsky, L.S. (1998) *The Collected Works of L.S. Vygotsky, Volume 5: Child Psychology* (trans. M.J. Hall, ed. R.W. Rieber). New York: Plenum Press.

Walkerdine, V. (1987) 'No laughing matter: girls' comics and the preparation for adolescent sexuality', in J. Broughton (ed.), *Critical Theories of Psychological Development*. New York: Plenum Press.

Walkerdine, V. (2000) 'Violent boys and precocious girls: Regulating childhood at the end of the millennium', *Contemporary Issues in Early Childhood*, 1 (1): 3–22.

Ward, J. and Robinson Wood, T. (2007) 'Room at the table: racial and gendered realities in the schooling of black children', in C. Skelton, B. Francis and L. Smulyan (eds), *The Sage Handbook of Gender and Education*. London: Sage. pp. 325–39.

Weikart, D. (2000) *Early Childhood Education: Needs and Opportunity*. Paris: UNESCO, International Institute for Educational Planning.

Wells, G. (1986) *The Meaning Makers: Children Learning Language and Using Language to Learn*. Portsmouth, NH: Heinemann Educational.

Wenger, E. (1998) *Communities of Practice: Learning, Meaning and Identity*. Cambridge: Cambridge University Press.

Wenger, E., McDermott, R. and Snyder, W. (2002) *Cultivating Communities of Practice*. Boston, MA: Harvard Business School Press.

Wertsch, J., Del Rio, P. and Alvarez, A. (eds) (1995) *Sociocultural Studies of Mind*. Cambridge: Cambridge University Press.

Wertsch, J.V. (1991) *Voices of the Mind: A Sociocultural Approach to Mediated Action*. Cambridge, MA: Harvard University Press.

Wertsch, J.V. (2007) 'Vygotsky on human nature and human development'. Keynote address at the 17th European Early Childhood Education Research Association Annual Conference, 'Exploring Vygotsky's Ideas: Crossing Borders'. Prague, Czech Republic, 29 August to 1 September 2007.

Whitbread, N. (1972) *The Education of the Nursery Infant School: A History of Infant and Nursery Education in Britain 1800–1970*. London: Routledge & Kegan Paul.

Wildy, H., Louden, W. and Bailey, C. (2001) 'High stakes testing in a low stakes environment: PIPS baseline assessment in Australia'. Paper presented at the Third International Interdisciplinary Conference on Evidence-Based Policies and Indicator Systems, July 2001, Durham, UK.

Wilks, A. (1993) *Assessment of Children in Kindergarten and Childcare Centres.* Report to the Ministry of Education, Palmerston North College of Education, NZ.

Williamson, D., Cullen, J. and Lepper, C. (2006) 'From checklists to narratives in special education', *Australian Journal of Early Childhood*, 31 (2): 20–31.

Wolfendale, S. (1993) *Baseline Assessment: A Review of Current Practice, Issues and Strategies for Effective Implementation*. Paris: Organisation Mondiale de l'Education Pré-scholaire.

Wood, D. (1986) 'Aspects of teaching and learning', in M. Richards and P. Light (eds), *Children of Social Worlds*. Cambridge: Polity Press.

Wood, D. and Middleton, D. (1975) 'A study of assisted problem-solving', *British Journal of Psychology*, 66: 181–91.

Wood, D., Bruner, J.S. and Ross, G. (1976) 'The role of tutoring in problem solving', *Journal of Child Psychology and Psychiatry*, 17: 89–100.

Wood, E. (2001) '"I know what I've got better at": young children's understanding of progression in their learning'. Paper presented to European Association for Research on Learning and Instruction, University of Fribourg, Switzerland, August.

Wood, E. (2007) 'New directions in play: consensus or collision?', *Education* 3–13, 35 (4): 309–20.

Wood, E. (2008) 'Conceptualising a pedagogy of play: international perspectives from theory, policy and practice', in D. Kuschner (ed.), *From Children to Red Hatters: Diverse Images and Issues of Play. Play and Culture Studies,* Volume 8. Lanham, MD: University Press of America.

Wood, E. and Attfield, J. (2005) *Play, Learning and the Early Childhood Curriculum*, 2nd edition. London: Paul Chapman.

Worthington, M. and Carruthers, E. (2003) *Children's Mathematics – Making Marks, Making Meaning*. London: Paul Chapman.

Wylde, M. (2002) 'Fulfilling needs and taking opportunities'. Paper presented at the European Conference on Educational Research, Lisbon.

Wylie, C. (1989) *Review of Research on Staff-Child Ratios and Trained Staff in Early Childhood Services*. Report prepared for the Implementation Unit, Department of Education, New Zealand.

Wylie, C. (1996) *Five Years Old and Competent. A Summary of the Main Findings of the First Stage of the Competent Children Project*. Wellington: New Zealand Council for Educational Research.

Wylie, C. (1998) *Six Years Old and Competent. The Second Stage of the Competent Children Project: A Summary of the Main Findings*. Wellington: New Zealand Council for Educational Research.

Wylie, C. (1999) *Eight Years Old and Competent. The Third Stage of the Competent Children Project: A Summary of the Main Findings*. Wellington: New Zealand Council for Educational Research.

Wylie, C. (2001) 'Early childhood education: an enduring legacy', *Early Childhood Folio*, 5: 3–5. Wellington: New Zealand Council for Educational Research.

Wylie, C., Thompson, J. and Hendricks, A. (1996) *Competent Children at 5: Families and Early Education*. Wellington: Ministry of Education and New Zealand Council for Educational Research.

Wylie, C., Thompson, J. and Lythe, C. (2001) *Competent Children at 10: Families, Early Education, and Schools*. Wellington: Ministry of Education and New Zealand Council for Educational Research.

Wynn, K. (1992) 'Addition and subtraction in human infants', *Nature*, 358: 749–51.

Yelland, N. (2000) *Mathematics and ICT*. Canberra, ACT: Department of Education, Training and Youth Affairs.

Yelland, N. (2005) *Critical Issues in Early Childhood Education,* Maidenhead: Open University Press

Yelland, N. (2007) *Shift to the Future – Rethinking Learning with New Technologies in Education*. London: Routledge.

INDEX

Added to a page number 'f' denotes a figure.